QUALITY PAYS

Companies can only be successful in the long term if they place quality at the core of their corporate philosophy and strategy. This was the major finding of the study 'Excellence in Quality Management', a joint study of the automotive supply industry by McKinsey & Company in Europe, the USA and Japan and the Technical University of Darmstadt, Germany, in close collaboration with many automotive suppliers. This book, based on the study, offers both a detailed analysis and a blueprint for success for manufacturers worldwide.

The level of quality demanded by the automotive industry from its suppliers has risen steeply in recent years. Quality, reliability and competitiveness are now the only sound basis on which to compete for new business. Customers expect zero defects: this demands the closest attention from every employee at every level of the supplier company along with a total dedication to continuous improvement.

Compromise is not an option. It will threaten the life of the company. Only companies dedicated to quality are successful, profitable and on the road to growth.

The authors are consultants with McKinsey & Company, the international management consultancy.

Quality Pays

Günter Rommel
Felix Brück
Raimund Diederichs
Rolf-Dieter Kempis
Hans-Werner Kaas
Günter Fuhry
Volker Kurfess

MACMILLAN
Business

English translation first published in the United Kingdom 1996 by
MACMILLAN PRESS LTD
Houndmills, Basingstoke, Hampshire RG21 6XS
and London
Companies and representatives
throughout the world

ISBN 0–333–68484–2

A catalogue record for this book is available
from the British Library.

This book is printed on paper suitable for recycling and
made from fully managed and sustained forest sources.

10   9   8   7   6   5   4   3   2   1
05   04   03   02   01   00   99   98   97   96

Copy-edited and typeset by Povey–Edmondson
Okehampton and Rochdale, England

Printed in Great Britain by
Mackays of Chatham PLC
Chatham, Kent

Contents

List of Figures

Foreword

In recent years quality has developed from a function of the production department into a corporate philosophy.

Companies can only be successful in the long term if they make this philosophy their own and master the three dimensions of quality: strategy, core process management, and staff motivation.

The level of quality demanded by the automotive industry from its suppliers has risen steeply in recent years. Quality, reliability, and competitiveness in German products are essential and are the only sound basis on which to compete for new business.

Our customers have a right to expect zero defects in our products, wherever in the world they are being installed. This demands the best attention from every employee in every position in the company, and a total dedication to continuous improvement in everything we do, to the point of perfection. Compromise is not an option; it threatens the life of the company and the livelihood of employees. That is why every employee in every area of activity must understand and adopt this principle. It is the most important task of management at all levels to make sure that this happens and continues to happen.

The McKinsey study 'Excellence in Quality Management', on which this book is based, demonstrates from the example of the 167 companies surveyed that there are still major differences in practice between quality companies and others. It also shows that the quality companies are the ones that are successful, profitable, and on the road to growth.

Every fault needs to be corrected. And the further down the product development and marketing process such faults are allowed to go unnoticed, the more expensive they are to correct. It is amazing how much effort is needed to reach a sustainable defect rate of zero ppm, even with relatively simple products. Piling up increasing controls and checks during and after the process are no solution; success can only be ensured if the whole process is perfectly mastered and the corporate organization and the mentality of the employees are directed toward the 'zero defects' goal.

The findings for automotive suppliers are equally applicable to the consumer goods industry and its suppliers, and likewise, of course, to the capital goods industry. Zero defects programmes can be used to good effect not only on automated mass production lines, but also with small lots and one-off production. The effort is well worthwhile, and this book provides some pointers on how to do it.

PROFESSOR KLAUS G. LEDERER
Chairman of the Board of Directors
ITT Automotive Europe GmbH

Acknowledgements

The underlying data for this book are the result of broad international collaboration. They were collected in the course of the study 'Excellence in Quality Management', a joint project between McKinsey & Company in Europe, the USA and Japan, and the Technical University of Darmstadt, Germany, in close collaboration with many automotive suppliers.

Above all, we would like to thank the many top managers who participated in the study on behalf of their companies and who went to considerable trouble to answer the many detailed questions and to make innumerable suggestions. We also thank around a thousand employees who helped us with the data collection in our factory visits.

Günter Rommel (initiator), Rolf-Dieter Kempis (responsible partner) and Hans-Werner Kaas (project manager), as well as authors Felix Brück, Raimund Diederichs, Günter Fuhry, and Volker Kurfess would also like once again to express their thanks to the members of the core McKinsey team: Matthias Pohl, Richard Wood, Marc Mayor, Christoph Schmid, Nicola Carbonari, and Kiyoshi Matsuura.

Our thanks also to our co-workers at the Technical University of Darmstadt, especially Professor Herbert Schulz and the other members of the core team, Ralf Augustin, Thomas Eller, Klaus Göttmann, and Ralph Wiegland, without whose untiring commitment the resulting database would never have been built and analyzed.

We would also like to thank the following colleagues at McKinsey for their contributions and support:

McKinsey Germany: Klaus Mund, Jürgen Kluge, Ulrich Fincke, Helmut Böttcher, Bertram Feuerbacher, Wolfgang Lindheim, Stefan Thomke, and Volker Württenberger;
McKinsey Great Britain: Mike Graff (project sponsor) and Mark Oliver;
McKinsey France: Philippe Bideau (project sponsor), Hervé Kerbrat, Zafer Achi, François Bouvard, and Yannick Sent;
McKinsey Spain/Portugal: Juan Hoyos (project sponsor), José Luis Cortina, Joaquin Capdevila, and Maria Teixeira da Motta;

McKinsey Italy: Francesco Baldanza (project sponsor) and Paolo Vagnone;

McKinsey Scandinavia: Bill Hoover (project sponsor) and Anders Kuikka;

McKinsey Japan: Tadaaki Chigusa (project sponsor), Tamotsu Adachi, Tadatomo Kato, and Ichiro Katagiri;

McKinsey US: Jeff Sinclair (project sponsor) and Glenn Mercer.

The data analysis and forwarding of individual feedback to the participating companies would have been much more difficult without the support of Reinhold Barchet, Christof Stierlen, and Jens Gollmer.

For process management, known to be an important quality factor, we thank Petra Ziemes, who always managed to make the impossible happen. Betty Stevens ensured a clean manuscript despite many rounds of amendments. And finally, we also thank Christel Delker and Jutta Scherer for their critical and creative editorial support.

The authors would, in short, like to say a warm thank you to all those who contributed directly or indirectly to *Quality Pays*.

About the Authors

Felix Brück is a director in the Cleveland office of McKinsey & Company. Felix joined McKinsey in Germany in 1983 and subsequently spent a year in Japan. He holds degrees in mechanical engineering from the University of Aachen and in business administration from the American Graduate School of International Management in Phoenix, Arizona. Before joining McKinsey, he worked for three years in production engineering at Robert Bosch GmbH. Felix is one of the authors of *Simplicity Wins*, published in 1995.

Raimund Diederichs is a principal in McKinsey's Vienna office. Raimund joined the firm in 1982. He holds a degree in mechanical engineering from the University of Aachen and an MBA from INSEAD. Before joining McKinsey he worked for two years as a process engineer at Procter & Gamble, spending one year in the United States. Raimund is one of the authors of *Simplicity Wins*, published in 1995.

Günter Fuhry is a principal in McKinsey's Vienna office. Günter joined the firm in 1987. He holds a degree in chemical engineering and in business administration from the University of Linz.

Hans-Werner Kaas is a consultant in McKinsey's Frankfurt office. Hans-Werner joined the firm in 1991. He holds a degree in mechanical engineering and business administration from the University of Kaiserslautern. Before joining McKinsey, Hans-Werner worked as a trainee for African Explosives and Chemical Industries (AECI) in Durban, South Africa, and as a consultant for Mercedes-Benz passenger car division developing a strategic and financial evaluation concept for new production technologies.

Rolf-Dieter Kempis is a director in McKinsey's Düsseldorf office. Rolf-Dieter joined the firm in 1983. He holds degrees in mechanical engineering and economics from the University of Aachen. Before joining McKinsey he spent two years with Thyssen Steel AG, using operations research methods to develop an automated, EDP-compatible production management system. Rolf-Dieter is one of the authors of *Simplicity Wins*, published in 1995.

Volker Kurfess is a consultant in McKinsey's Stuttgart office. Volker joined McKinsey in 1992. He holds degrees in engineering and business administration from the University of Karlsruhe. Before joining McKinsey, he spent one year with Daimler-Benz to develop a knowledge-based project management system.

Günter Rommel is managing director of McKinsey's Tokyo office. Günter joined the firm's German office in 1980 and subsequently spent a year and a half in Tokyo. He holds degrees from the Technical Universities of Stuttgart and Munich in electrical engineering, business administration, economics and law, and obtained his PhD in investment planning. Günter is one of the authors of *Simplicity Wins*, published in 1995.

1 Introduction: Why and How Quality Pays

If you're not cheaper, you have to be better. But in today's tough and increasingly international competitive arena, even this plausible rule is at best only half the truth. Many players have to lower their costs even to get the chance of proving their superior quality. And high quality, properly understood, also helps cut costs. Finally, there will soon come a day when 'cheaper' is no longer a viable option: cost competition is inevitably turning into quality competition. A comparison of automotive industry suppliers around the world has now proved that quality pays, and that it can be measured, learned, and does not depend on location.

European car manufacturers are struggling with costs 30 to 50 per cent higher than the world's best – by the normal definition of 'costs'. But the term has to be widened in the automotive industry to include, for example, all warranty and ex gratia costs. This can soon double or treble the actual 'manufacturing costs', particularly since the extended warranties offered by a few pioneers are likely to trigger widespread reaction. In this situation, the recently emergent sweeping restructuring of the supply industry was unavoidable.

If manufacturers feel themselves under pressure to tap all cost reserves over the entire value chain, from raw materials purchasing to delivery and customer service, the performance of their suppliers is also put to the test. If international competitors offer higher value and/or better prices, a significant share of supply industry sales may migrate to them. This process of concentration will mean that ultimately only a few direct suppliers and some 'secondary suppliers' will survive, while many players not offering cost or value advantages will be squeezed out of the market altogether. Even today, for example, the leading supplier in one segment has an average growth rate of 20 per cent and a 12 per cent return on sales, while its keenest international rival has to be content with only 5 per cent growth and 2 per cent return on sales.

In this struggle for survival, cost-reduction programmes alone are unlikely to provide an answer: they will not help a German supplier, for example, to close its (partly location-dependent) cost gap, particularly since competitors' cost positions are unlikely to remain where they are. If those of us in the old industrialized countries, and especially Germany, want to maintain our prosperity, we need to earn a high markup which, in turn, depends on delivering superior value.

What is happening here is a kind of life-cycle of industrial regions. A similar phenomenon occurs in the development of individual industries. It starts with a technological breakthrough or technical innovation; the first company to use the new technology to provide a marketable benefit to the customer wins a superior position with the best market share and return. Even at this early stage in the life-cycle, quality, in the sense of generating value to the customer and mastering technology, plays an important role.

Once the technology has been proven, several competitors typically come on the scene, and an oversupply often occurs within a short space of time. As further product differentiation on customer value becomes increasingly difficult, a price war develops and, as a rule, the industry consolidates. Only suppliers with superior cost structures survive. Outstanding process quality achieved by stable R&D and production processes is the precondition for this kind of cost position.

At the end of the life-cycle, competition once again focuses more on quality. Superior service and sales become the decisive factor, especially since global distribution allows further improvements in the cost position. In addition, at the end of the cycle the winning companies are still earning such attractive returns that they can finance the development of replacement technologies, to achieve higher value and/or lower costs.

So quality plays an important role at the beginning of the industry life-cycle, by creating new value, and at the end of the cycle; in the middle phase it is almost taken for granted. Today, Germany and the rest of Europe are in the same position as a mature industry; price competition still prevails, but in the long term competitiveness will depend on quality. While in some individual cases, such as turn-around situations, other measures like site concentration or mergers with competitors may initially seem more important, in the medium or long term a company will only succeed if it leads the field on quality.

Even today, customers explicitly reward quality. There is, for example, a close correlation between the American J. D. Power Index (customer satisfaction with automobiles) and growth in the sales figures of different makes of car.

In the area of fast food, McDonald's has demonstrated how a consistently high standard of quality can bring phenomenal world-wide success. Founded in 1954, McDonald's now has 14,000 outlets and franchises in 70 countries; in the last twenty years alone, sales have increased almost ten-fold. The decisive factor in this success was the company's focus on the customer's perception of quality, which is by no means limited to the product. Only around 40 per cent of customer satisfaction in fast food restaurants is determined by the food itself; 20 per cent depends on cleanliness, and about 15 per cent on the friendliness of the staff – all elements of the 'total quality package'.

Citibank was able to build its customer base four times faster than the German *Sparkassen* (savings banks) and to double its balance sheet growth rate by concentrating on improved service: 24-hour telephone banking 6 days a week, automatic teller machines with a wide range of facilities (making cash deposits, ordering checks, setting up standing orders), and higher interest on current accounts. Citibank bet successfully on service quality in this service industry.

All very plausible, but how far can we generalize from these observations? A group of McKinsey consultants were keen to investigate this point, and so began the international study on 'Excellence in Quality Management' (see the insert, 'Project Description', pp. 21–5).

Two questions were uppermost in their minds: 'What role does quality play in the success of a company?' and 'What, in concrete terms, makes quality companies different?' The automotive supply industry in Germany, Japan, and the US was chosen for a number of reasons: first, because, in this sector, objective customer requirements are comparable worldwide; second, because the product spectrum ranges from simple components to highly complex systems. This means that results can by and large be transferred to other industries as well.

The results of this long-term global study form the analytical basis of this book:

- *Quality is measurable,* although it is in no way the same as merely fulfilling technical standards. Above all, the results of quality can be measured; they can be read off straight from the company's balance sheet.

- *Quality is at home everywhere,* as proved by companies from all segments and regions.
- *Quality can be learned.* The most successful 'quality companies' provide a role model for those wanting to catch up.

QUALITY IS MEASURABLE AND WORTHWHILE

High quality is the best road to corporate success. The results of the long-term study show that quality companies delivered twenty times fewer faulty products[1] on average than poorer quality companies, and almost twice as many of their products are considered superior to the competition. These companies from levels III and IV, roughly the top 40 per cent according to a weighted quality benchmark, achieved much higher returns on sales and growth rates than their competitors at the bottom end of the quality scale. Moreover, both the 'good' and the 'less good' show the direct impact of quality performance on returns and growth.

Quality Leaders Are Also the Most Successful Companies

Two benchmarks for process and design quality were created in the long-term study as comparable quality parameters across different business segments (see the insert 'Project Description', pp. 21–5).

The resulting quality scale revealed four typical levels of quality management (Figure 1.1):

- *Level I: Inspection.* Companies at this level achieve quality primarily by interim and final inspections followed by elimination of defects. The quality function works separately from other functions and is almost solely responsible for quality. These companies' end products are prone to significant defects: their ppm rate is about 4,800, their reject rate is over 5 per cent and their rework rate over 3 per cent; process, service, and design quality are generally not even measured. R&D and production mostly operate in isolation from each other. Of the companies studied, about one in four are still in this stage of ex-post defect elimination and rejection.

---

[1] Measured in faulty parts per million (ppm).

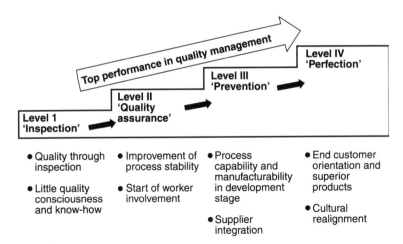

Fig. 1.1 *Four levels of quality*

- *Level II: Quality Assurance.* Even at this next quality level, quality objectives are mainly focused on production, which is also the function driving the optimization and stabilization of the processes. The ppm rate is about 900, and reject and rework rates are about 3.1 per cent and 2.7 per cent respectively. Many of these companies are beginning to measure their process stability, but their C_{pk} ratio[2] is usually still under 1.33, and therefore below the threshold for quality processes. The service quality is known, a quality benchmark for design has not yet been set. The largest group of the companies studied (36 per cent) were at this level.

- *Level III: Prevention.* At this third level, product design interacts with production processes ('robust design'), and, for the first time, a clear customer orientation emerges in the product features. The proportion of competitively superior products is correspondingly high, at over 25 per cent. The ppm rate falls to 300, and reject and rework rates are 1.5 per cent and 1.7 per cent, respectively. The processes reach a C_{pk} ratio of over 1.67 and are thus highly stable; it is not uncommon for production to achieve zero defect rates. To optimize costs and quality, these companies work in closer cooperation with suppliers. About a quarter are at this level.

---

[2] This ratio (quotient of the allowed production tolerance and actual process scatter) measures 'process capability'. The higher the C_{pk} value, the stabler or more quality capable the process is (see also Appendix A, 'Top Quality Tools').

- *Level IV: Perfection.* This fourth level describes the – by today's standards – ultimate 'quality company'. It has internalized a culture that generates quality in all areas. Every employee is aware of the importance of quality for the success of the company, searches for improvement opportunities, and strives for perfection in terms of the 'zero defects principle'. A prerequisite for this is a good relationship with internal customers/suppliers. But a consistent orientation to external customers and optimization of the most important processes from supplier to customer in the business system also characterize the level IV company. This customer orientation is needed in order to recognize added value and translate it into practice through superior design quality.

Quality companies try to keep raising their standards in a process of continuous improvement. Accordingly, over 35 per cent of their products are superior to the competition, their ppm rate is less than 100, and reject and rework rates are less than 0.8 per cent. Processes are highly stable, the C_{pk} ratio is often more than 2.0. Only about 13 per cent of all the companies in the long-term study have reached this quality level.

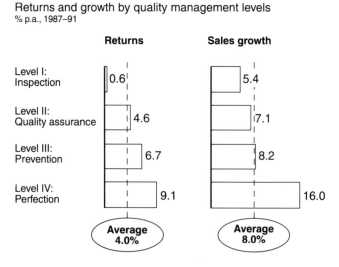

Fig. 1.2 *Companies prosper as they move toward quality*

From the findings of the long-term study, improving quality performance over the four levels contributes directly to growing financial success. At the top of the pile are level IV companies, which grew between 1987 and 1991 by an average of 16 per cent per year and earned an average annual return on sales of 9.1 per cent (Figure 1.2).[3] Companies at level I trail behind with an average annual return on sales of around zero per cent and falling market shares; unless they dramatically improve their quality performance, these companies will soon go under.

Stable Processes for Returns, Value to the Customer for Growth

An examination of the development of returns and sales growth over the four levels of the quality scale reveals two discontinuities. When level II is reached, return on sales jumps to about the industry average. At the transition from level III to level IV, the growth rate doubles. This is because returns and growth are influenced in different ways by quality management.

Return on sales can be improved by a price premium and above all by competitive cost structures. Companies that achieve stable processes have 6 to 8 per cent lower costs than competitors that do not. The saving comes from the direct cost of quality (3 to 4 per cent) and from significantly higher labour and machine productivity. Process quality has a fundamental influence on the total cost structure, both directly and indirectly. Companies with superior process capability as a prerequisite for high process quality have a return on sales of around 11 per cent on average (Figure 1.3).

Strong *growth* comes from a better understanding of customer requirements and the world's best competitors, which in turn is expressed in superior product features and outstanding service. Companies that consistently achieve this orientation, partly by using relevant tools such as Quality Function Deployment, grew in the period of the study by 13–15 per cent per year (see Figure 1.3).

---

[3] All figures refer to the period of the study, i.e., 1987–91, when average returns for the sector were around 4 per cent. In the last two years (situation in 1994), average returns have been around 0 per cent; while the really top companies are still making a profit (3 ro 5 per cent), a large proportion of the companies have gone into the red.

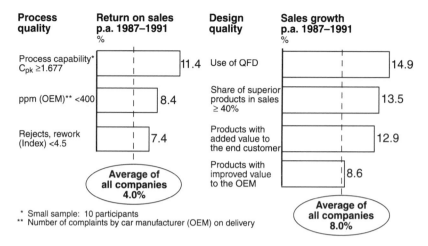

Fig. 1.3   *Process quality drives returns, design quality fosters growth*

This explains both the jump in returns between levels I and II and the jump in growth between levels III and IV. Process quality at level I is totally inadequate. Companies at level II then concentrate their quality endeavours on stabilizing production processes, resulting in a significantly lower ppm rate and a jump in return on sales of about 4 per cent. The quality performance and financial results of these companies are about average. Companies at level III pursue preventive quality assurance strategies and are differentiated from their weaker competitors mainly by their superior cost structure and preventive quality policy. At level IV, the focus is outwards, with a high proportion of competitively superior products. As masters of 'design to market', these companies are the real winners. During the period of the study, they grew twice as fast as the market, were thus able to win significant market shares, and earned at least double the industry average.

The difference in orientation is demonstrated by other ratios as well: for example, capital intensity (fixed assets per capita) reaches its highest point at level III and then remains constant at level IV, although the good companies do use their higher returns to invest in new technologies and extend their competitive lead. But here, purely technological optimization is supplemented by intensive investigation of customer requirements and their translation into labour-intensive service.

Labour productivity (value added per capita) shows the highest increase between levels II and III, at +35 per cent. Productivity growth slows a little between level III and level IV, to +20 per cent. Capital productivity (the ratio of value added to fixed assets), on the other hand, declines slightly but steadily from level II to level IV. This confirms the supposition that the quality companies may be raising their labour productivity at the expense of capital productivity – a phenomenon which has also been observed in studies of the automotive and mechanical engineering industries.[4]

The study also confirmed another of our experiences as consultants – that improvements in quality do not have to be paid for by extra time or costs. To the contrary, leading companies manage to be superior in all three dimensions. At levels III and IV, development times are about 30 per cent shorter than at level I, development costs are about 25 per cent lower; in terms of production, the series startup times of companies at levels III and IV are about 20 per cent shorter for full-scale production, their labour productivity rate is 75 per cent higher and, of course, their process quality is considerably higher.

QUALITY IS AT HOME EVERYWHERE

In the long-term study, the majority of very high quality companies were located in Japan – but Europe and the US were present as well. Such companies are to be found across all sectors and regions; a company is obviously in the 'right' sector and at the 'right' location if it understands and fulfils the specific quality demands of its market.

These quality demands differ significantly from segment to segment, depending on whether competition is mainly based on price, the OEM's total costs, technology, or value to the end customer. This tends to mean that quality demands – and thus the risks of failure – are higher in the more sophisticated segments (e.g., systems, complex components). A regional imbalance and different catch-up needs in the individual dimensions of process and design quality are evident here. On the whole, an understanding of how to meet the demands of the most sophisticated segments was found more frequently in Japanese companies than in others involved in the study.

---

[4] See G. Rommel *et al.*, *Simplicity Wins*, Harvard Business School Press, 1995.

The More Promising, the More Sophisticated

An automotive supplier delivering screws or insulating material to an OEM must compete first and foremost on price; success depends on its own in-house cost efficiency. The supplier that develops and produces complex modules or systems more or less independently, on the other hand, will find that its competitive advantage depends on how effectively it holds down costs in the OEM's value chain and/ or improves the value to the end customer.

These examples demonstrate the two extremes in the strategic position of the supplier relative to the OEM, simply defined as the supplier's contribution to assembly and to R&D. A matrix based on these two features can be used to describe the entire span of the supply segment with its differing success factors and quality demands (Figure 1.4).

The strategic position of the supplier vis-à-vis the OEM is determined by its development contribution and assembly contribution

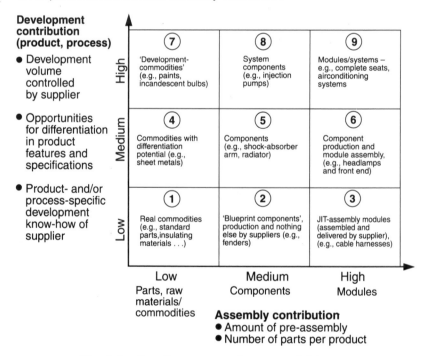

Fig. 1.4 *Supplier segments by scope of delivery*

Roughly speaking, the performance profile runs from the bottom left to top right with increasing and interdependent demands. Moving from the 'commodity area' to the 'module/system area', new and usually more demanding success factors are added (Figure 1.5). The long-term study confirms that the 'higher' segments have a greater potential for returns and growth, but also carry the highest risks. How well a company performs depends primarily on its quality performance.

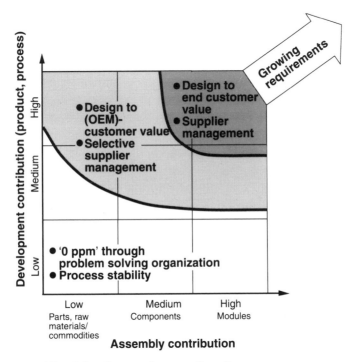

Fig. 1.5 *Success factors of quality management*

Parts manufacturers, for example, can never be content with level III quality performance. While it is true to say that they do not need to focus much on the end customer, they still need to reach level IV in the other 'perfection' features (broad-based employee responsibility, internal customer/supplier principle, zero defects attitude) to ensure superior quality. It should always be remembered that in every segment, not only the systems segment, the company with superior quality earns higher returns (Figure 1.6).

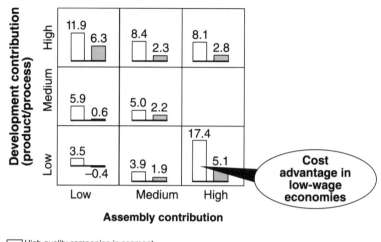

Return on sales and quality
% p.a. 1987 – 1991

Fig. 1.6 *Quality pays in all supplier segments*

Segments with only a small contribution to R&D (and thus only a small design differentiation potential) range from commodities via blueprint component production to 'just in time' assembly modules. In these segments, it is essential to aim for low reject and rework rates and to minimize the ppm rate of the end product.

In the *commodities* segment, then, product design should facilitate automated production with stable processes and economies of scale; in the *assembly intensive* segment, ease of assembly and low labour costs are the key factors for success.

In terms of returns, the *assembly modules* segment (low R&D contribution, high assembly contribution) proved particularly interesting. Suppliers in this segment achieved the highest individual returns of any segment (average 9.5 per cent). None of them was making a loss, and the best had returns as high as 17.4 per cent. This success is based on a unique competitive position, temporarily at least, based on a superior cost structure rather than technological differentiation. A good example is provided by cable harness manufacturers who moved their production to countries such as Portugal and Spain in the mid-1980s and were able to gain a clear labour cost advantage. However, an unrivalled cost structure cannot be achieved without high process quality, i.e., a ppm rate approaching zero.

But it is extremely doubtful whether pure assembly segments will continue to enjoy high profitability and high growth in the future. Because of their small contribution to R&D, suppliers in this segment have no real opportunity to influence the OEM's time requirements, quality, and costs, i.e., product complexity and product/process fit.

And in the case of pure JIT assembly, their contribution to value generation is so small that their labour cost advantage relative to the OEMs is not reflected to any great extent in the end product. Suppliers in this segment therefore run the risk of having their business taken over by 'real' module/system suppliers who make a high contribution to R&D, especially when technological discontinuities or technology leaps appear on the horizon, such as the change from traditional cable harnesses to networked bus systems with glass fibre cables.

Components suppliers must ensure that their own in-house processes are stable, but also have to offer an OEM solutions that are technically superior to its specifications. The product design should help the OEM to control complexity better (use of identical parts) and should secure manufacturability or ease of assembly through stable processes. It is imperative here to be integrated into a customer's development process and to master and/or understand its development concept. Focus on the end customer also becomes more important here. This segment grew by the market average, with a return on sales of about 3 to 5 per cent.

Suppliers of sophisticated, technology-intensive parts with a low share of assembly are operating in a segment where attractive returns of about 8 per cent on average can be earned. Superior technology is the key factor for success here; high investment in building product and/or process know-how can lead to an extremely profitable value-based monopoly – but also to substantial losses: among the companies studied, the results ranged from a 26 per cent profit to a 7 per cent loss.

Module/system suppliers also have to meet all the demands mentioned so far. But they also have to generate added value in design, such as a lighter, quieter, safer or more durable product. This basically involves developing better concepts and problem solutions than the OEM itself. Suppliers can only do this if they know both the OEM and the end customer inside and out and have sufficient R&D capacity and competence. In addition, supplier management, once principally the domain of the OEM, is being transferred more and more to these system suppliers, who also use sub-suppliers to manufacture their components. Quality management during development and supplier integration become the most critical tasks for these suppliers.

Only companies at quality level IV will succeed in this segment in the long term. A comparison of some key ratios shows how demanding this quality level is, and thus how hard it is to compete in this segment:

- The share of superior products was 60 per cent for good systems manufacturers as opposed to 35 per cent for component manufacturers and 12 per cent for parts suppliers.
- This product lead is achieved without high labour intensity. At around US$100,000 per employee, labour productivity is around 30 per cent higher than in the parts segment. The decisive factor here is optimized vertical integration, i.e., important components are purchased from sub-suppliers.
- Systems suppliers have to put substantial resources into development to build the necessary know-how. Development costs are about 5 to 7 per cent of turnover and around 9 per cent of employees are R&D workers. For components manufacturers, the corresponding values are about 4 per cent for development costs and 5.6 per cent of employees in R&D, and for commodities manufacturers, the figures are about 2 per cent for development costs and about 3.5 per cent of employees in R&D.

Concentration on system suppliers, restructuring vertical integration in value added and R&D, closer cooperation with suppliers – these are all significant trends in the automotive and automotive supply industries. The module/system segment is becoming a particularly desirable objective for suppliers' attempts at repositioning, which is hardly surprising in view of average returns of about 5 per cent and an average growth rate of about 11 per cent per year. But if a company wants to be successful, it is precisely here that it has to be particularly good. These high average figures should not disguise the fact that heavy losses can also be made, both in the module/system segment and in technology-intensive parts. And companies can never afford to rest on their laurels; it is very difficult to sustain a competitive advantage over time, because even highly differentiated products are constantly being pushed aside by new technical solutions offering new or better customer value.

Different Catch-Up Needs for Different Regions

It is not possible to draw up in-depth industry profiles by country on the basis of our study, since the number of participants varied too widely from country to country and in some cases was too small. Some interesting patterns are, however, perceptible. For example, if all the companies involved are grouped into the supplier segments with their own particular quality demands, and this classification is compared with the quality level each company has reached, it becomes evident that the gap between aims and achievements – between the targeted segment and the quality level reached/quality skills mastered – is much wider in some countries than in others (see also Chapter 5 and Appendix B).

- The *Japanese participants* have the highest share of quality companies, with 85 per cent in phases III and IV. The Japanese companies largely fulfil the demands of the highly differentiated segments (top right area of the matrix), even though, for historical reasons, they have room for improvement in some areas of their design quality.
- There seems to be a contradiction between the standard of segment and level of quality with the Italian and German participants. *Italian suppliers* take the highest share of the systems segment (25 per cent), but only 8 per cent of these companies are at level IV, while nearly 60 per cent are still at levels I and II. In *Germany* as well, about 15 per cent of the companies are trying to stake their claim in the systems segment, yet only 5 per cent have realized the quality of level IV; over 70 per cent are still at levels I and II.
- Sixty-seven per cent of the participating *British* companies were at levels III and IV, giving them, in total, the highest quality level in Europe. It is, however, surprising to note that they also have the third lowest share of the systems segment, above France and Spain/Portugal. With their excellent mastery of their processes, the British seem well equipped to become stronger competitors there.
- Most of the *French participants* are on the level of parts suppliers; 64 per cent are at quality level II.
- In international terms, quality is least developed in *Spain/Portugal*. None of the participating companies is at level IV, while

about 80 per cent are still at levels I and II. Iberia undoubtedly still benefits from low factor costs, but since more Eastern European companies are entering the market, only a dramatic improvement in quality will be able to secure competitiveness over the longer term.

- After Japan and Great Britain, *US suppliers* provide the third largest share of quality companies, with 44 per cent in phases III and IV. The increasing technology orientation of US suppliers is demonstrated by the presence of about 30 per cent of companies in the systems segment.

With the exception of Spain/Portugal, therefore, all participating countries have a number of companies at quality level IV, the present world-class level of process and design quality. In our consulting experience, the reason why such widely varying clusters of these excellent companies appear in different regions can basically be attributed to the fact that conditions in the industry (above all the relationship between suppliers and OEMs) have led to differing *quality and production philosophies.*

Different industry conditions

The highest quality level is quite clearly to be found where the customer (be it the OEM or end customer) demands it and the OEM is ready to translate these high demands into action in collaboration with its suppliers. This applies both in Japan and Britain, where new Japanese factories have established very high quality demands. Other countries which have so far had less demanding customers in some areas (e.g., Spain and Italy) have stuck at a lower average quality level. Exceptions to this rule are companies that wanted to play an important international role and have adapted to the demands of the world's best OEMs.

Optimum customer value and products designed for manufacturing, in other words stable processes, can only be achieved if suppliers and customers work closely together across the entire business system. Japan, with its *Keiretsu* system, the broad vertical association of companies, definitely has substantial advantages over the West with its traditional approach of supplier changes, price competition and price squeezing (see also Chapter 5, 'Japan, Europe and the US').

Different quality philosophies

Western companies often optimize their quality costs by trading off the costs of avoiding faults against the costs of their consequences. The optimum is therefore reached at a certain fault rate. Japanese companies, on the other hand, want to avoid these kinds of tradeoffs as much as possible, since the consequential costs are much higher than the direct cost of quality, not just in the company's own production process more expecially in the form of lost customer loyalty, as well as warranty and *ex gratia* costs. For this reason, Japanese companies aspire to a 'zero defect rates' – or absolute perfection in process quality. With continuous improvement processes, they have been so successful in reducing the costs of fault avoidance, even or particularly in the situation of zero defect production, that a tradeoff has become superfluous. Both the consequential and the preventive costs are minimal.

On the other hand, European, and US companies have focused strongly on value to the end customer, without having a fixed relationship with a specific purchaser. They lead the world in this dimension of design quality.

Despite all the differences in customer requirements, production philosophies, optimization processes, and general business conditions, a quality culture can be created anywhere, and quality leads everywhere to enduring and outstanding corporate success in international competition.

QUALITY CAN BE LEARNED

Whether suppliers of systems or parts, whether Japanese, European, or US, quality companies (i.e., companies we would position in levels III and IV) have different regional strengths, but they agree on the most important features of their quality management. Their impressive success is reason enough to study these typical features in more detail.

The most obvious feature is that quality companies do not see the achievement of high quality as the domain of any particular function, but rather as the responsibility of the whole company. They have long since discarded the belief that quality is ultimately created in the production process – they know that the seeds of good or bad quality are sown as early as the R&D stage, and that all must pull together to

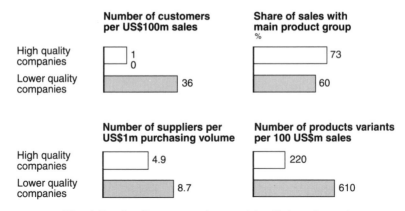

Fig. 1.7 *Quality companies are 'simplicity winners'*

achieve high quality. Quality companies have also recognized production and R&D as 'core processes' that carry the company and also have a decisive influence on quality. But they do not look on these processes as merely the internal business of the R&D and production functions; rather they view them from a cross-functional perspective as 'market-oriented, manufacturable design' and as 'zero defect production and focus their internal organization accordingly. In addition, neither of these processes is confined within the company's gates: both customers and suppliers are an integral part of the process and are closely involved in it.

It is also striking that the quality leaders are characterized without exception by simplicity (Figure 1.7).[5] They earn 80 per cent of their sales from relatively few products, variants, and customers, require just under half as many suppliers for a comparable purchase volume as lower-quality companies, are characterized by simpler processes, and have on average one less hierarchical level (see also Chapter 2, 'Strategy and Organization').

Genuine top quality is only possible through simplicity, and simplification can accelerate and ensure sustainable quality improvements. High process quality improves a company's cost position and thus its return on sales, but it will only have its full impact if the criteria of simplicity are also observed. This principle is even more apparent when it comes to design quality; companies with high design quality and simplicity grew during the study period about two and a half times more quickly than the more complex companies. For

---

[5] See G. Rommel *et al.*, *Simplicity Wins*, Harvard Business School Press, 1995

example, if development volume is spread out over too many product families, whose profit impact is all too often not reliably known, development volume will drop below the critical mass per product family. As technical development races ahead, a company runs the risk of not being able to keep up and its future is placed in jeopardy.

A company can only effectively and efficiently become a 'quality company' by taking the simplicity route. The analyses from the long-term study also confirm this; virtually every company at quality level IV is also largely guided by the rules of simplicity.

How can a company achieve this 'core process orientation'? How can it integrate customers and suppliers? How can it ensure stable processes and a greater focus on the customer? How do all these elements interact? In short, what are the distinguishing features of a quality company and how do you become one? The successful examples from the long-term study provide concrete pointers. These pointers form the subject of the following chapters of this book.

- *Strategy and organization: Think quality.* Outstanding companies have systematically acted on the realization that things will only move if everyone pulls together. For them, quality management involves the whole company. They set specific targets for each function and for each level of hierarchy, which together support the overall quality objective. In addition, they provide each individual with the information and skills he or she needs to perform his or her duties. Top management is personally involved in developing and implementing the quality strategy. The operative[?] level is given a major share of the responsibility for quality, and the mobilization of employees is taken correspondingly seriously; skills and readiness to produce quality are supported by training and team competition. In this environment, the scope of quality assurance narrows. The structures are generally simple, with flat hierarchies.

- *The R&D process: Value to external and internal customers.* Quality companies have recognized that a total orientation to the customer – and therefore ultimately growth – can only be achieved through dialogue with the customer. They use tools and techniques in a targeted manner to ensure this customer focus in their product design. This applies both to close cooperation with the direct customer – the OEM – and to efforts to comply with the end customer's understanding of value. At the same time, these companies never forget that the quality of production downstream will depend on the process capability of the products; their quality assurance strategy focuses on fault avoidance and they are bold enough to make frequent changes. Because they treat their suppliers as their development partners, quality and technical competence are usually more important than cost as criteria for supplier selection.

- *The production process: Zero defects at source.* The overriding goal of the production process is to minimize faults in the delivered product. To this end, quality companies not only employ quality assurance techniques that ensure stable processes, but have also recognized that the contribution of the employee on the shop floor is of decisive importance. In quality companies, operative quality assurance is the task of the workers – they have the skills to intervene in the process to correct faults; their motivation to do so is enhanced by an entrepreneurial, high-performance environment. In addition, the production function also collaborates closely with the suppliers: joint, tightly managed improvement projects together with the suppliers ensure that quality is delivered to the production line. Short response times and perfect fault elimination lead to a process of continuous learning.

- *Japan, Europe, and the US: Learning from the strengths of others.* The Japanese do not always come out on top in comparisons of quality companies in these three regions. While the Japanese do have significantly better process quality, the Europeans and the Americans show certain strengths in the customer value dimension of quality. This bi-polarity has developed for historical reasons and is partly structure-dependent. The quality methods of each region can also be transferred to the others: the greater emphasis given by the Japanese to fault prevention, 'continuous improvement', and supplier integration; the Europeans' and Americans' leaner organizational structures and greater focus on the end customer; the additional, specifically American, far advanced mobilization concepts in production.

- *The road to becoming a 'quality company'.* Where 'quality companies' and 'lower quality companies' are referred to here and in later chapters, the conclusions and data refer to levels III/IV and level I, respectively. However, the highest quality level reached so far is undoubtedly not the end of the story; the last chapter therefore considers the question of where companies go from here, beyond level IV.

On the way to top quality, the best companies do not compromise on costs and speed. They want to achieve excellence in all three areas, and they can do it, too, not least because the best achievements in each area are often mutually reinforcing.

PROJECT DESCRIPTION

Excellence in Quality Management
The McKinsey [long-term] study on quality management

Conducted by: McKinsey & Company in collaboration with the Department of Production Technology at the Technical University of Darmstadt, Germany.

Objective: To investigate the importance of the 'quality' factor worldwide and the success profiles of quality management, from R&D to the manufacturing and delivery of the product.

The rapidly globalizing automotive supply industry is particularly suitable for a study of this kind. Not only is quality measured very strictly and objectively by the direct customer, the car manufacturer, but competitive conditions in the global market also offer the comparability for a comprehensive analysis. And finally, the product segments of the automotive supply industry (such as mechanical, electronic, electromechanical, and process-manufactured products) covers a broad spectrum, so that findings should also be transferable to other sectors.

Time-scale: Trends from 1987 to 1991 and forecasts to 1997.

Scope of the study and regions covered: 167 companies were included in the study from countries in the three Triad regions of Europe, the US, and Japan – 122 in Europe (62 of which were German), 25 in the US, and 20 in Japan (this last group includes one Korean and one Australian company).

The product range of the participating suppliers included all major systems, components, and parts of a car. The study did not deal with large corporations as a whole, but with business units and individual operating companies, and, within a business unit or individual company, the main product group and the main factory or factories. The study did not include in-house production of systems, components, and parts by the car manufacturers themselves.

Coverage of the industry: Of the 20 largest automotive suppliers in the world, 75 per cent participated in the study. In Europe, almost 90 per cent of the top 20 participated, in Japan 45 per cent. But mid-sized and smaller companies also took part (particularly in Europe), as can be seen from the average figures for sales and workforce size (Figure 1.8). In Germany, participants accounted for about 30 per cent of total industry sales, in the other participating countries for between 10 and 20 per cent.

Participating companies by sales volume 1991	Number of companies by supplier segment	Average values			
		Sales 1991 US$m	ROS 1987–1991 % p.a.	Sales growth 1987–1991 % p.a.	Employees
US$ m Number 122	Total 167	233	4.0	8.0	1,820
>700 21	Systems 37	300	5.5	11.4	2,060
200–700 41	Components 58	340	5.1	8.2	2,930
<200 60 25 4 17 4 20* 8 9 3	Parts/ commodities 72	112	2.4	7.2	805

Europe US Japan

* Including 1 Korean and 1 Australian company

Fig. 1.8   *167 companies in Europe, US and Japan were surveyed*

Project approach: Information about the success patterns of the leading companies in quality, the 'quality companies', and about the behaviour of lower quality companies came from the evaluation of an extensive questionnaire, detailed on-site interviews, broad discussions at nine international participants' conferences, and the experiences from McKinsey consultancy projects.[6] To achieve valid international comparisons, non-monetary yardsticks were used in most cases (e.g., project resources in terms

---

[6] Unless stated otherwise, all analyses and findings are based on the data collected in this study.

of person days per supplier or R&D costs as a percentage of sales). In cases such as value added per employee, where monetary values could not be avoided, official OECD exchange rates for the periods in question were applied.

Analytical method: To discover successful approaches to quality management it is necessary to look at companies with the best quality performance. Our first task, then, was to define quality as a quantifiable value and to measure it for each participating company. It was then possible to investigate differences in quality management between high and low quality companies to identify the factors for success.

Indicators of design and process quality were used as benchmarks (Figure 1.9):

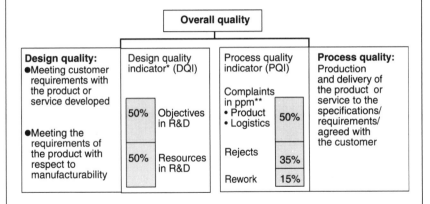

* Scoring model
** This covers complaints due to defective, missing or wrongly delivered products from the supplier on delivery at the automotive production plant

Fig. 1.9 *Definition of quality*

- *Design quality:* Quality of design[7] is a company's ability to develop products that meet the demands of the customer as closely as possible (in the case of automotive suppliers, the requirements of both the OEM and the end customer) and to manufacture these products with the lowest possible defect rates. To determine design quality, for which there are no

---

[7] See also 'Integriertes Qualitäts-management in der Produkt- und Prozessentwicklung' ('Integrated quality management in product and process development') by Hans-Werner Kaas, PhD thesis in preparation, planned to be published in 1997.

absolutely objective benchmarks, we developed the Design Quality Indicator (DQI). This uses a scoring model to determine the *quality objectives* for development (e.g., orientation to the most demanding customers and world-class benchmarks, manufacturability targets) but also to evaluate the use of *quality assurance tools* such as QFD and FMEA (see Appendix A, 'Top Quality Tools'). These figures are then used to calculate an index of design quality.

- *Process quality:* Process quality is a company's ability to manufacture and deliver a product to the specifications agreed with the customer. The process quality indicator (PQI) captures clearly quantifiable values that are valid throughout the industry:

  - Complaints from the automotive manufacturer about defective parts on delivery by the supplier (the *ppm* – i.e., *parts per million* – *rate*, the number of defective parts per million delivered) were given a 50 per cent weighting. These *complaints* were not just about product faults, but also errors or delays in logistics e.g., too small, too large, or incorrect deliveries.
  - Internal process quality was also given a weighting of 50 per cent. 35 of these percentage points were allotted to the cumulatively measured *reject rate* on a unit basis. Reject costs were not considered, as methods of evaluating them differed widely between companies. Rework time was considered as the rework share of the total working time, with a weighting of 15 per cent. No cost parameter was calculated because of the above evaluation problems.

As well as these quality indicators, a full understanding of quality also has to consider the quality of the company, i.e., the professionalism of interactions within the company and relations with customers and suppliers. This dimension of quality was not included in the quantitative part of the study because of the lack of objective benchmarks.

The quality ranking of the participating companies was calculated according to their PQI and DQI values (the PQI calculations took into consideration the different requirements and levels of difficulty of various production processes and products (e.g., processing glass as opposed to machining mechanical

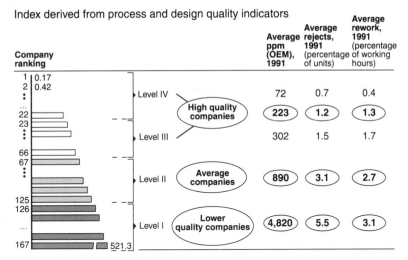

Fig. 1.10 *Quality indicators by quality levels*

components). The outcome was four groups of companies ranked according to their quality performance, as illustrated in Figure 1.10 according to the defect rate in ppm, reject rate, and reworking.

To identify the *success factors*, quality management approaches in the 'quality companies' (levels III and IV) and 'lower quality companies' (level I) were then examined. Companies with average quality (level II) served, so to speak, as a 'statistical buffer'. This method of analysis ensured that the quality management procedures had a direct correlation with quality performance in each case. The quality approaches used only by quality companies (levels III and IV), or used more by quality companies than by lower quality companies, must therefore be considered the success factors.

✳　　✳　　✳

The conclusions from the long-term study have been confirmed in many discussions with participants from industry, academia, and management consultancy. A number of publicly available individual examples further support the observed correlation of behaviour with quality success or failure.

2 Strategy and Organization: Think Quality

Eight out of ten 'quality' campaigns undertaken by companies come to nothing or, at best, produce unsatisfactory results for their initiators. The reasons behind this are just the same as those that cause corporate strategies to fail: a hostile external environment accounts for the failure in no more than a quarter of all cases. Often, corporate and quality strategies get in each other's way. Or – most typically – the organization is quite simply not in a position to internalize the new strategy and therefore to implement it on a day-to-day basis. Top quality has to be firmly embedded in a flexible, fast-learning, high-performance organization.

When the brakes are applied, the driver's head has to be jerked back slightly – then he or she perceives the brakes as 'good'. Conversely: the brakes are 'bad' if the head is thrown up. Car designers are aware of this subjective 'braking sensation' from statistical surveys, and they approach their work with this in mind. In contrast, manufacturers of brake callipers and linings have remained largely indifferent to it, as it does not really matter to their design. Unless, of course, they decide to reposition themselves as suppliers of braking *systems*. Once they take that decision, the interaction of their own system with chassis and bodywork becomes part of their quality strategy.

As suppliers of brake parts, these manufacturers selected only raw materials and individual parts, strictly on the grounds of price and adherence to simple quality standards. As suppliers of systems, they have be able to integrate outside components and sub-systems into a total system, for which they will have to take responsibility. Their own supplier management will have to look far more closely at the products and production processes of their sub-suppliers. In product design, they will have to coordinate with the chassis manufacturers – i.e., the OEM and possibly another system supplier as well – and, of course, they will have to understand the end customer. The 'OEM' as customer, previously satisfied merely with delivery of good quality brake callipers or linings, now also expects minimization of braking noise or optimization of the braking sensation, for example. If the supplier's quality strategy is not equal to this challenge, then its strategic reorientation will fail.

Corporate strategy considerations can be reduced to two key questions: How do we want to compete? and Where do we want to compete? For a German component manufacturer, the 'how' question might be: 'Should our competitive difference be cost leadership or superior product concepts? Should we remain component suppliers – and perhaps become a sub-supplier to a system supplier – or should we include more value added stages and development work in our business, and market ourselves as a system supplier?' The 'where' might be: 'In future, should we stay with Germany, or should we make a greater effort to sell our products on other European markets, or even go global?'

The ensuing moves on the 'strategic game board' (Figure 2.1) will invariably have implications for the company's quality strategy, whether on the 'how' axis, as in the brake manufacturer's case, or on the 'where' axis. The decision to become a system manufacturer, for example, which is probably the most frequent 'how to compete?'

Corporate strategy options for an automotive supplier

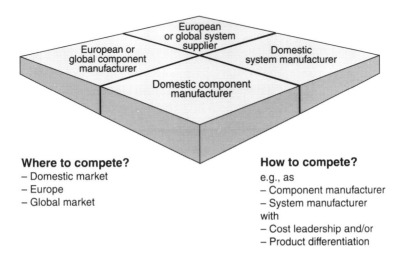

Fig. 2.1 *Strategic game board*

consideration in the automotive supply industry today, also surfaces a whole range of questions relating to quality requirements and capabilities (see 'How to Compete' on pp. 53–4). The same applies to the 'where' axis, if new quality requirements or a completely different quality assurance system are needed to capture new markets. Japanese suppliers, for example, see the introduction of the ISO 9000 system primarily as an additional entry barrier to the European market, above all because of what they see as excessive documentation.

The right quality strategy is therefore an absolutely essential prerequisite for a successful business strategy. However, merely deciding to take action in either area is of little use, unless the organization is in a position to carry them out. This was what the majority of participants in the long-term study found to be the greatest hurdle. Eighty per cent of them had already abandoned a quality improvement programme or were dissatisfied with the results achieved. Although the programmes had given employees some further training and made them aware of the importance of quality, measured by hard quality ratios the projects had to be labelled as failures.

On closer inspection, the failures could in the main be traced back to similar causes (see Chapter 6, 'The Road to Quality'):

- *Lack of direction*: If you don't know where you are heading, only chance will put you on the right road. Credible strategic objectives can only be set by top management. However, their targets are often not concrete enough for assembly workers, sales staff or development engineers. Or input rather than output ratios are measured: instead of registering improvements at the customer and over the entire value chain, records show only how many teams are taking part, how many meetings are held, and how many ideas are collected. While this approach may well ensure general enthusiasm at the outset, the tangible results are more sobering. Finally, top management often confines itself to firing the starting pistol, without actively contributing to the implementation of the programme.
- *Underskilling of the workforce*: 'Not another staff exercise!' – the value of quality programmes often escapes employees, particularly if they have no mastery of the quality improvement tools or their effects, and if they also do not know how what they are doing is contributing to the success of the company. In these

circumstances, a drastic improvement in quality seems neither very realistic nor likely to bring about a sustained improvement in competitive position. They equate higher customer value with over-engineering, and consider 'zero defects process' as inconceivable – especially one with lower costs into the bargain.

- *Organizational barriers*: Even highly motivated staff lose their enthusiasm in the jungle of a bureaucratic organization. Change processes often fail because an excess of hierarchy and functional interfaces makes decision paths too long. And one should not underestimate the barriers that are sometimes erected in decentralized production areas when a highly centralized quality management function sets out to make changes commando style.

Top companies overcome these problems. They have moved the traditionally functional organization forward in three dimensions: they set stimulating quality objectives 'top-down'; they mobilize the will and the skill of employees toward continuous improvements 'bottom-up'; and, with simple, targeted structures and processes, they create the organizational conditions for flexibility and independent initiative.

STIMULATING OBJECTIVES

A quality strategy will only be realized if corporate management gives it explicit support. It therefore cannot be left solely to the Quality Assurance Manager to decide on this strategy. Accordingly, top management in quality companies is much more involved in developing the quality strategy, and is more likely to play an active role in its implementation (Figure 2.2).

Here, commitment does not mean just signing an information sheet to be hung on the noticeboard, but active participation in an ongoing process. At top companies, members of the top management team give more than moral support: they often take part in working sessions to keep abreast of individual topics and contribute to concrete solutions. And they realize that staff are unlikely to make a firm commitment to strategic objectives which they themselves have not understood clearly and accepted. Therefore, excellent companies take communication of the strategy just as seriously as its development.

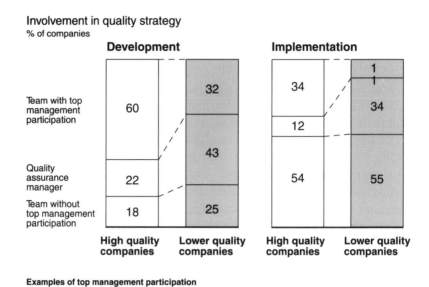

Fig. 2.2 *Quality on the top management agenda*

When setting objectives, quality companies differ from others mainly in two points: They set their standards at as high a level of aspiration as possible to stimulate constant efforts. But at the same time, they ensure that they can be implemented by 'operationalizing' the objectives into concrete tasks on a time scale that staff can relate to.

High Level of Aspiration

'So you think 99.9 per cent is good enough? Just 0.1 per cent error means no fresh water for one hour a month or one crash landing per day at Frankfurt Airport.' This was the striking example used by one top company from the long-term study to promote the zero defects objective to its employees. This is the usual objective set by level III and IV companies for process quality, which after all can be definitively measured. Being aware that every defect is one too many keeps the will for continuous improvement alive.

High objectives, signalling a new start, are essential to focus and mobilize staff. If the defined objective is set too low, resulting in constant modifications or even a change of direction, management will soon lose credibility. Therefore, quality companies steer by global 'best practice', or set ideal figures beyond it. The most effective landmarks lie outside their own organization; for example: 'We want to be OEM XY's best supplier in five years', or: 'We want to be leaders in technology Z by the year Y.'

The high level of aspiration implies that the quality strategy of top quality companies is designed for prevention rather than cure. This can be expressed in hard figures. One quarter of all quality costs goes toward fault prevention – particularly toward preventive quality assurance tools in R&D; in companies of lower quality the amount is only 13 per cent (Figure 2.3). With this focus on prevention, successful companies achieve lower quality costs, namely 3.4 per cent instead of 5.1 per cent of sales. (At many lower quality companies, there was no quality cost accounting – the actual cost of quality may therefore be even higher, possibly around 7 or 8 per cent.)

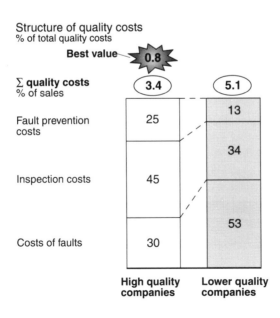

Fig. 2.3 *Quality companies invest in prevention*

Clear Tasks and Time-scale

Setting the strategic direction and defining high quality objectives are the first steps. But even convincingly formulated and communicated objectives are of little use if the individual does not know what personal contribution he or she can make.

Quality companies are therefore especially thorough in the next step: the medium-term objective, formulated for the entire company, is detailed for each function/department and for each hierarchical level, and is broken down into concrete sub-objectives. Whether these are met is then systematically tracked. Right through to the employee on the shop floor, each individual knows exactly what (clearly measurable) target he has to achieve by when, how this target fits into the overriding objectives, and where he stands at present.

Objectives for all functions and levels
Quality targets for production are set in practically every company nowadays. However, this still does not apply in research, development, service or purchasing. Here, quality companies differ considerably from the others – they formulate their quality targets for the *entire* business system (Figure 2.4).

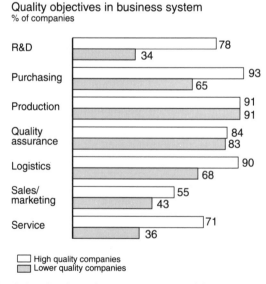

Fig. 2.4 *Quality objectives over total business system*

For example, this is what one Japanese supplier does:

- The *marketing department* has recently been given the target of making the end customer's requirements transparent and formulating them as concrete requirements for QFD analysis.
- In *research and development*, the product developers are set targets for the stability of the production processes which will later be used to manufacture the parts they design; the figures have to be confirmed by colleagues in production or in test or pilot series.
- The aim of the *purchasing department* is to push the defect rate (ppm rate) of sourced parts down below a certain percentage, possibly by setting different priorities per supplier group.
- The *customer service department* must process customer complaints within twelve hours and ensure satisfying solutions.
- The *sales department* is obliged to measure customer satisfaction at the OEM continuously, and also to collect information about OEM development projects as early as the concept stage, so that it can pick up on opportunities for its own participation in good time.

At the various hierarchical levels, the 'tailored' objectives might, for example, be as follows:

- The *production manager* is responsible for halving the ppm rate for outbound goods; the individual *works managers* are set the same target for their own units.
- The *cost centre managers* in the production function are given targets for ppm rates and also for rework and reject rates; the same applies to the *teams* of individual production groups.

Personalized responsibility is fundamental here. In quality companies, the objectives are assigned to names in 56 per cent of cases all the way to floor supervisor levels and in 46 per cent right through to employees on the factory floor. At lower quality companies, this figure falls to only 20 per cent that assign responsibility at individual floor supervisor level, and 10 per cent that vest such power in individual employees on the factory floor (Figure 2.5).

This kind of differentiated system of objectives for all functions and levels would represent a huge step forward for companies at quality level II. However, companies at quality level IV are already thinking beyond this: they try to set targets for entire process chains in a process-oriented organization (see pp. 46–52, 'Orientation to processes').

Operationalization of quality objectives
% of companies

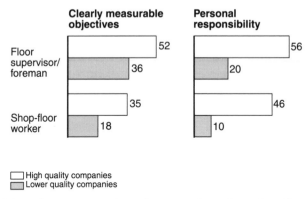

Fig. 2.5 *Short-term quality objectives through to shop-floor level*

Track progress
ABB bóss Percy Barnevik is credited with the statement: 'Only things
that are measured actually get done.' This certainly does not refer to
pure 'top down' control; it is rather that each individual who can
identify with a target, and wants to achieve it, needs information about
the remaining gap to guide his actions in the right direction and, where
necessary, to correct them. Therefore, the members of a production
team aiming to halve the ppm rate of finished products depend on
constant feedback about the current figures, perhaps via a noticeboard
at the workplace (see Chapter 4, 'The Production Process').

If targets are longer term, then 'milestones' must be set over the
period in question. This applies, for example, to R&D, with its very
long time horizons. One manager recently made this clear with a vivid
example: in the Stone Age, man's time horizon covered the period
between hunts – when he had caught game and had enough to eat
then he was satisfied for a while; shortly before the food was finished
he went out again to catch some more. The transition to farming –
and thus from a nomadic to a settled form of existence – was very
difficult for man, partly because, even in the best case, the period
between sowing and harvest was going to be three to six months.

Staff in the development department are often required to work
toward targets which lie three, four or even six years on – and to
remain highly motivated throughout. Without positive feedback,

perhaps at the end of each phase, the momentum can scarcely be sustained.

MOBILIZING EMPLOYEES

One company introduced 'Wanted'-type posters into its offices and factories: 'This is the person most important to the quality of our company'; below the text is a mirror. In another company, large posters remind each employee of the requirements of the next department down the line: 'If you've no internal customers, you're not needed.'

Such campaigns ensure the right attention level. However, on their own they would probably achieve little. Quality companies therefore combine them with carefully planned programmes that strengthen the 'will' and 'skill' of employees, i.e., simultaneously arouse enthusiasm and impart skills (Figure 2.6). Most of us would acknowledge, looking back on our schooldays, that only a combination of the two achieves results: we were always best at the subjects we were most interested in, and where we had excellent teachers who could put the material across in a well structured, logical, and attractive way.

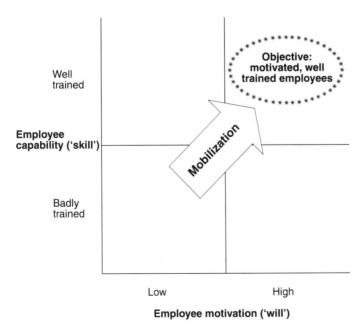

Fig. 2.6 *Mobilizing skill and will*

Enabling 'Skill'

Quality companies invest considerably more in staff training. They spend an average of US$470 per capita per year on training pro-grammes – compared to only $180 at companies with lower quality. This ratio is informative in itself. However, more significant are the areas of training and the methods involved at the quality companies; along with intensive training in quality tools, informal approaches which further develop the quality and cost awareness of employees play an important role:

Training in quality tools

One manager trying to get an overview counted approximately 200 quality tools (admittedly including some variants) in the relevant literature. Faced with an abundance of terms like Pareto diagram, Fishbone diagram (cause–effect diagram), SPC, Taguchi or Quality Function Deployment he drew a sobering balance: assuming a developer has to master 20 to 30 tools, and assuming an average training period of at least three days for each tool, then every developer would have to be trained for about 60 to 90 days. If we include follow-up training, which, according to experts, is needed six months or at the latest one year later, then the average time spent on training would be in the region of 140 days – just to introduce these tools. To shunt employees through university-style seminars about all of them therefore seems rather pointless – especially since they need some of the information so rarely that, when the time comes to use it, it has been long forgotten.

Quality companies aim for a small number of tools which are really relevant to the team, and hold the appropriate training during the tool's actual introduction phase. Fundamental to the selection is that each individual employee learns exactly the skills he or she needs to use all the time in his/her day-to-day work.

The top companies heed Confucius: 'I forget what I hear, I remember what I see; I truly understand what I do.' Consequently, the focal point of the training method is 'learning by doing'. This is why some top companies take a conscious decision to have the diagrams relating to statistical process control (see Appendix A, 'Top Quality Tools') compiled by hand by the employees working on the machine instead of entirely by computer. The workers use the techniques routinely, get to know them and accept them. And one of the most important factors is their sense of achievement when consistent application of the techniques produces better results.

To disseminate the quality tools further after the introductory phase, successful companies use selected employees who are intensively trained for the purpose and who function as 'missionaries' or 'know-how centres': they look at which workplaces could usefully employ particular tools, and train the employees concerned in applying them. And when they do that, the rule is 'the closer to the application the better'. A German electronics company therefore had two staff from its production function trained as quality trainers – this ensured that production personnel were trained in the application of quality tools in 'their own language'.

Sharpening quality and cost consciousness

An engine manufacturer shows his production team very graphically the additional costs that arise through quality problems – e.g., rejects. There is a display in the hall showing that a casting of a cylinder head costs DM120; next to this is the scrap value of the same part – DM20. This makes it clear: 'For every badly cut cylinder head, a DM100 note lands in the garbage can.' In other companies there are display cases containing consumables such as gloves or cloths or small tools such as hammers or screwdrivers, complete with their prices. This is also a continual reminder to avoid waste. Quality for these companies means not only the quality of the end product, but also the quality of the production process.

Some suppliers confront their staff with customer reactions to quality defects: parts that customers have complained about are displayed next to the 'culprit' production machines, stating the fault. At other companies there are notice boards – sometimes actually at the relevant workstation – with customer letters containing either praise or complaints.

Many are also starting to send production staff to the customer in problem cases. An Italian manufacturer of plastic parts explains why he consistently employs this policy: it is not so concerned about having the problem parts fixed on site; instead it is more important that the production employee is familiar with 'his' customer's production process and learns to understand the customer's problems from personal experience. This applies similarly to 'internal customers' – the better an employee understands the requirements of the next stage in the work process, the more he can contribute to improving the entire process (see Chapter 4, 'The Production Process').

Finally, the good companies do not confine themselves to work-place- and function-specific messages, but also inform their employees about general company and market information. Here, too, it is not the amount of information that counts – indeed, too much can be counter-productive – but the right choice and the right form of display. Information about the market share of the company or about the large orders won or lost from OEMs displayed graphically on information boards in the factory hall create awareness amongst all employees that the company does not have a licence to print money, but has to earn it from the customer against tough competition – that, ultimately, it is the customer who pays the wages! Individual companies have very creative ways of doing this; one German tyre manufacturer uses the reverse side of wage slips to inform its employees regularly about current quality issues and company data.

Mobilize the 'Will'

Employees who come to work reluctantly or who have inwardly handed in their notice are every company's nightmare. The mountains of books about incentive systems testify to this. Quality companies make a conscious and differentiated effort to deal with this problem, as the following impressions from the long-term study and consultancy projects show.

Money has only limited power as an incentive, provided that a reasonable salary level can be earned. This was confirmed by the study. It is particularly doubtful whether a company's quality standard can be improved by cash bonuses: if staff are not interested in earning high bonuses, producing poorer quality will not have much impact on their income – or in any case, too little to give quality the priority it should have.

Something very similar applies to absolute output targets. It is like the REFA piece rate system, where the maximum bonus is awarded for a performance level of 140 per cent measured by the target time: a 'quality target' is an excellent way of achieving a one-off jump in performance. But it is less appropriate as an incentive for constant improvements, as the system offers no rewards for performance better than the target. A bonus system will therefore contribute little to the process of continuous improvement that marks a genuine quality company.

The strongest performance motivator, according to all the studies, is personal recognition and approval: although fair pay is a basic requirement of employee satisfaction, pride in an achievement and perceived acknowledgement of it are the fundamental incentives for making improvements. Similarly, the wish not to be disapproved of by others is the strongest motivator for avoiding under-achievement.

This is why quality companies instal an integrated system of incentives and – indirectly – pressure to perform: by giving recognition and strengthening the employee's identification with his own product they promote employees' pride in their work; forming teams and promoting internal competition in and between teams brings a certain group pressure to bear as well as a sense of belonging to a unit.

Recognition
In many hotels or fast food restaurants there are noticeboards where the most enthusiastic or friendly employee of the month is depicted and mentioned by name. Quality companies have adopted this approach and use it to distinguish employees who, for example, have contributed a good idea towards eliminating quality problems. The works manager gives them a small gift, their picture appears in the works paper. The bottleneck with this kind of recognition is that it can only be given to small number of employees – the majority of the staff have to be reached by other means.

Encouragement of 'pride of ownership'
During discussions at top quality companies, employees always remarked with pride that the control panel or the fuel injection pump for car XY originated from them. This identification with the product is naturally easier to create at the OEM, where the whole car is made; but it can also be achieved by the component manufacturer who knows how to associate its own product with the end product, and how to recognize the individual's contribution to this achievement. For example, it helps to show the function of the components in a display car in the factory. One cable harness manufacturer 'sliced open' a chassis to show the course and the technical interfaces of the finished cable harnesses.

Integration in groups
Quality companies rely very heavily on group structures: more than half of them have organized their production into self-managing

teams with broadly defined responsibilities such as setup, maintenance, and quality assurance. In our opinion, the fact that the
employees' skills complement each other in a group is a secondary
aspect. The separation of the individual from the anonymous mass
and his integration into a considerably smaller community, where he
is unmistakably of decisive importance, is more important. The
encouragement of colleagues ('We need you') and mutual and
personal responsibility are the actual performance drivers.

Quality circles are used in 87 per cent of top companies, as
compared to only 45 per cent of weaker companies. The differences
in the scope of commitment and output are more drastic still: at top
companies, some 56 per cent of production staff are organized in
quality circles; at the poorer companies it is only 9 per cent. The good
companies produce an average of 90 suggestions per circle per year;
at lower quality companies the figure is all of 11. More extreme still –
by a factor of more than 1:100 – are the differences between the
financial impact of the suggestions (see Chapter 5, 'Japan, Europe
and the US').

Promotion of internal competition
Quality companies have often institutionalized group pressure as the
counterpart to the sense of belonging by making transparent the
contribution of the group to total corporate performance, and, if
possible, the contribution of the individual to the group's performance as well. At one Japanese transplant in England, there are
noticeboards at each group workstation displaying the performance
of the group concerned for all to see (Figure 2.7): a table shows
the development of the group's ppm rate and; directly next to this the
development of corporate performance is shown. The noticeboards
also show the skill profile of the individual members – what jobs each
individual can handle – and a further table gives information on each
employee's attendance record.

Understandably, it is impossible to transpose every detail to a
different environment. German industrial law, for example, would
not allow personal attendance rates to be publicly available. The
basic idea, however – institutionalization of a kind of sporting
competition – can undoubtedly be adopted. For example, individual
performances might be only discussed within the team, but all the
more frankly and constructively for that.

Performance chart

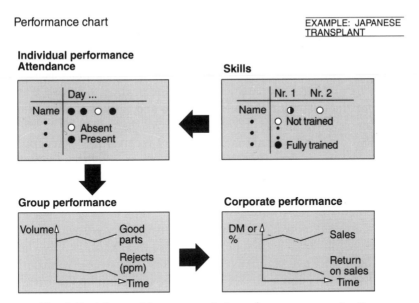

Fig. 2.7 *'Competitive pressure' through open communication*

The common argument that such approaches are bound up inextricably with the Japanese mentality is not true, at all events – for example, there was only one single Japanese employee in the English transplant (see Chapter 5, 'Japan, Europe, and the US'). And one German tyre manufacturer provides a successful example of how the principle of the sports competition can also be used across all teams: a 'league table' of all the teams in order of their quality ratios hangs on its wall.

ORGANIZATION BY SHORT PATHS

Suppose that a highly motivated employee is trained in problem-solving skills, and now finds a recurrent quality problem in his working environment. As he knows the material in detail, he has an idea on how to solve it: a minor tool alteration would eliminate its source.

In traditionally organized companies, the process would then go as follows. The employee tells his floor supervisor, who passes on the improvement suggestion to his colleague in toolmaking. As he cannot take sole responsibility for the alteration, he goes to the planning department. The employee there who receives the suggestion cannot make the decision and informs his superior. The head of the planning department covers himself by asking around his colleagues in the R&D and sales departments. The sales director gives the salesperson responsible the task of discussing the change with the customer's purchasing and R&D departments when he next calls, in two weeks. Assuming the customer responds quickly and authorizes the altera-tion after one week, the information flow then goes into reverse internally, and the toolmaking department receives the order for the change about ten weeks after the idea was first conceived (Figure 2.8). In the meantime, many containers' worth of rejects have been produced, and the worker will perhaps be less inclined to suggest improvements in the future.

Not that that consultation with the R&D department and the customer would have been superfluous – all this specialist knowledge has to feed into a tool change if mistakes are to be avoided. But whether the decision process has to be so complex is open to question. Feedback loops in traditionally organized companies are typically too long and too sequential, technical competence and decision-making power too fragmented, and hierarchies too deep. What took ten weeks in our example should be possible in just a few days by combining specialist and decision-making competence, pro-vided that the customer agrees quickly.

And as anyone familiar with large organizations knows: our worker could have fared worse. In companies with a strongly functional organization he would probably have received a discreet hint from a superior to get on with his own job and leave improving tools to the toolmaking department – he is, after all, only paid for churning out volume. In this extreme case the good idea would have got stuck in the organizational channels. At this type of company, all attempts at setting and operationalizing objectives, upskilling and motivating employees can be written off in advance.

Problems of this kind are rare in quality companies, as they have systematically broken down the organizational barriers – hierarchy, functional orientation, and excessive centralization.

Flat Hierarchy

The quality companies from the long-term study stand out from the other participants because of their leaner organization: on average,

Decision-making paths for tool alterations

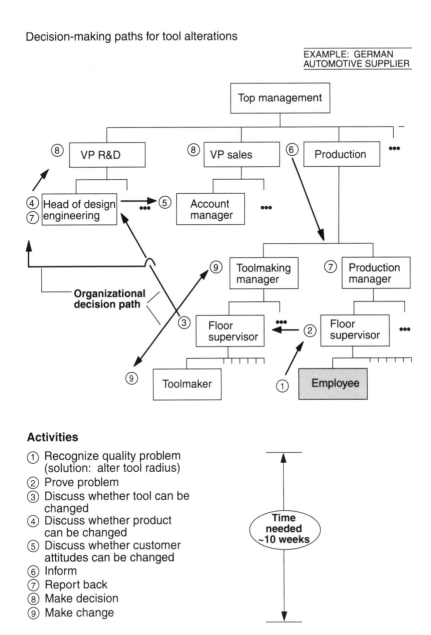

Activities

1. Recognize quality problem (solution: alter tool radius)
2. Prove problem
3. Discuss whether tool can be changed
4. Discuss whether product can be changed
5. Discuss whether customer attitudes can be changed
6. Inform
7. Report back
8. Make decision
9. Make change

Fig. 2.8 *Bureaucracy – a brake on motivation*

Vertical organization (for comparable sizes of company)

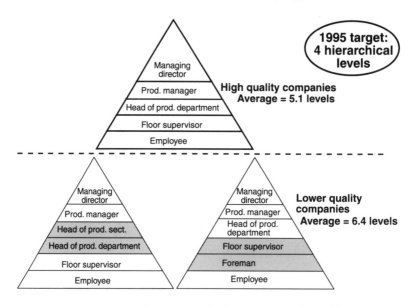

Fig. 2.9 *Quality companies have flatter hierarchies*

with 5.1 hierarchical levels, they have one level less – usually due to merging the group manager and department manager levels, or the floor supervisor and foreman levels (Figure 2.9). In the longer term they want to shrink further to four levels.[1] (The perhaps surprisingly small difference of only one hierarchical level is explained by the fact that Japanese companies – exemplary in many other areas – are still relatively hierarchically organized and therefore raised the average of levels III and IV in our analysis.)

By streamlining their hierarchies, quality companies also achieve completely new reporting structures: the senior ranks are given wider spans of control (on average five to six people instead of three to four); the dubious practice of one-to-one and one-to-two subordination in particular is thus avoided. At the base, conversely, spans of control are smaller than in companies of lesser quality (average of 14 to 19) – this creates tighter on-site management, more personal contact, and greater transparency (Figure 2.10).

---

[1] Basis is always a company of average size, i.e., with approximately 800 employees.

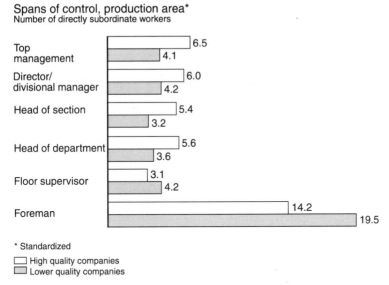

Spans of control, production area*
Number of directly subordinate workers

Top management: 6.5 / 4.1

Director/ divisional manager: 6.0 / 4.2

Head of section: 5.4 / 3.2

Head of department: 5.6 / 3.6

Floor supervisor: 3.1 / 4.2

Foreman: 14.2 / 19.5

* Standardized

☐ High quality companies
▨ Lower quality companies

Fig. 2.10 *Wider spans of control in management, tighter control on the shop floor*

One UK automotive industry supplier has just completed this streamlining process. Six years ago the company still had eight hierarchical levels and was very similar to the example mentioned earlier; lack of flexibility and preoccupation with internal affairs were an increasing irritation to customers. After the company was taken over by a foreign investor the turnaround was achieved: in four years the traditional structure was transformed into an efficient 'problem-solving organization' with only five hierarchical levels. Team organization took the place of the floor supervisor/foreman/employee structure; middle management – traditionally structured by functions and areas of responsibility – was changed into a cost and profit centre-based organization. The number of managers in production dropped accordingly from 168 to 98 (Figure 2.11).

The results speak for themselves: now almost 80 per cent, as opposed to 40 per cent previously, of all suggestions for improvements are implemented; the time for evaluation of the suggestions has been reduced to a third. In addition, employees say that the working atmosphere between management and operative levels has improved noticeably.

The immense effort has obviously been worthwhile. However, this example also demonstrates what you have to be prepared for in an

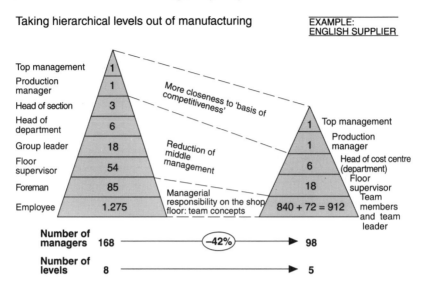

Fig. 2.11　*From traditional structure to problem-solving organization*

organizational renewal of this kind. First, the change process needs to be clearly driven from the top; in this case the takeover by the foreign investor spurred it on. Second, the change process takes time. Necessary employee skills have to be developed from scratch in some cases – a technically skilled section manager is often a long way from being an entrepreneurial profit center manager. The previous management may even have to be supplemented by outside hires. A Taylorist and autocratically inclined middle management may be the fundamental block to the change process. Moreover, demotivation is most likely in this area, as it is here that most jobs are lost and the most radical rethink is needed. Finally, the following success factors have to be added: the solidarity of the management, intense communication with the staff (to convince them of the competitive necessity), and top management's will to put the project in place.

Orientation to Processes

Quality companies are tackling the other major barrier to progress just as resolutely as the excess of hierarchy: the vertical organization, structured by functional criteria. This is giving way to a system of

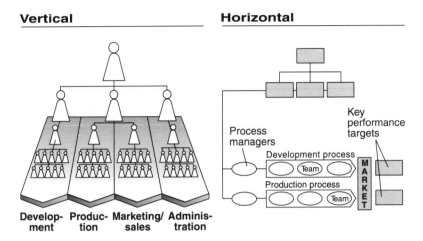

Vertical	Horizontal

Fig. 2.12 *Horizontal instead of vertical organization*

organization that is horizontally structured according to the company's most important, customer-oriented value adding activities – or 'core processes' (Figure 2.12).

The basic idea is that a core process of this kind should ideally be generated by one source – functional authority and execution would be agreed upon and there would be no decision-making or communication problems. In the real world the 'single source' – the 'process owner' – can only be a group of people. In contrast to the classical functions, it has to produce a whole bundle of complementary skills so that it can take full responsibility for a core process in the company – for example, the entire manufacturing process from receipt of the raw materials to delivery of the finished product to the customer.

What a core process consists of can differ from company to company, and even more so from industry to industry. Defining these processes correctly is decisive for success in the automotive supply industry as in others. And it is no less important to find the optimum design for the remaining interfaces between these processes and to allocate responsibility correctly.

Defining the core processes
By definition, a core process consists of tasks which form the core of the business, are decisive for its success, and serve customer satisfaction in the broadest sense. Which activities these are for individual

automotive suppliers depends – as shown – on their contribution to
R&D for the OEM: at one extreme, the company that works to the
blueprints of the OEM or a design company and *produces* parts as an
'extended workbench'; at the other, the manufacturer with its own
development competence – which thus offers comprehensive technical
solutions – for a component or a system (and which sometimes
subcontracts parts of its manufacturing).

On this basis, the R&D and production processes can be derived as
two core processes of the supply industry. Added to this is the fact
that the two processes pursue different, clearly definable objectives:
the primary aim of the *production process* is to ensure that the
required quality is achieved at the lowest possible cost. The primary
function of the *R&D process* is to ensure that a product is generated
which offers the customer – not only the OEM, but in particular the
driver as the end customer – a benefit and therefore creates a demand
for this particular product.

Production and R&D processes can only achieve their objectives if
both the customer and sub-suppliers are fully-fledged 'process stages'
– neither value nor cost can be optimized without consulting their
needs and know-how. It is here that the process-oriented mentality
differs from the functional approach, in which production and R&D
are treated as purely in-house units.

The functional structure too, its advocates claim, is always much
concerned with further developments to benefit the customer and
investment in rationalization to reduce production costs; it is just that
coordination procedures are needed where functions intersect. However, it is precisely these coordination processes and particularly the
time they take that are fatal. They make the conventional form of
organization too sluggish for the development times, the speed of
improvement, and above all the speed of learning required today.

*Management of the interfaces between the R&D and production
processes*
Even in an organization totally structured by the two core processes,
one important interface remains. The development process and the
production process themselves do not, of course, operate completely
independently of one another: it is a known fact that about 80 per
cent of downstream production costs are already decided in R&D.
And an excellent quality standard as early as the pilot phase of a new
product can only be achieved by good coordination between product
design and production ('robust design').

So even the most up-to-date, process-oriented organization cannot manage without coordination processes. In quality companies, however, coordination does not turn into a brake on efficiency and progress. These companies involve the production process experts in every new development project at an early stage (see Chapter 3, 'The R&D Process').

These companies have developed staff rotation into an extremely effective tool for interface management. Japanese companies, in particular, consistently start new development engineers off in the production department. Staff who know the production process personally in this way will, in their later role as design engineers, be less likely to transgress against the laws of 'manufacturability', and will independently seek production-friendly solutions. As far as possible, they will also gear their new designs to the available production capabilities. This saves unnecessary investment in new plant, and by using known and controlled production processes the startup quality is improved (see Chapter 5, 'Japan, Europe and the US').

Responsibilities and yardsticks
The responsibility for the R&D core process and the production core process, which the top companies at quality level IV place in the hands of individuals teams, is dealt with in more detail in the following chapters, 'The R&D Process' and 'The Production Process'. The performance yardsticks for the managers are invariably output parameters such as ppm rate, manufacturing costs, and development time. It is here that the great advantage of process organization becomes clear: those responsible for processes possess practically all the levers they need to influence these yardsticks. There is no need for the somewhat pointless discussions about accountability, responsibility, and decision-making authority that seem common elsewhere.

Interestingly, in quality companies, independent 'quality responsibility' loses its central role. Where, as is the rule at the top companies, top management is heavily involved in setting quality targets and designing the quality strategy, and where, at the same time, inspection work and accountability for it are moved to the operational level, the traditional quality function will shrink. The quality assurance function at one large automotive manufacturer, for example, which only a few years ago was an independent division headed by a vice president and employing 10,000 people, is gradually changing into a 'lean' staff department with planning, consultancy, and training responsibilities.

The quality function is becoming a mentor, actively promoting the quality ethos in the company, responsible for building the tools, application training, and consultancy, with its only remaining independent task the performance of works and divisional quality audits. In Figure 2.13 this principle is outlined using the example of an international quality leader:

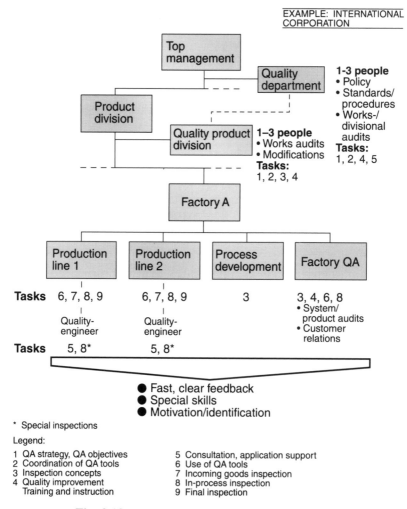

Fig. 2.13 *Many quality tasks are decentralized*

- Reporting to the board is a quality staff unit with one to three employees. This unit deals with quality strategies, quality objectives, the coordination of quality tools and inspection concepts, as well as with overriding training and consultancy.
- At the level of the (product) business units, there is a further staff unit of one to three people, which adapts these general quality targets to specific products and proposes initiatives for quality improvement for the individual business units.
- One quality assurance department per factory concentrates on performing system and product audits.
- The application of quality assurance tools, incoming goods inspection (if still needed), and final inspection are tasks for the production lines and the quality engineers assigned to them, who function as consultants and experts, i.e., do not intervene on the operational level.

Top companies need considerably fewer quality function staff in total (Figure 2.14). On average, only 4.5 per cent of their employees are entrusted with quality tasks; at poorer companies this figure is

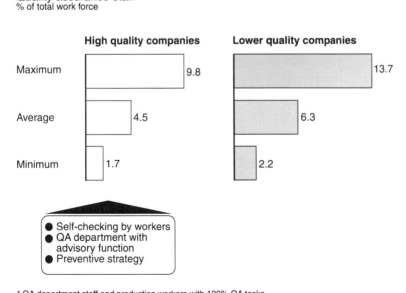

Quality assurance staff*
% of total work force

	High quality companies	Lower quality companies
Maximum	9.8	13.7
Average	4.5	6.3
Minimum	1.7	2.2

- Self-checking by workers
- QA department with advisory function
- Preventive strategy

* QA department staff and production workers with 100% QA tasks

Fig. 2.14 *Quality companies have fewer quality assurance staff*

6.3 per cent. Naturally, there are differences from segment to segment – a foundry makes different demands on quality assurance from a manufacturer of electric motors. However, if the minimum and maximum figures for comparable segments are compared, similar relationships are also found between quality companies of level III or IV and the quality laggards, i.e., level I companies.

Summary

Only organized quality is good quality – where initiatives to improve quality fail, or do not come up to expectations, the source can normally be traced to significant weaknesses in the corporate organization. And conversely, top companies at levels III and IV on the quality scale, who score big wins in cost efficiency and customer value, have provided the right organizational framework. Here the popular recipe of 'an atmosphere of quality throughout the company' is visible and effective in quite concrete actions, procedures, and structures in day-to-day activities:

- The target quality level is set by corporate management in clearly defined, challenging objectives which directly and obviously match corporate strategy. This overriding level of aspiration is broken down into comprehensible, logical individual targets for departments and hierarchical levels, and into comfortable periods of time.
- That all employees can and want to get involved with their own personal quality contribution is taken seriously in the form of the practical management tasks around 'skill and will'. A broad spectrum of formal training, information, and recognition, but also informal communication, incentives, and acknowledgements, is therefore a part of everyday life.
- Simple, clear structures ensure short paths in communication and decision making. The organizational structure follows the core processes of R&D and production, with customers and suppliers as integrated stages in the process. Spans of control are wider than usual at the top management level, and, conversely, considerably narrower at the operational level. Responsibility and decision-making authority are always vested in one person or group, and verifiable quality parameters are the performance yardstick for both management and employees.

'HOW TO COMPETE?'

Questions on Potential as a Systems Supplier

Seven questions help to decide whether entry into the systems business makes sense for an automotive industry supplier. They take into account the close relationship between corporate and quality strategy.

1. Is the planned product scope relevant to several customers, now and/or in future?

This question is important, as the specific situations of individual manufacturers sometimes lead to scopes of modules which cannot survive in the market – for example, because they are determined in individual cases by particularly complex interfaces or a large number of necessary technologies.

2. Have we mastered the necessary central R&D know-how and the necessary quality management in R&D for the targeted product scope, or can we build it?

Here the possibilities of cooperations, joint ventures, and mergers or acquisitions should be considered.

3. Have we mastered the cost- and quality-relevant processes in R&D and production?

The basic assumption here is that your own value added (or that achievable through cooperation) should, in our experience, be greater than 40 per cent in order to be able to actively influence product/process, complexity, and cost-structure potentials.

4. What kind of sub-supplier structure do we need, and how can we train sub-suppliers?

Where a major share of value added comes from sub-suppliers, the tools and skills of supplier management are also needed – above all to secure and promote the quality management competence of the sub-suppliers in both the development and production processes.

5. Are our management capacities adequate?

Companies should not underestimate the management resources needed for the internal redesign of functions such as purchasing, sales, and R&D to fit them for collaboration in joint ventures or cooperations, particularly with suppliers from the East, as well as for the design of the systems integration role.

6. Do we have sufficient financial resources?

Additional financial requirements arise particularly from up-stream and concept developments independent of the OEMs, but also from new assembly sites which are often needed to supply modules on a large scale.

7. Who are the existing or potential competitors and how can we maintain sustainable differentiation?

As with question 1, the geographic sphere of activity has to be examined. A leap into the systems business must be based on core competences superior to those of competitors – for example, in technology integration (as system leader), in supplier manage-ment, or in that knowledge of end customers which is vital to design quality.

*　　*　　*

This checklist is not intended to deter potential systems suppli-ers. It should, however, encourage them to be clear about the basic strategic issues in good time and with all due realism:

Is a position in the new target segment really more attractive than what we could achieve by improving our current segment?

3 The R&D Process: Value to the External and Internal Customer

The outstanding quality to which top companies owe their success is mostly generated right up front in the product development stage. It is here that they ensure that both the customer and their own in-house production function will have every reason to be satisfied with the product. It goes without saying that the R&D process also has to meet the highest standards; not only are its end products better than those of the competition, but the better design and process quality costs less time and money.

Top companies do not buy their quality successes by throwing money at R&D. Thanks to a leaner product range, their R&D costs are actually an average of 20 per cent less than those of lower quality companies, although they take development costs a lot less seriously as a control parameter than, for example, process stability. At the same time, the low-friction organization of the top companies allows them to complete the entire development phase up to the start of series production in about three-quarters of the time taken by lower quality companies (Figure 3.1).[1]

All this is achieved together with excellent design quality which is clearly rewarded by the market. Customers are evidently so impressed by the products that they even prefer them to competitors' offerings despite sometimes higher prices: quality companies steadily increase their market shares. They also earn higher returns than competitors, partly due to price premiums, but primarily because of cost advantages over the entire value-adding process. The foundations for this

---

[1] See also G. Rommel *et al.*, *Simplicity Wins*, Harvard Business School Press, 1995.

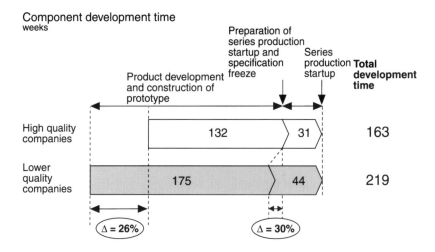

Fig. 3.1 *Faster overall development and shorter preparation time for production start-up*

are laid by high standards in the R&D process: maximum value to the customer and production-friendly 'zero defects design'.

- Top companies take the initiative in looking for a customer focus; not content merely to meet the demands of OEMs, they also help them to understand the requirements of the end customer better and to translate them into product features.
- All top companies are characterized by their continuous striving for perfection. From the early concept phase up to a short time before the start of series production, measures to prevent, identify, and eliminate faults are the order of the day.
- To fulfil customer wishes efficiently, suppliers work closely with their own sub-suppliers. Quality companies select these sub-suppliers more carefully and support them with targeted qualification measures and joint projects.

Responsibility for quality does not rest with a member of the quality assurance department, even though development teams generally include someone from QA; in top companies, the project leader is responsible for the *total* success of the project – not only cost and time, but also quality. However, he can also count on the unqualified support of top management.

MAXIMUM VALUE TO THE CUSTOMER AS GUIDING PRINCIPLE

Many automotive industry suppliers have done pretty well in the past by understanding the wishes of the OEM's development engineers precisely and converting them accurately into good technical solutions ('cooking to the recipe'). These suppliers managed an annual growth in turnover of about 6 per cent and returns of 2 per cent during the period 1987–1991 covered by the study. Although these figures were below the industry average, many companies considered them acceptable. The average was reached by those suppliers who could achieve lower defect rates and closer tolerances than the car manufacturers asked for.

However, those companies that were keen to offer their automotive manufacturer customers higher value in the face of all cost pressure fared significantly better. These suppliers earned average returns of 7.3 per cent, almost double the industry average. By bringing attractive products to the market earlier, they were not only in the position to demand price premiums, but also to convert learning-curve effects into cost advantages or other improvements, while poorer competitors were still scrabbling to come up with imitations.

One supplier, for example, developed a self-tightening hose clamp which, compared to traditional screwed models, drastically reduced the OEM's high assembly costs. The saving was a multiple of the actual cost of materials, with the result that the supplier earned far higher returns in the first years after the product's introduction than other hose clamp manufacturers. The company achieved this considering both its own manufacturing costs and the installation costs for its product when developing the product concept. This consideration also induces good suppliers to send their development engineers to visit not only their own production function, but also that of the OEM.

Superior value offered to the OEM can, then, have a significant impact on a supplier's profits. However, it seems that such an approach has hardly any effect on growth rates. Only a handful of suppliers in our study were able to seize bigger market shares from competitors with solutions aimed only at OEMs. Growing market shares went to those companies that looked beyond the automotive manufacturer to the end customer. They recognized early, often before the OEM, what the car buyer wanted, were first to the market with the right products, and were thus able to capture a monopoly position until competitors followed with similar products.

To give an example: in surveys, car drivers repeatedly criticized the noisiness of one electro-mechanical component. Most suppliers tried to convince the car-makers that the requirements were excessive and that the problem could be alleviated by putting in cladding. However, one of their number immediately set about finding a technical solution which would satisfy the end customer without incurring too much extra cost. The supplier's subsequent success showed that it had done the right thing; when it launched the improved component, it was able to snatch even models already in production away from their former suppliers. For the OEMs, which were hearing more and more customer complaints, any other modification would have required a significantly higher one-off expense than switching suppliers, which was possible in this case without modifying the technical concept of the vehicle. Suppliers who created superior customer value in this way grew during the period of the study by almost 13 per cent per annum, compared to an average of 8 per cent (Figure 3.2).

Superior end customer value is rarely created by a supplier that confines its consultations to the OEM. Quality companies identify the needs of the end customer at first hand, translate them into technical solutions and include future market trends in their evaluation of the cost/benefit ratio.

Sales return and growth as a function of different quality objectives
% p.a., 1987–1991

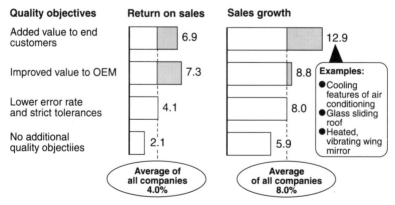

Fig. 3.2 *Market success through value to the customer*

Remove Filters on End-Customer Requirements

Its quite possible, of course, to seek ideas for added customer value by asking development engineers to assess their own product critically and creatively. But because these engineers are not objective, the right criteria probably may not even occur to them ('What does the typical end customer consider good or bad?'). Concrete and reliable information can only be gained straight from the horse's (or end customer's) mouth. What are the characteristics of the average car buyer at the top end of the medium segment, what does he use his car for, what criteria are important to him? And does this description also apply to typical buyers at the other end of the medium scale, or are their demands very different?

Standardized consumer surveys are not very suitable as a first step; the range of options that can be included on a questionnaire is typically too rigidly structured to allow improvement ideas to come to light. Joint discussion with a number of end customers has proved much more fruitful. Further ideas can be found by giving prototype end customers a sense of what it is like to use the product. A few top companies go as far as manufacturing enough prototypes to have them tested intensively by the target groups, so as to get a direct assessment of the advantages and disadvantages of the technological concept. While such methods are hardly used in Europe because of the high cost of manufacturing prototypes, they could become more important in the future as a result of rapid prototyping techniques or technological progress in the area of simulations (cyber graphics).

A counter-argument much in vogue today is that the customer does not have the vision to anticipate his own requirements accurately five years in advance, so the developer is still a much better source of information. It would undoubtedly be wrong to develop a product the consumer can visualize today; new technical solutions call for creative ideas from experts. Yet it is equally true that a consumer test in the development stage can help point the way for these creative solutions. In our experience, the most innovative companies get their ideas from the customer; their special achievement is to translate these ideas quickly and rigorously into new products.

Considering customer requirements means more than just determining technical function values: beyond functionality, *perception* plays a vital role. The best known example of this is that many consumers consider that a car door that closes with a nice solid thud is an indicator of a soundly built car. But how can a value of this kind, which cannot be measured in decibels or Newtons, be defined for the development team? To quote two of the most interesting ideas: some manufacturers get the target customer to compare a number of their own in-house solutions; others ask the target groups to assess several technical solutions offered by competitors, and take the preferred solution as a reference model.

Transform the Desirable into the Technically Feasible

Clearly defining the end customer's preferences (At what point does a fan become too loud? How important is an infinitely variable gear change rather than a stepped change?) decides many technical solutions. The project will run into trouble, however, if different customer requirements make conflicting demands on the technical concept. In these cases, it makes sense to use Quality Function Deployment (QFD) – a technique which translates the elements of value to the customer into functional characteristics and pinpoints where trade-offs have to be made (see Appendix A: 'Top Quality Tools').

One of the best documented examples of QFD is probably the assessment of different car door designs described by Hauser and Clausing in a *Harvard Business Review* article in 1988.[2] Their analysis found that two elements of customer value made conflicting demands on design; on the one hand, the door had to close as easily as possible, but on the other hand, it was considered desirable for it not to close on its own when the car was parked facing uphill. One requirement needs the weakest possible spring, the other the strongest possible spring.

This example demonstrates the strengths and weaknesses of QFD. On the one hand, it shows the developer that his concept has to reconcile two conflicting demands. On the other hand, the basic technical principle, in this case a traditional door, is not challenged as long as the strength of the spring is seen as the only variable (with folding doors, for instance, the tradeoff described would not be needed). In most cases, however, this restriction on the problem-solving scope is acceptable. In addition, because the QFD analysis reveals the limits of a technical concept, it may inspire the engineer to get round the compromise between product features by making a fundamental change in the concept.

---

[2] John R. Hauser and Don Clausing, 'House of Quality', *Harvard Business Review*, May-June 1988, pp. 63–73.

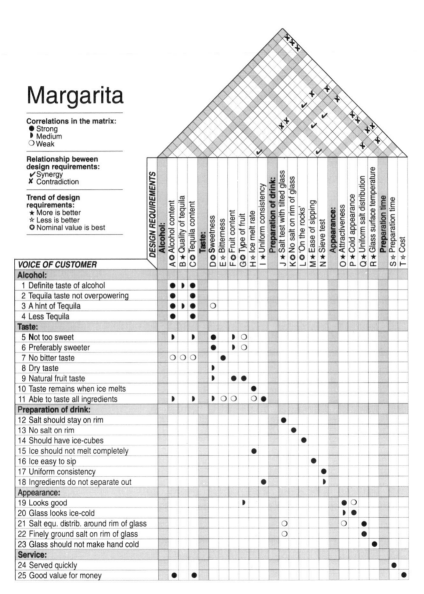

Fig. 3.3 *Example of QFD application*

The technique and detailed structure of the four-step QFD method are described very precisely in an amusing example generated at a seminar at the Massachusetts Institute of Technology: the QFD for the well-known Mexican cocktail 'Margarita', as illustrated in its core elements in Figure 3.3. In the summary diagram, also known as the 'House of Quality', the customer requirements are listed on the vertical axis, while the resulting technical design requirements are listed on the horizontal axis. The developer gets off relatively lightly if a customer benefit only matches against one technical requirement; for example, the customer requirement that 'Glass should not make hand cold' (23) requires merely the regulation of 'Glass surface temperature' (R). It is a different matter when customer requirements are in conflict, for example 'Definite taste of alcohol' combined with 'Good value for money', requirements that demand different strengths of Tequila or different proportions of Tequila in the cocktail. In this case, the optimum from the customer's point of view should be identified, or possibly various options should be offered.

Intensive use of QFD in the early stages of the development process marks quality companies out from the others. However, the approach consumes considerable resources: beginning with the customer survey, eight to twelve person weeks have to be budgeted just for the 'House of Quality' (step 1 of the method), depending on the database and product complexity. Consequently, it cannot be applied to every product. It is best to reserve QFD for basic considerations of the product philosophy and to build on these findings in later designs. It should, however, be impressed upon all developers that they should not just rely on 'gut feel' in determining value to the customer, but should get additional impressions from customer surveys and targeted analyses of the market.

Consider the Realities of Tomorrow

Everyone in the automotive and automotive supply industries knows that the issue of weight is becoming increasingly important, driven by the issue of fuel consumption. But this knowledge is not much use to the developer if lighter components are not allowed to be more expensive. It is, however, hard to tell what additional costs can be passed on to the customer.

One automotive supplier who manufactured a 10kg module had often considered various lightweight concepts, but rejected them every time as too expensive. An analysis of life-cycle costs based on various fuel price scenarios finally put the issue in perspective. To 'drag' the component 100,000 km, the driver had to buy 60 litres of fuel, corresponding to an extra DM90 at DM1.50 per litre of fuel. If the weight of the component could be reduced by one third, the driver would save DM30 over 100,000 km; he should therefore be prepared to spend DM30 more – without even taking the time value of money (interest, inflation) or ecological responsibility into account. In other words: since the component cost about DM80, a weight reduction of about 30 per cent was worth as much attention (and effort) in the medium term as a direct reduction in product cost of about 35 per cent.

Yet few suppliers will believe that they could ask the car manufacturer for a 30 per cent higher price in exchange for 30 per cent less weight and get it, and so most suppliers prefer to give priority to cutting costs. This rationale is probably still valid today. But how about in a few years' time, when the '3-litre-per-100km car' becomes a serious aim?[3] The first signs are beginning to appear that OEMs are changing their buying criteria: one seat manufacturer recently won a contract because his lightweight seat weighed about 15 per cent less, although admittedly its price was only 3 per cent more than that of competing products.

Weight is only one of many issues where totally new demands can be expected in future from the end customer, and also from the car manufacturer – which will adopt them only when the customer says so. Other examples include minimal noise, lowest possible maintenance, more comfort, better ergonomics and even greater vehicle stability. Good product concepts are not just based on the customer's requirements today; the priorities of the future have to be recognized early, extrapolated, and acted on. A supplier can only create the well-known 'temporary monopoly', during which it earns sales growth and a temporary premium on returns, by perceiving trends before competitors do.

---

[3] Tr. note: '3 litre' in terms of petrol consumption – the Germans measure consumption in petrol used per 100 km, not miles per gallon.

PERFECTION ABOVE ALL, AND IN ALL THINGS

The straightforward goal of 'zero defects' is not in itself difficult to achieve – just depend on traditional procedures and processes and gradually eliminate more and more 'old faults'. But quality companies are aware that end customer value would lose out under such an approach; such gradual improvements could hardly keep pace with the constant development of customer requirements. For this reason, top companies define quality as 'high end customer value with zero defects'.

The sales department often demands 'aggressive' concepts, but with a 'zero defects guarantee'. The most important prerequisite for this is adequate upstream development: this is where the developer can afford to 'take a chance' on concepts that might prove unworkable, but could equally well lead to a breakthrough. For this reason, quality companies safeguard their technology upstream – their development budgets allocate more than 20 per cent of the resources to preliminary development, giving it far more weight than in poorer quality companies.

These high standards are continued all through the development process. The top companies are able to prevent most faults in advance, to recognize the remaining ones at an early stage, and to correct them quickly. Design reviews, regularly performed by 70 per cent of the good but only about 30 per cent of the poorer companies, serve as a controlling tool throughout the process.

Avoid Faults

In many companies, customer preferences and demands only become gradually apparent in the course of development projects. A lot of time goes by before the realization dawns that some part 'is a bit heavy' or 'needs to be easier to adjust'. The concept is then often quickly changed, but the series production date is not. This approach can only work well if the development time allowed was overgenerous in the first place; otherwise, necessary tests will have to be shelved, making it highly unlikely that 'zero defects' will be achieved in series production. This is the classical tradeoff between quality and time. Quality companies avoid it by conducting end customer surveys and studies early and feeding the results into their production concepts.

Once this information is available, it is important to calculate design parameters correctly (metal thickness, shaft diameter, etc.), but not to knock something quickly together that later has to be optimized by trial and error. Quality companies use CAE and CAD/ CAM much more consistently, and optimize these methods on the basis of their practical project experience. Lower quality companies, on the other hand, often 'park' their 'number crunchers' in a service function far removed from actual project activities, so that they are unable to further refine their tools in response to on-the-job discoveries.

At this point, the 'internal customer' enters the picture – the production department. Development engineers in quality companies explicitly consider production's requirements from the very beginning. One hundred per cent of the good companies claim to keep a very careful watch on the process capabilities of developed products, compared to only about 70 per cent of the poorer ones (Figure 3.4). An exchange of experiences with production is a matter of course; the developer gets information from the relevant employees themselves (not from the production managers), and is familiar with the machine on which 'his' components will be made. As a result, he is not later tempted, for example, out of sheer ignorance and overcaution, to apply 'just-in-case tolerances' that cannot be realized by the available machines.

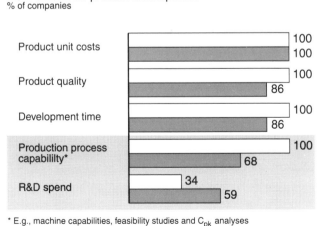

Main criteria for product development
% of companies

Product unit costs	100 / 100
Product quality	100 / 86
Development time	100 / 86
Production process capabililty*	100 / 68
R&D spend	34 / 59

* E.g., machine capabilities, feasibility studies and C_{pk} analyses

☐ High quality companies
▓ Lower quality companies

Fig. 3.4 *Process capability more important than development cost*

To keep within car manufacturers' ppm requirements, outstanding suppliers do not trust to manufacturers' reports on the first samples, which is the usual acceptance procedure in the car industry. Statistically speaking, this procedure is not particularly meaningful. The interaction of the different process tolerances may cause the product to perform perfectly on one occasion by pure chance, but it does not necessarily follow that this will also happen in subsequent series production. Quality suppliers want their development concepts to prevent downstream manufacturing faults as far as possible and create the conditions for stable processes. To this end, they make intensive use of techniques such as C_{pk} analysis, Taguchi, and Poka-Yoke. (An overview of how these approaches work and where they are used can be found in Appendix A, 'Top Quality Tools'; the following descriptions are therefore restricted to their main applications.)

C_{pk} analysis

In simple terms, the C_{pk} value reflects the ratio of design tolerance of a product parameter to its actual standard deviation in the manufacturing process, and is thus the most important parameter for robust 'design to process'. In production, quality companies track this figure almost routinely in their statistical process control (SPC). But it is also a useful means of safeguarding concepts early, in the development phase; the designers are given a minimum C_{pk} value (between 1.33 and 3.0) and product and process design are then harmonized (taking into account the essential demands of the customer) until the required C_{pk} value is sustainably achieved.

Poorer companies often argue that this kind of procedure is pointless, as process tolerances in production are sometimes not even known. On closer examination, many production processes do not actually have process capability in the true sense of the word, but are prone to stochastic fluctuations. But this attitude is wrong: 'flying blind' in the development phase is more than likely to lead to substantial faults in series production. For critical series processes at least, a C_{pk} analysis should be required for the pilot series; for new processes, this requirement should be extended even to test series (which can, for example, be limited to 50 units). Instead of a statistically meaningless first sample, a 'sample series' should be used (i.e., more than 1 unit).

With one client, we became aware during the development stage of the problem of process stability, and were informed that the process tolerances were not precisely known. Measuring systems were promptly installed and showed within four weeks that the processes were not sufficiently stable. Furthermore, even supplied components were subject to deviations far beyond acceptable tolerances. A number of suppliers were then asked to correct their production tools immediately. So the initiative that started in the development process led to a dramatic improvement in process stability, and therefore quality, in ongoing production. At the same time, of course, valuable insights were gained into how higher process stability could be achieved in new development by using design to manufacture.

Taguchi

The Taguchi Method belongs to the school of statistically planned experiments ('design of experiments'). Using a skillfully selected series of experiments, the free parameters of a product are set in such a way that disruptions in the production process cause as little variation in performance as possible, which means that the product is largely resistant to fluctuations in the process parameters ('robust').

A famous example of this method comes from Dr Taguchi himself, who saved himself the need to build a new brick kiln by systematically varying the process parameters. The uneven temperature distribution (i.e., disruption of the production process) led to substantial reject rates with the existing kiln. Instead of building a new one, Taguchi established in a series of experiments that there was a material compound (i.e., free parameter) which was significantly less sensitive (i.e., more robust) to uneven kiln temperatures. Using this new compound, he was able to significantly reduce the proportion of rejected bricks.

Careful performance of the 'design of experiments' procedures requires an investment of several person weeks. For this reason, quality companies use them very selectively. We were able to observe this when we visited the major Japanese car manufacturers in the course of a 'best practice' study. We had indicated in advance in an interview guide that we wanted to talk about the use of the Taguchi Method. To our surprise, one of the 'Big Five', particularly known for its product quality, first had to ask what the Taguchi Method was. Our contact proved to know the term 'design of experiments', however, and later, during an exchange of experiences, we were given an example of its application – but only after some research in the company.

Poka-Yoke

To realize process stability in the broader sense in production procedures as well, the product design itself must ensure that an employee cannot make any production mistakes under normal conditions. Tools such as Poka-Yoke, with 'design for assembly' (DFA) and 'design for manufacture' (DFM) as the most important versions for the development process, are useful here. The solutions are often very simple: an assembly fault might be avoided by marking or milling grooves. Since even creative people do not usually possess enough imagination to envisage every possible assembly fault, the application of this technique in the early concept phases is difficult. Experience with the current series or the analysis of competitors' products offer starting points.

Recognize Defects Early

Even the most careful fault prevention procedures using all the tools mentioned (and more) will be powerless to eliminate every defect from the development process. For this reason, quality companies make every effort to track down any remaining faults as early as possible, in order to leave enough time to find and thoroughly test alternative solutions. Here, a difference in actual 'philosophy' between high and lower-quality companies comes into play, and can be illustrated by the following simple example. Two companies were manufacturing similar products. The quality company said that it normally found about 100 faults in the first prototype, while the lower-quality company only admitted to around 10. The reason was that, in the quality company, faults were recognized at an early prototype stage, at a time when the other company did not see them as such ('You can't really know what such fine details will lead to this early').

To meet their own quality standards at this stage as well as later, top companies make more intensive and skilful use of systematic fault recognition through interfunctional 'simultaneous engineering' teams and relevant analysis techniques.

Interfunctional teams

In recent years, it has become increasingly established practice to pull together employees from upstream development, series development, production, purchasing, and controlling in so-called 'simultaneous engineering teams', in order to carry out product and process development as far as possible on a parallel, integrated basis. For the good of the whole, all the team members are expected to contribute their complementary experiences and special knowhow. This concept is known to most companies and is used by many.

But the key to success with the approach lies in how it is implemented. For example, each individual function is often required to send one employee to work full-time in the team. Solutions of this kind are often a disaster, however, because the individual functions are involved deeply in some phases of the project and hardly at all in others. In really effective teams, the project leader therefore has a contact in each individual function at all times, but the time each contributes to the team is flexible.

An even more critical factor is the dilemma of ensuring the autonomy of the teams while at the same time using the experience of the whole company. To this end, quality companies mainly use design reviews, described later, because even the most sweeping use of CAE, simulations, and other quality techniques is no substitute for the accumulated experience of the 'old guard'.

Techniques for recognizing sources of faults
Fault recognition techniques are similar to interfunctional teams in as much as their impact depends on their correct application. Quality companies use such techniques much more intensively, particularly FMEA (failure mode and effect analysis) (Figure 3.5) but also FTA (fault tree analysis). But they also select the components to be analyzed very carefully.

The practicalities of this became clear in a detailed discussion with a leading car manufacturer in Japan. The head of the current development project told us that the application of FMEA was mandatory for all new technology. When asked how many FMEAs were performed in the course of a typical project, he replied that between five and ten were normal for a completely new vehicle.

This figure seemed extremely low to us, but was soon explained: as Japanese car manufacturers always test new technologies at the upstream development stage, the corresponding FMEAs also run in this phase. The first prototype experiments are also concluded then, so that concept issues cannot arise in series development. In addition, many designs are carried over from earlier or other models, so that risks here are limited and a detailed FMEA would be far too costly. The approach is only applied to those systems representing a genuine technical innovation and therefore greater and unpredictable risks.

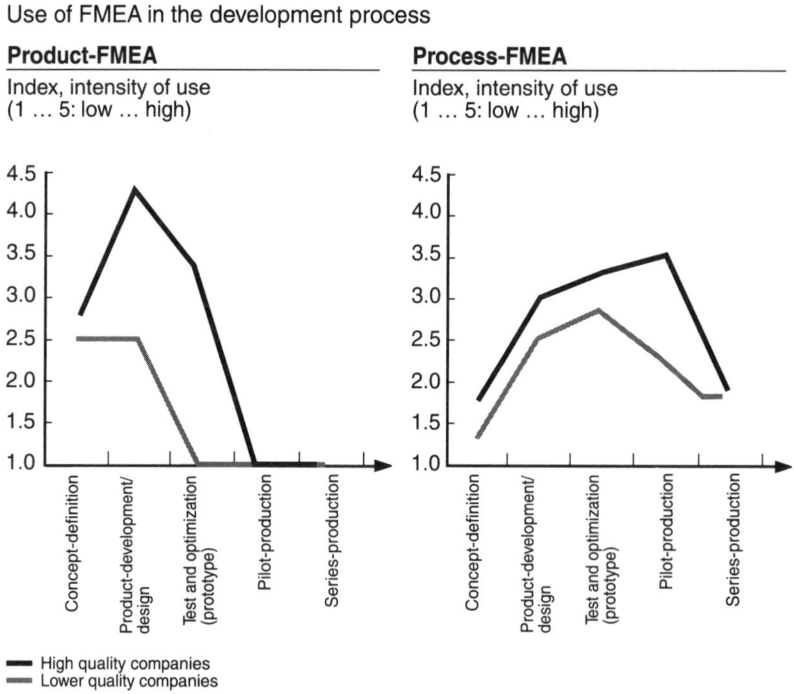

Use of FMEA in the development process

Product-FMEA

Index, intensity of use
(1 ... 5: low ... high)

Process-FMEA

Index, intensity of use
(1 ... 5: low ... high)

■ High quality companies
■ Lower quality companies

Fig. 3.5 *Quality companies have more rigorous troubleshooting*

Things are, of course, different for companies at levels I and II. They need to make more intensive use of techniques such as FMEA, not only in upstream and concept development, but also in series development. However, there is small point in the requirement often stipulated by OEMs – and often observed – that an FMEA should be carried out on all sub-assemblies; a detailed procedure yielding meaningful results is only possible at three to ten person days per instance. Instead of applying FMEA indiscriminately as a let-out, the analysis should be limited to clearly identifiable potential problem cases breaking new technological ground. And in these cases, the FMEA should be carried out all the more thoroughly and intensely.

Eliminate Mistakes Fast

Quality companies make more alterations than lower-quality companies, not fewer (Figure 3.6). This fact is often disputed, even by the quality companies themselves, since they watch their modification

Design changes in the development process

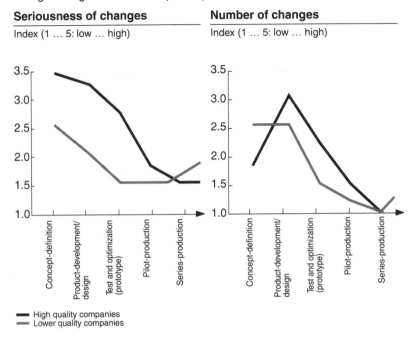

Seriousness of changes

Index (1 ... 5: low ... high)

Number of changes

Index (1 ... 5: low ... high)

- ■ High quality companies
- ▬ Lower quality companies

Fig. 3.6 *Quality companies make more changes before pilot production*

rate keenly and are always eager to reduce it. Yet it stands to reason when you consider their higher standards.

Top companies never let even tiny quality problems slip through the net in the hope that they may solve themselves at a later stage ('By the time the parts are produced, it'll have improved anyway') or because they can be easily remedied by minor corrections during the final review. They are not content to produce most of the parts for the first prototype in-house because the suppliers are not ready to deliver; nor do they accept the production of parts by auxiliary tools in the pilot series. They meticulously check at relatively short intervals whether their hard quality targets are being met, and do not wait till disaster strikes before implementing crash measures.

For the same reason, quality companies also make product alterations through to a much later stage. Other companies introduce (or at least try to introduce) a design freeze weeks before the start of series production, because they worry that every alteration could bring more quality problems in its train. Top companies, on the other hand, allow alterations right up to the last minute if a potential quality problem is discovered. The fact that they still go into series production with much better ppm rates can be attributed to more efficient execution. Top companies have developed a systematic procedure for design changes which allows them to achieve much shorter modification cycles. And anyway, these changes are not 'complete' concept revamps.

For example, a car manufacturer known for its 'zero defects' mentality found out during pilot series production that there were still three actual defects in the handbrake and that the stroke time was higher than planned. Reaction was swift; a quickly formed expert circle – the simultaneous engineering team drew on supervisors from the relevant production areas – worked out 25 improvement measures which were introduced into the assembly process within days. After a week, only one fault remained; after a further two weeks, not only were all the faults eliminated but the time needed for this assembly stage had been reduced by about 20 per cent (Figure 3.7). Of course, such excellent performance is only possible if the number and seriousness of cases is limited. This, in turn, is achieved by greater 'modification-friendliness' in the early stages of the process. Another obvious prerequisite is that the team must be autonomous and not bogged down by a constant need to ask for permission before taking action.

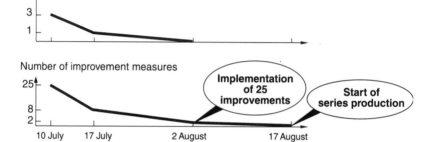

Case example: pilot production at a Japanese OEM – handbrake assembly

Fig. 3.7 *Large number of changes managed efficiently*

In one company, analyses showed that the average time taken to implement a modification was over eight months. This high average was partly due to maverick cases where complex tool modifications had taken up a huge amount of time. But the main cause was something else, as a detailed examination revealed: fault reports and change applications were just left to pile up. When dealing with changes, every developer decided for himself whether the fault in question was 'urgent' or could be corrected at a later date. Nobody systematically maintained the speed of the process. Each individual set his own priorities – one of the major causes of poor quality.

One simple measure relieved the problem considerably: each department had to state within 24 hours the deadline by which the alteration would be completed. This enabled at least an early synchronization of the important activities. A reporting system now tracks whether the answers are really being given within 24 hours, as well as monitoring the modification times proposed and what proportion of deadlines is met. As a result, every participant in the development process knows that changes are a matter to be taken seriously.

Reinforce Quality Culture with Design Reviews

Many of the quality problems occurring in a company will have been met before in a similar form but in a different place. Some of the employees could probably have picked them up at an early stage, if they had only been told. With the new – and undoubtedly correct – approach of simultaneous engineering teams, this particular phenomenon tends to occur even more often. This is because the traditional intensive quality control by the technical or functional bosses is no longer carried out, because too much interference 'from above' or 'from outside' would demote the project team to the role of a committee on functional interests, whereas its main purpose lies in crossfunctional optimization.

The downside of this independence is that managers often do not take an interest in projects until they are well down the track; by this time, the degrees of freedom for optimization are already severely restricted, and the experience available in the company is not used to the full.

Quality companies overcome this problem with design reviews, a concept used by around 70 per cent of them, but only around 30 per cent of the poorer companies. These reviews are much more than just information meetings at which the team reports on the progress of the project; they are clearly structured processes linking exchange of experience with control. It is important that the development team should never lose sight of its objective, despite the long time horizon to the start of series production and the multitude of new techniques and wealth of information that has to be taken on board during this period. That is the main purpose of the design review, assured by three features: the overall project perspective, quantified progress control, and consultation of experts at need.

Overall project perspective
The design review tracks adherence to schedule (e.g., the number of sub-suppliers decided on, the percentage of parts already manufactured using series tools). It also monitors adherence to budgets, strategic objectives (e.g., number of variants, number of individual parts, weight), the requirements of the end customer, legal regulations, and the use of quality methods (Figure 3.8). This overall perspective obviates the need to hold three separate meetings with almost the same participants: one to elaborate quality standards, one to discuss costs, and another to discuss whether the start of series production could possibly be brought forward.

Examples of topics included in design reviews

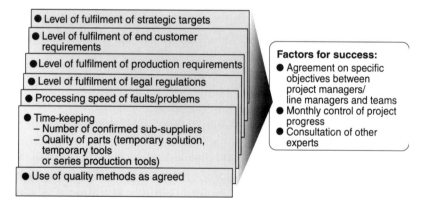

Fig. 3.8 *Extensive project support with design reviews*

Quantified progress control

The team prepares quantitative data on stated criteria to provide the meetings with a complete overview of progress. With some criteria, this is relatively simple (e.g., a plan/actual comparison of the number of parts already manufactured by series tools or a cost or weight comparison). With other criteria, such as 'Fulfilment of legal requirements', it might be, for example, that only one out of ten criteria remains to be met, but that this criterion is of outstanding importance.

In cases of this kind, the scientifically oriented developers may well try to find a correct weighting by a complex procedure such as utility value analysis. But this would involve unnecessary effort; in practice, a broad categorization is usually quite sufficient: completely fulfilled, mostly fulfilled, half fulfilled, only very partially fulfilled, or not fulfilled. If the corresponding percentages (100, 75, 50, 25, or 0 per cent) are then applied, the original 'soft' criteria are quantified. The task of the project leader is to indicate cases where critical points are not sufficiently transparent, or if individual evaluations seem more dramatic than they really are.

Of course, quantification becomes more and more important as the project progresses. In the initial phases, the design review serves more to ensure that the experience of the advisory committee is used. However, as the work advances, it becomes a controlling tool requiring careful quantification.

Expert participation

The entire procedure described above has failed in its purpose if it is guided exclusively by controllers. It is important to have the participation of other experts who can assess content and make practical suggestions about preferred technical solutions, in addition to the simultaneous engineering team and the controllers, who of course do have a right to be there. This expert committee should, naturally, include the functional managers and specialists in specific technological subjects; but experts in the various quality tools should be represented as well.

The 'quality tools expert' will, for example, explain why he or she considers a specific tool particularly promising for a specific product group, and the participants will agree, if they are convinced, that the technique should be used. In subsequent implementation, the same expert should direct and support the project team. Experience shows that the team will not easily forget the technique concerned once they have used it in their own project and grappled with its strengths and weaknesses. The design review therefore ensures that sustainable skills are built.

It goes without saying that the success of the whole process depends on the capabilities of the participants. This is particularly true for the participating experts and the Design Review Board made up of line management staff from the various departments, who check on the project's progress and make suggestions for improvements.

With its overall perspective, quantified progress control, and use of experts, the design review makes possible very sensitive quality control and thus timely initiation of corrective measures. The right supervision frequency is important in this context; there should be a gap of three, or preferably six, months between major design reviews, to keep the cost/benefit ratio at a reasonable level. However, the project team should update the key ratios every month, and pass these data on to the project leader or the responsible person on the Design Review Board; in other words, internal design reviews should be held at shorter intervals.

Beyond these groundrules, a design review must be individually tailored to every company and every project. It always takes considerable resources. Depending on the complexity of the product, a design review takes at least half a day and sometimes up to two days, and preparation can often take five to ten person days. But this time is well invested, not only because the design review drives project progress, but also because it makes the project more transparent and provides the project leader with better insights for decision making.

SUPPLIERS AS DEVELOPMENT PARTNERS

High-quality products can only be manufactured if the company uses quality suppliers and integrates them as partners in the development process. This is nothing new for most automotive industry suppliers – where their relationship with their immediate customers is concerned. But in the suppliers' relationship with their own sub-suppliers, this wisdom has, in the past, been much less widely applied. Because of enormous cost pressure, they are turning in increasing numbers to low-wage economies, where labour costs are lower by a factor of ten, but where quality standards are often not met.

Quality companies set their priorities differently. They organize supplier collaboration right from the start in such a way that their suppliers can deliver the quality required. For every scope of delivery, the method of sourcing (and thus the role of the supplier) is chosen in such a way as to open up the most attractive long-term cost and value potential. Quality companies tend to give their suppliers more responsibility for development than lower quality companies. At the same time, their narrower range of products and suppliers allows much more individual support for each supplier. Finally, quality companies consider it important to transfer their own development philosophy – especially the targeted use of preventive tools – to the suppliers and invest accordingly in suitable training programmes.

Sourcing Decisions Made on Long-Term Potential

Many automotive industry suppliers can hardly bring themselves to entrust their sub-suppliers with development tasks. But here in particular, quality companies stand out because of their greater ability to carry their actions through to their logical conclusion. With a quarter of their suppliers, they rely on full technical competence, and purchase 'black box solutions' for sub-systems;[4] if they see no opportunity for this, they usually set up joint development teams. Only a third of all top companies give suppliers specifications for their detailed engineering. But the majority of lower quality companies still control their subcontractors in this way (Figure 3.9).

It is almost impossible to agree on 'black box' sourcing with a supplier in a low-wage economy. Buying sub-systems from low-wage economies is therefore an option that has to be assessed in each case according to hard criteria. If the best solution is to be found in each case in the face of extremely divergent demands, neither the purchasing nor the development department can take the decision in isolation.

---

[4] Black box sourcing may, of course, refer to components as well as sub-systems. For the sake of simplicity, we will only discuss sub-systems here.

Type of development cooperation between suppliers and their
sub-suppliers
% of companies

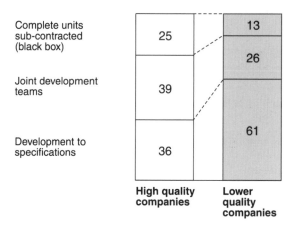

Complete units
sub-contracted
(black box)

Joint development
teams

Development to
specifications

High quality
companies

Lower
quality
companies

Fig. 3.9   *Suppliers as competent development partners*

Sub-system sourcing

Taking outsourcing of sub-systems to its logical conclusion means
placing a contract that includes every aspect of the complete unit. The
customer stipulates the desired functionality based on a list of
objectives, but does not specify how this is to be achieved technically.
The supplier also undertakes the lion's share of development. If a
sub-system, including its interfaces with other components, is properly defined (i.e., large enough to allow optimization covering more
than individual components, but still small and homogeneous enough
for appropriately qualified suppliers to be found), this decision in the
development phase can cut total costs by 30–40 per cent compared to
in-house production.

- The sub-supplier can significantly cut its internal *complexity costs*
  by using existing standard components and also by designing the
  product as simply as possible. Variants are produced so close to
  the end of the overall process that they do not put a strain on the
  entire production process and are limited to those production
  steps where they will incur only relatively low incremental costs.
  The sub-supplier will also often suggest removing certain 'exotic
  variants' from the programme completely. Its customer will be
  well advised to follow this advice or obtain the 'exotic' parts
  elsewhere (at appropriate price premiums) instead of burdening

the main sub-supplier's process with it. A 10 to 15 per cent reduction in costs can often be achieved just by optimizing complexity in this way.

- The sub-supplier can achieve a better *product/process fit* because it knows its production processes and their costs much better than the customer does. Since the sub-supplier is in control of the design concept, it will search for solutions that facilitate favourable and stable production processes. At the same time, it can make suggestions about optimizing outdated specifications. In many cases, such levers can also bring about cost cuts of 10 to 15 per cent.

- As a rule, sub-system outsourcing also brings about a *shift of vertical integration* from the direct supplier to the sub-supplier. Detailed analysis has shown that there is often a 30 per cent difference in labour costs between 'primary suppliers' (most with sales in excess of DM500 million) and their sub-suppliers. If 40 per cent of the total manufacturing cost of a sub-system is labour cost, then this effect can reduce total costs by a further 10 per cent.

- Finally, outsourcing sub-systems leads to elimination of *coordination procedures* in the company, so that corporate structures can often be simplified. The savings here vary widely from company to company, but have been in the order of 5 to 10 per cent in individual cases.

Sub-system outsourcing is obviously an issue primarily for manufacturers of large systems: classical component suppliers with a relatively small share of assembly and their main value added derived from a few mechanical processes will, as a rule, derive less benefit from it. Yet, in our experience, many automotive industry suppliers are too quick to dismiss this solution as unnecessary, when some of them could profit considerably from it.

This was confirmed in a workshop with potential sub-suppliers at which, initially with a great deal of scepticism, participants investigated opportunities for collaboration on a metal casing for a component. The outcome was that complexity was halved (from 30 to 15 variants) and superfluous boreholes and plastic coatings were eliminated – yielding a saving of DM1 million per year by reducing unit costs from DM0.87 to DM0.66. And the new trust-based relationship opened up possibilities for further quality and cost optimization in the future (Figure 3.10).

Results of a workshop with sub-suppliers

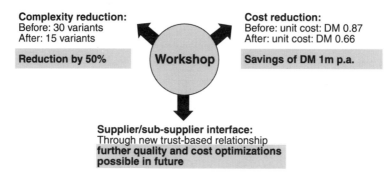

Case example:
Metal housing for component X
Elimination of:
• Superfluous holes
• Plastic coating
• Exotic variants

Complexity reduction:
Before: 30 variants
After: 15 variants

Reduction by 50%

Workshop

Cost reduction:
Before: unit cost: DM 0.87
After: unit cost: DM 0.66

Savings of DM 1m p.a.

Supplier/sub-supplier interface:
Through new trust-based relationship
further quality and cost optimizations
possible in future

Fig. 3.10 *Joining forces for higher quality and lower costs*

The most important condition for success is always to find – or develop – a qualified supplier, who understands and controls its own production processes and the associated costs well and also has the necessary development skills.

Outsourcing in low-wage economies
Where 40 per cent of the manufacturing cost of a component is spent on labour, total manufacturing costs can theoretically be cut by over 30 per cent if production is moved to a low-wage economy with a 90 per cent lower wage level. Does this mean, as is occasionally claimed, that the entire Western European supplier structure will inevitably collapse and be replaced by Eastern European suppliers?

Eastern Europe will undoubtedly become more important. But such sweeping statements are undoubtedly just as false as the assumption that changing to a low-wage supplier will always be financially more attractive than sub-system outsourcing, for instance. If the company in our example had decided to go for a low-wage economy rather than buying sub-systems, it would probably have gleaned similar cost advantages to start with. But not for long. Unlike the sub-system supplier, the low-wage supplier would have been unlikely to be able to achieve improvements in the product concept and thus make a further leap forward in savings, within a fairly short time; it is more likely that it would have had to pass on wage increases in the future. It makes much more sense to outsource sub-systems to high-wage specialists, at least whenever a high share of development suggests opportunities for design optimization.

Outsourcing to low-wage economies is usually the better option if the technology of the components purchased is fundamentally stable, the ratio of labour cost to total cost is high, production cannot be further automated, and even the most creative minds cannot come up with more than a sparse crop of optimization opportunities. If a company chooses this option for a large number of components, however, it should draw up a well-considered, integrated concept and concentrate on partner companies where it is prepared to make major investments in training.

Focus for More Intensive Supplier Care

One company had major problems with the quality of its supplies, even though it employed an above-average number of staff in purchasing and 'supplier quality assurance' (goods inward inspection and supplier quality management). It soon started to think that none of its German suppliers was good enough, and that the purchasing department was too concerned with costs at the expense of quality.

An analysis of the facts found the root of the problem: too many components and suppliers. This led to high staffing, but also meant that much less management capacity was available for each supplier than was the case in higher quality companies. A member of staff in purchasing or quality assurance was responsible for about 30 different suppliers, and had no time to do anything but scheduling and selective troubleshooting. In a comparable high-quality company, on the other hand, each employee was only assigned two large suppliers which he could, of course, look after much more thoroughly. The same applied to the products – the quality company could afford to invest five times as much time per component. It was a 'simplicity winner'.

Supplier development measures will fail if components and suppliers are allowed to proliferate. This is another reason why it is so dangerous to seek a panacea in buying from low-wage economies, and to source different components from Poland, the Czech Republic or the former Soviet Union piecemeal, depending on the price. It is important in these countries, too, to select a small number of partners and then bring their quality, as well, of course, as their productivity and on-time delivery capabilities, up to the required standard. The choice of these strategic partners cannot be left to the sole discretion of the purchasing department.

One tyre manufacturer restructured its purchasing strategy on this basis. It had previously purchased its rubber on the commodities exchange, at the lowest possible price. Today, it purchases only from audited rubber plantations, one of which is assigned to each of its factories. The advantage is consistently high quality and a consequently lower risk of defects in production.

One particular extreme form of supplier concentration is gaining in importance: 'single sourcing', which limits a company to one sub-supplier for a particular family of parts or for an entire process technology. This form of sourcing is particularly suitable where lower variety promises high savings, such as in processes where resetting procedures are associated with considerable startup problems.

Take the casting industry as an example. Many casting processes today suffer from enormous overcapacities, and foundries, with their very high fixed costs, are often ready to offer products at far below full cost. The result is that the automotive industry supplier gets far better prices than in the past, but its sub-supplier is unlikely to survive in the long term. For this reason, many suppliers purchase from a number of foundries to ensure that they can still deliver even if a sub-supplier goes bankrupt. But in many cases the alternative course of action would have produced better dividends: concentrating on one foundry, ensuring its survival by placing very large orders, and working with it to optimize complexity. As complexity costs are high in casting processes because of the high tool costs, both parties could benefit greatly from this collaboration.

With a streamlined supplier structure, a company can obviously afford to invest significantly more in supplier development. However, even quality companies do not carry out indiscriminate qualification measures, but are very selective in picking out those suppliers that have the potential to become high quality partners in the future. Having selected a particular supplier, they then try to transfer to it their own development philosophy: the supplier is integrated in the simultaneous engineering teams and involved in the design review process. At over 30 person days per core supplier, high quality companies devote about twice as much time to this as do lower quality companies. This joint problem solving brings both parties more benefits than generalized qualification programmes.

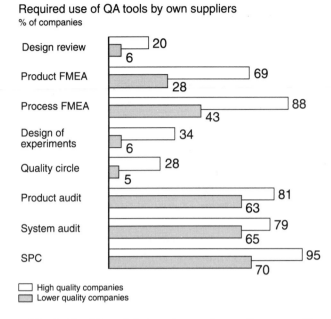

Required use of QA tools by own suppliers
% of companies

Design review — 20 / 6

Product FMEA — 69 / 28

Process FMEA — 88 / 43

Design of experiments — 34 / 6

Quality circle — 28 / 5

Product audit — 81 / 63

System audit — 79 / 65

SPC — 95 / 70

☐ High quality companies
▨ Lower quality companies

Fig. 3.11 *Use of QA tools at sub-suppliers as well*

Of course, top companies insist that their suppliers master and apply techniques such as FMEA and FTA (see Appendix A: 'Top Quality Tools') as well as they do themselves (Figure 3.11). They invest considerable effort in training their suppliers, particularly those from low-wage economies, but generally expect suppliers in high-wage economies to learn the necessary techniques, processes and procedures for themselves. But work still has to be done on these more capable companies. Quality companies see their role here more as requesting, or at least suggesting, that the techniques be applied, and giving support where needed.

Summary

Quality companies at levels III and IV view research and development as a core process of the utmost importance to returns and growth. They achieve better results faster and more economically than poorer companies because they invest more per project, are less hampered by organizational barriers, and structure the entire development process more intelligently.

- Their development perspective extends beyond their own organization. They have translated value to the OEM, as the direct customer, and likewise value to the end customer into explicit, operationalized development objectives. Sub-suppliers also collaborate as partners in the development process, but only after careful examination and, if necessary, qualification.
- They apply quality tools earlier and more intensively in development, emphasize process capability, and, as a result, also allow modifications right up to pilot series production.
- The responsibility for quality is taken by individuals and teams to whom the projects are directly entrusted, objectives are clearly defined, and progress is tracked systematically and with short feedback loops.
- Quality companies create continuously and rapidly learning organizations by giving development teams frequent suggestions in design reviews, and they pay just as close attention to skill building as to development progress.

4 The Production Process: Zero Defects at Source

Defect rates below 100 ppm: automotive industry suppliers expect this to be the target set them by OEMs as early as 1995. To ensure this level of quality by control and rework would explode any conceivable schedule or budget: it has to be produced, and not 'inspected into' the product. As outlined in the last chapter, manufacturable design makes a considerable contribution here. However, the production process itself also faces a huge challenge in the quest for zero defects: a challenge that demands a sweeping reorganization of tasks, competences, and working practices from many companies.

In the long-term study, companies at quality levels I and II, with defect rates still at about 4,800 or 900 ppm respectively, were still above the future target of 'less than 100 ppm' by a factor of 10 to 50. This gap is all the more serious as the front runners among the quality companies, at approximately 70 ppm, are already one-third ahead of the future target. Furthermore, the good companies achieve this with about 30 per cent lower quality costs in production, and in such areas as planning effort, test equipment, and quality assurance staff.

However, perhaps the greatest strength of the top companies at quality level IV is that they are not satisfied with having produced excellent results. With the ideal of perfection constantly before them, they work tirelessly toward reducing defects still further – not only in the product, but in the entire production process as they understand it: the chain from supplier to customer. To learn from these companies means, above all, taking on board this holistic view of the sources of defects and approaches to problem-solving (Figure 4.1):

- *Minimization of employee error*: employees in the factory have to be trained in the appropriate methods and motivated to recognize faulty products or work processes and to introduce improvements.

85

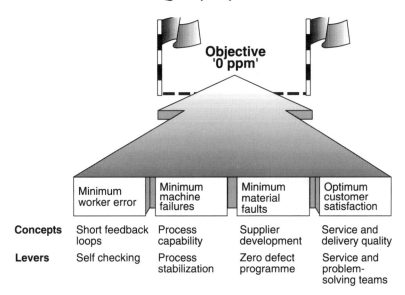

Fig. 4.1 *Four levers to achieve the zero defects objective in the production process*

- *Minimization of machine error*: the greatest possible stability must be ensured for machine processes.
- *Minimization of materials defects*: external suppliers should meet the same high level of quality as demanded of the in-house value adding process.
- *Minimization of delivery and service faults*: as delivery time, on-time delivery, and quality of service are often just as important to end customers and OEMs as the actual product quality, quality companies set and achieve demanding targets in these areas, too.

MINIMIZED EMPLOYEE ERROR WITH INCREASED SKILLS AND ACCOUNTABILITY

In recent years, leading companies have drastically reduced or even totally eliminated post-production inspection by the 'men in white coats'. One German car manufacturer integrated most of the final inspection into the assembly team in a new assembly line, and one company in the plastics extrusion industry even transferred the inspection of machine process stability entirely to employees.

Such a radical step, of course, cannnot be made overnight and by fiat. First, production employees have to be put in a position in which they are able to ensure high product quality and process. Employees and shop-floor supervisors have to be able to act responsibly on the basis of extended decision-making powers and technical capabilities; timely, need-oriented information has to support the essential good eye for problems and will to perform; and a quality-related evaluation system (not a bonus system!) and direct feedback on faults have to support the spread of a 'zero defects mentality'.

Delegation of Tasks and Accountability

'The material just wasn't right.' 'The machine just produces x per cent scrap.' 'The inspector at the end of the assembly line will sort it out.' Low-quality companies all say the same: you cannot expect the production department to react to quality defects any other way. Or, perhaps: 'The staff are simply not interested enough and don't try.'

But experience shows the reverse: lack of employee commitment is often primarily due to lack of management commitment. Why should the man on the machine make a particular effort if his only experience of management's commitment is new time targets or time and motion studies? Instead of simply making demands, management has to demonstrate the will to change by example, and it also has to arm employees with the necessary tools and new decision-making powers. One such tool is the establishment of self-managing production teams and quality circles, which are much more widespread at high quality companies than at lower quality ones (see Chapter 2, 'Strategy and Organization'). They serve as platforms for problem solving.

The gap to be closed in the area of team structures in particular does not only exist at the poorer companies. Even at the quality companies, not even a quarter of the employees were organized in self-managing manufacturing or production teams until the early 1990s. And this is not merely because not every area is suitable for teamwork in terms of functions, tasks or even physical environment. A more important factor is that setting up functioning, self-managing production teams is a long process: the change process has to be intensively accompanied and supported – by every level up to top management. In the team itself, the necessary intellectual, technical, functional, and interpersonal skills have to be present, or have to be 'trained in'. Mutual and personified responsibility must be in place, and commitment to shared (!) targets, a shared approach, and a hands-on, value-driven system must be created. It takes a major effort to set up a truly functioning team. And it is therefore impossible to organize all production staff into such teams in a short space of time.

The formation of quality circles is, in contrast, further advanced. However, wide disparities exist between successful and less successful companies in both the number and the results of such circles (Figure 4.2). If the leading companies generate almost 90 suggestions per quality circle year on year and the poorer ones, by comparison, only manage eleven, this naturally also affects the improvements actually made. At high-quality companies, quality circles are a key lever for increasing productivity and quality. At lower-quality companies, in contrast, they only occur in the form of token employee involvement; truly measurable successes from delegating responsibility to quality circles have not been observed at these companies so far.

The same applies to company suggestion schemes – their mere existence will not make them successful. Short decision-making and implementation times are the most important thing; quality companies are one and a half times as fast as lower-quality companies. The best get there in five to ten days. To reach this standard, quality companies have decentralized decision-making powers. Managers in production, supported by team leaders and floor supervisors (depending on the organizational structure) make the decisions. More harm than good is done by central approval committees with complex, intransparent rules for making decisions and awarding bonuses,

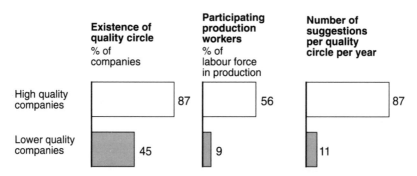

Fig. 4.2 *More problem-solving by workers in quality companies*

where several months often elapse before decisions are made or measures implemented (see Chapter 2, 'Strategy and Organization').

Here, the key to success is once more to delegate responsibility, which encourages commitment with short, fast feedback loops. With this approach, quality companies use their suggestion schemes and quality circles as valuable collecting points for ideas on improvements, large and small, from *individual* employees. And they achieve results to be proud of: savings of around US$125 per capita, in comparison to approximately US$70 at poorer-quality companies.

Whether inside or outside team structures, top companies always put much more faith in their employees' capabilities than level I or II companies: every one of them has enlarged the responsibilities of the worker (teams) to allow them to ensure quality independently, and they have raised the decision-making powers of the floor supervisors to a real management role. And the employees respond well to these approaches: in almost half the quality companies employees – according to their own statements – see their relationship with management as based on partnership; at lower-quality companies this figure dwindles to just under one-quarter.

Enlarged responsibilities on the shop floor
For the employee in the factory to be 'educated' about quality production, he needs constant direct feedback about the quality of his work. If a fault in a part is not noticed until three or four operations later, on a completely different machine, the original culprit scarcely feels it is any concern of his. The part has gone through further value-adding stages and the fault becomes expensive, as the reject costs are higher or reworking has become more difficult than if the problem had been corrected immediately where it occurred.

The quickest and most effective feedback comes from self-checking: as soon as the part has been processed or assembled, the employee checks it over at his own workplace so as to be able to remedy possible faults immediately. Sooner or later, he will try to prevent the need for reworking from ever arising – he can no longer afford to take the attitude that 'someone will sort it out'. In the last six years, the share of self-checking by employees has increased sharply at quality companies – from about 70 to 90 per cent of the total inspection work on the product. The trend is also rising at lower-quality companies, but they still trail well behind, with about 60 per cent (Figure 4.3).

Share of self-checking by workers in ongoing production
% of cost of inspection by workers

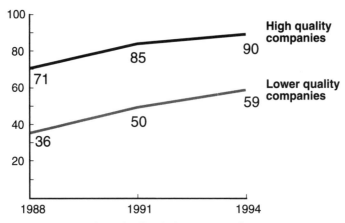

Fig. 4.3 *Short feedback loops in quality companies*

One participant in our study had long tried in vain to minimize rework costs. His assembly costs had risen dramatically because of high rework requirements; a special rework shop was staffed to make corrections. But then the company focused its efforts on the sources of faults – the employees on the assembly lines had to rectify their own errors themselves. Faults detected at the end of the assembly line were 'personified', i.e., assigned to individual assembly groups wherever possible. Training programs and factory-wide information sessions were also used. After only a few months, reworking due to assembly faults fell to a minimum and reworking capacity could be slashed.

At top companies, employees not only carry out quality inspections themselves, they also adjust machines, carry out minor maintenance jobs, and intervene in the process to make corrections. It is of decisive importance that employees or employee teams are well trained and that decisions are clearly delegated to them. For example, at over 50 per cent of quality companies, employees can order a block on incoming goods independently – this is only allowed at 20 per cent of poorer companies. Similar policies exist for stopping the assembly line or independently introducing measures to eliminate faults. This was also confirmed by the workers interviewed: at about 50 per cent of the quality companies they said that they had the authority to implement improvements in their units. At lower-quality companies, not even 20 per cent of the employees could claim this freedom.

Exactly which tasks and decisions employees should undertake independently and using their own technical judgment differs from company to company and from factory to factory. It is management's task initially to identify the most important process chains along the materials, information, and decision flow and to organize them in such a way that the employee can genuinely take entrepreneurial action. Then, the delegation of tasks and decision-making powers has to be completed step by step, accompanied by continuous training and coaching by superiors – foreman, floor supervisor, factory manager or team spokesperson – according to the organization structure chosen.

Once the decision is made on what to do, how much to do, and by when to do it, the superior has to describe, or at least help to describe, how to get there. Not every employee will immediately arrive at the best decision on his own. Here, teamwork helps to spread competence widely in the organization. Teams at top companies have nine to ten members (including the team spokesperson) and their area of responsibility covers self-responsible quality assurance for setting up, adjusting, operating, and even servicing the machines.

One Japanese transplant in England introduced the '5 S' concept from Japan as a creative approach for the workers to set objectives and map out routes. Under this concept, excellent product quality begins with quality at the workstation. Abstract figures, percentages, and ppm data are not used – instead, quality requirements are based on the state of the workstation as directly perceived by the employee, and on his working style (Figure 4.4). The five 'S's stand for *Seiso* (tidiness at the workplace), *Seiri* (using only the necessary working materials), *Seiketsu* (proper maintenance of working materials and of exchanges of information), *Shitsuke* (adherence to working regulations) and *Seiton* (correct positioning of all working materials at the workplace).

The third 'S,' which emphasizes the importance of maintaining an exchange of information, is put in place at all the survey's Japanese participants by institutionalizing internal customer/supplier relations between upstream and downstream process stages. This takes the form of, for example, daily discussions at the start of a shift or so-called complaint or comment boxes which are hung on the wall in the meeting room of every workstation or group of workstations. Only two-thirds of the European companies practised such forms of internal customer relations.

The 5S concept

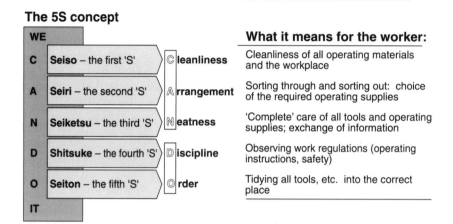

WE			**What it means for the worker:**
C	**Seiso** – the first 'S'	ⓒ **leanliness**	Cleanliness of all operating materials and the workplace
A	**Seiri** – the second 'S'	Ⓐ **rrangement**	Sorting through and sorting out: choice of the required operating supplies
N	**Seiketsu** – the third 'S'	Ⓝ **eatness**	'Complete' care of all tools and operating supplies; exchange of information
D	**Shitsuke** – the fourth 'S'	Ⓓ **iscipline**	Observing work regulations (operating instructions, safety)
O	**Seiton** – the fifth 'S'	Ⓞ **rder**	Tidying all tools, etc. into the correct place
IT			

Fig. 4.4   *The 5S concept involves every worker in thinking and acting quality*

Generally, creative, motivating approaches were still thin on the ground at the companies studied – often TQM (Total Quality Management) programmes are equated with capturing all quality-relevant data and measuring them intelligently. Such data are undoubtedly extremely important for management to be able to recognize, prioritize, and control quality problems and targets. But applying these findings and figures to the behaviour of the men on the machines or on the assembly line calls for more: it calls for an understanding of the quality problems and grievances of the workers on the shop floor, and of their know-how and training requirements. This is the only viable basis for initiating the necessary process of change, improvement, and – ultimately – motivation.

Upgrading of the floor supervisor's role

The floor supervisor, as the employees' direct superior, has a crucial role to play in an efficient factory. In many companies, his work mainly consists of tracking down missing assembly parts, ordering changes of schedule at short notice, or dealing with cover for absent staff. But in top-quality companies he is one of the problem solvers in questions such as the organization of operational sequences, required rigs and tools, and for the working style, results, and targets of the staff directly reporting to him. Of course, administrative tasks are still a part of the job, but they do not take up the 70 per cent of his time that they do in many companies.

With the introduction of the team concepts increasingly practised by participants in our study and also by other industries, the role of the floor supervisor will certainly change for good; particularly where teams are given a high degree of self-determination. A team leader with planning and management skills in his specific work area can make the traditional floor supervisor, not to mention the foreman, superfluous. At the same time, the team leader continues to contribute to day-to-day operations, just like his colleagues.

This development leaves two options for the present floor supervisor. First, he may compete with qualified workers and possibly foremen (if this level exists) for a team leader's job. Direct hands-on involvement in production will be new to the floor supervisor; it does, however, promote team spirit and the team leader's job usually involves a wide and highly challenging array of tasks. Alternatively, he may become the manager of a production department. This means – assuming he has adequate management and leadership skills – that he will act as a coach for several teams whose leaders report back to him. In this role the 'new' floor supervisors will also be competition for the existing production department managers. As they advance into this hierarchical level, at least one level can be eliminated as a net effect.

The 'new' floor supervisor with enhanced management skills, properly employed, has to motivate his staff and serve as their role model. His position will therefore be clearly upgraded and associated with a broad range of management tasks.

- The floor supervisor will be given real *people management responsibility*; i.e., he will be involved in the personnel selection process, he will evaluate the employees in his group and lead them by means of delegation and personal responsibility. The aim is for the team to work as independently as possible: it should recognize minor problems itself, find possible solutions quickly, test them, and, if they are found workable, put them into effect immediately, monitor success, and set the next target. In one company a floor supervisor told us: 'I try only to hire people for my area who strengthen the knowhow of our team. With our customers getting more and more demanding, I can't use anyone without the relevant skills. In addition, each individual must be prepared to learn fast and contribute to the team, i.e., be able to work as part of a team. As his superior, coach, and trainer it is up to me to supply all the help and training possible.'

- The floor supervisor is *responsible for the process*; with his team he decides on procedures, times, and tools. At quality companies, operating procedures change frequently; in the context of continuous improvement the ideas of shop floor workers, superiors as well as ideas from other functions (development, purchasing, logistics) force – or rather, allow – manufacturing or assembly processes to change. Of course, the floor supervisor draws on support from other functions such as toolbuilding, maintenance or production planning in all these process adaptations, but he is the driving force. He is the 'Manager' of continuous improvement.

- Finally, he is *responsible for the results*; this means he has to steer by concrete targets – above all in quality and productivity – and, together with his colleagues, he has to decide on where investments are to be made in his area. In addition, he has to find tools and methods to communicate the improvement programme and its success regularly and universally to the workforce, for instance, by targeted selected visuals in the factory.

- At one company, each team was given a budget of a few thousand DM for minor machine modifications and operating materials purchases. The teams were then able to make their own decisions about such small investments, on three conditions: the expenditure had to be exclusively for the improvement of the working environment; at least half of the team members had to agree to the investment; and the change had to be completely in place within ten weeks. As a result, motivation and speed in the implementation of improvements increased enormously. Instead of going through long processing times and approval processes as before, the team met after work to decide on the priorities for allocating the budget, and they also regularly measured the improvements achieved.

There are many examples to illustrate the fact that fresh improvement ideas are continually developed in this kind of environment. At one German radiator manufacturer, the team on a tube welding plant independently developed a new model for work breaks which made it possible to operate the production plant continuously. The result, in addition to better capacity utilization, was that the rejects decreased as the machine did not have to be started up so frequently. Another team tightened up working procedures in the production hall: previously, workers had slowed one another up at the soldering furnaces as each person simply helped himself to the carrying frames nearest to hand. At the suggestion of the workers, the frames were colour coded and each was allocated to a furnace, and the search and grab approach came to an end.

Timely and Accurate Information

Top companies also train the quality consciousness of frontline employees by keeping them up to date on the current status of quality (see Chapter 2, 'Strategy and Organization'). Naturally, this information does not only relate to company-wide quality data or the reactions of the OEM customers. Direct feedback from superiors or 'internal customers', i.e., the upstream or downstream assembly stage, is just as essential and useful. This feedback helps to pinpoint and prevent quality defects in good time, and therefore cost-effectively.

The ability to have information ready 'just in time', to pass it on to employees immediately, and therefore induce them to react immediately if necessary is the core of good information management. Complete but complex computer listings do not usually reap the expected benefits here. They sometimes entail too long and complex feedback loops; days or even weeks sometimes pass before they are evaluated. These lists – too long and complicated for direct use by the employees in any case – can normally only be analyzed at higher levels. Accordingly, the entire control system works slowly: by the time faults are corrected, problems and priorities have already changed.

Thus, it is a key task of the floor supervisor or team leader and management to process quality information in a comprehensible form for the individual workers or the team, and to enable them to counter problems 'just in time'. This was done successfully in one company, for example, which had successfully introduced a TQM project and achieved huge company-wide improvements in quality, cost, and time. The top management team and the controlling function kept up to date on the actual progress of hundreds of measures against plan through skilful aggregation. Ongoing, clearly expressed feedback to the shop floor employees was, however, taken just as seriously.

Almost 70 per cent of all employees in the factories had been involved in developing the measures; now they had every right to be shown how implementation was progressing monthly and quarterly. Noticeboards were put up illustrating the targets, actual performance, and key actions for the individual factories, production teams, and departments. By this means, not only was the workforce highly motivated to put the TQM programme in place, but the foundations of continuous improvement were also laid.

Quality Performance Through Targeted Personnel Development

People who produce quality and keep making improvements like to be praised. Financial incentives are only one way of rewarding good achievements; they must be supplemented by explicit personal recognition. Quality companies therefore have evaluation systems, which, for shop floor workers too, go much further than the definition of pay grades and piece-rate allowances or bonuses. It is not a question of handing out school-type grades; the evaluations are used for targeted personnel development. Floor supervisors and employees are assessed in this way in half of the quality companies, but only in a fifth of the others.

At one company, where this kind of evaluation process is actually performed every six months, a detailed development plan is drawn up for each employee, which also includes his or her own personal input. This plan is divided into three parts:

- In the *work evaluation* section, manager and employee describe the employee's detailed tasks, the most important quantitative objectives per task area are defined, and the basic requirements (e.g., tool modification, training) for the achievement of the targets are discussed. The objectives are given different priorities according to their importance for quality results at the workstation concerned. In this process, the worker is asked for his own assessment in comparison to that of the foreman, floor manager or team leader (depending on the form of organization) and both assessments are explicitly taken into account. In the next evaluation session, the extent to which the targets have been achieved is discussed with the employee, and further improvement levers are agreed upon.
- The *personal evaluation* covers workstation-specific and general knowledge, planning ability, creativity, and decisiveness. In addition, the teamwork capabilities, cost-consciousness, and problem-

solving abilities of the employee are assessed, for example, by looking at their contribution to team discussions and at the suggestions for improvements that they have offered.

- The third section deals with *future prospects* for the employee. Here, a 'career' and training plan is drawn up, used as a basis for promotion but not for monetary evaluation. Individual opportunities for extending responsibilities or for promotion are discussed and upskilling measures are agreed upon. This plan contains the worker's previously demonstrated ability to master his workstation's and team environment's tasks, as well as his personal desire to expand the scope of his responsibilities.

Comprehensive personnel development at the shop floor level therefore depends on individual and detailed evaluation of workers and individual definition of training requirements. Both are the task of the employee's superior. Forms should be prepared to facilitate operationalization (Figure 4.5).

Assessment of performance (index: 1, 2, 3 – very good, good, satisfactory)

Performance plan				
Objectives and quantitative criteria concerning	Priorities (1 - 2 - 3)	Assessment of performance by		Comments
		Worker	Superior*	
Drilling and turning a shaft				
● Reduction of reject rate by 25% from January 1993 to April 1993	(1)	2	2	● Improvement levers – Training in techniques – Technical improvement in machine
● Correct stacking of all finished goods on transport pallets	(3)	3	3	● Worker demands functioning transport pallets
Capturing and analyzing SPC data				
● Workers to carry out SPC-data analysis themselves by July 1993	(2)	2	2	● Further improvements possible after 2 SPC training units
Preventive maintenance				
● Changing tools in the correct way and in the given time (<20 seconds)	(2)	3	3	● One week's training in maintenance needed to improve skills
● Machine servicing once a month	(2)	3	3	

Signature

Worker: ....

Superior: ....

Purpose:
– Personal development
– Basis for promotion
– No assessment for bonus purposes

* Floor supervisor, foreman or team leader if applicable (depending on chosen form of organisation in the factory)

Fig. 4.5 *Performance-based personnel development*

The widespread fear that the introduction of strict performance-based principles will demotivate employees was not confirmed by the long-term study. The opposite is true: in companies with stringent employee evaluation, the employees interviewed were much more positive about the working atmosphere than at companies with no individual evaluation. Evaluated employees identified more strongly with their company's objectives, their quality awareness was considerably higher, and they had a more holistic orientation, than people at less stringently managed companies.

Another element which undoubtedly contributes to a positive atmosphere is the fact that evaluation is not a one-way street in quality companies, and the employees' opinions are also considered important. In some 60 per cent of the quality companies examined – at companies of lower quality the figure is only about 15 per cent – there is a feedback system to gauge employee satisfaction. Typical themes are job content, workplace design, the opportunity to apply their personal knowledge, decision-making powers and participation in decision making, the overall working atmosphere in the group and at the workplace in general, and finally – particularly important – support from management.

All in all, important as work groups and employee teams undoubtedly are, the widespread conception that they in themselves are enough to effect a comprehensive, results-oriented cultural change at the grass roots has proved here to be another myth. Employee mobilization is a top management task – that applies to the initial stimulus for culture change as well as to sustaining the improvement process or giving support in setting objectives.

In our experience, culture changes have to be generated 'top down'. The seed of culture change is not the work group or the employee team, but the management. Innovative concepts for which management has to provide the role model are the driving force behind the continuous improvement process – employee participation cannot compensate for neglected management tasks. The greatest incentive to top performance comes from ambitious objectives set 'from the outside in' with an eye to competitors or customers. An objective chosen in this way from the outside has to become the self-selected goal of a work team. This does, however, require a proper understanding of the competitive situation and identification with the company. To generate such understanding and identification should be a primary management task (see Chapter 2, 'Strategy and Organization').

Quality companies do not rate quality bonuses highly, i.e., extra financial rewards for quality performance – quality is, after all, the core of performance, to which the customer is entitled. However, quality companies do involve their employees more in the improvements derived from company suggestion schemes and quality circles. Of the savings achieved each year, they pass on 40 per cent more to employees than companies of lower quality. Where quality companies work with variable compensation at all, they use it to reward either individual strengths (e.g., problem-solving ability, creativity) or team performance.

At quality companies, intangible recognition is much more important. It guarantees the commitment of the team in the long term – the fact that energy and initiative are there to be tapped is constantly proved by many employees in their leisure activities.

Short Feedback Loops as a Result of Process-Oriented Organizational Procedures

A traditional workshop organization with its separation of departments and stringent demarcation of tasks does not ensure direct feedback, and internal customer/supplier thinking is also difficult to establish. In addition, companies find themselves struggling with the costs of high buffer stocks between departments. This reasoning induced one German component manufacturer to introduce a process-oriented organization by production cells (Figure 4.6). The employees in each cell then had an overview of the entire process, their customer – the employee standing next to them – gave them direct feedback, for example on the correct assembly of two elements. In a short time stocks decreased and above all internal quality (measured by rejects) improved noticeably.

MINIMIZING MACHINE ERROR BY PUTTING PROCESS STABILITY FIRST

An ordinary internal combustion engine for a passenger car will run for well over one million kilometres – if used like a generator. That is, if it runs without stopping for weeks and months – with high 'process stability'. Ordinary driving is a different matter – starting at a cold

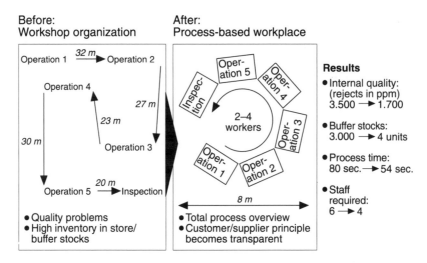

Fig. 4.6 *Introduction of a process organization for the manufacture of mechanical components*

temperature and with less-than-perfect lubrication, frequent gear changes, acceleration, and braking mean considerably greater wear and tear, pushing performance well below such record levels. This is an extreme example, yet it shows quite realistically how important the phenomenon of 'process stability' is to machine availability.

The top companies therefore make every effort to work with the most stable, constant machine processes possible; i.e., to minimize any kind of interruption and other negative influences, for instance, frequent setups. Using this approach, some Japanese companies achieve machine operation or availability of over 90 per cent on a daily basis. Productivity increases accordingly, since one employee can operate – or, more accurately, monitor – up to ten, and sometimes even more, machines at a time.

One fundamental requirement for stable processes is, of course, the standardization of parts, as this allows larger lot sizes. 'Simplicity wins' here, too. However, quite apart from complexity of products and parts, the most stable processes are achieved by those companies that meet two requirements before and during production: optimization of design tolerances and minimization of process variance around the expected or target figure (see Appendix A: 'Top Quality Tools').

Optimization of Design Tolerances

The tolerances set by design engineers are sometimes the most important lever for improving process capability: if the design drawing specifies a tolerance so narrow that it can scarcely be achieved by man, machine or materials, then high reject rates are a foregone conclusion.

In this case, the design tolerance is in an unfavourable ratio – in mathematical terms, less than 1 – to the deviation of the process figures around the desired mean. This means that the variance is greater than the region between the upper and lower tolerance limits – the probability that the physical deformations to which the blanks are subjected (e.g., diameter) will lie outside the allowed tolerances is relatively high. This relationship is the C_p value, which many companies measure regularly: the permitted tolerance of a quality-related parameter, divided by the variance or standard deviation in the production or assembly process (see Appendix A: 'Top Quality Tools').

The C_{pk} value, which goes a step further, is also frequently used. It not only measures the relationship between the design tolerance and process variance, but also the 'centering' of the variance in the process values, which usually approaches the standard distribution of a Gaussian curve, in comparison to the upper and lower tolerance limits. The poorer, i.e., smaller C_p value is the C_{pk} value (shown in simplified form in Figure 4.7). Quality companies often set themselves a target C_{pk} value in the medium term of 1.33 and in the long term of 2.0 or more. The statistical ppm defect rates are then more likely to remain in two figures, at 64 ppm or lower.

Of course, dimensions, fit, and tolerance limits are often givens, because of either physical characteristics or performance specific design and the requirements on a part, component or product. However, experience also shows over and over again that the real consequences of setting specific dimensions on the drawing board are often not known. Thus, a control panel manufacturer had considerable reject problems with a certain type of product because the designers had put in too many air ducts packed too tightly together in the parts – clearly a poor product/process fit, caused by the designers' lack of understanding of the needs of production.

Lack of knowledge of the manufacturing processes and their process stability drives up reject costs and defect rates. When the processes are taken into account, 'Design to Cost and Quality' is

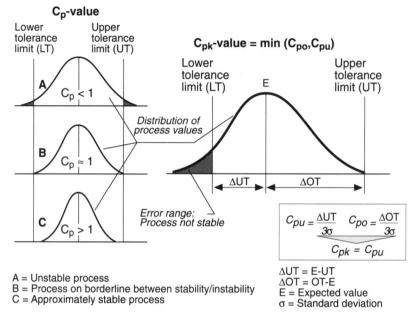

Fig. 4.7 *C_p and C_{pk} as indicators of process capability*

called 'Design to Manufacture'. To achieve it, the designer needs a precise knowledge of his own and his supplier's manufacturing processes, in order to derive the optimum from the performance characteristics of the product and the process capability of the machines and assembly processes.

Excellent companies use every means in their power to try and anchor and further develop this know-how in their development departments. For example, by ensuring short paths – one supplier has put the designers' offices right beside production, to bring development engineers into direct contact with the production function. For the same reason, a manufacturer of wing mirrors makes his designers work on the assembly line for a while at regular intervals; the idea is to sharpen their sense of the extent to which product design influences the attainable productivity and reliable manufacturability.

Minimization of Process Variance Around the Target Value

Within the production and assembly process, five parameters basically decide process stability; these are also analyzed in 'cause–effect' diagrams (Fishbone diagrams) as the sources of faults (e.g., process instabilities):

- *Materials*, i.e., the quality and consistency of the raw and semi-processed materials, assembly parts, components, and modules to be machined and processed.
- *Machinery*, i.e., the precision of the production plant in maintaining target dimensions and values.
- *Man*, responsible for the correct operation of plant and use of tools and materials, and for following operating instructions and assembly rules properly.
- *Production methods*, which should of course be optimally geared to the requirements of the value-adding process – and often are not.
- *Environment*, above all influences such as fluctuations in temperature, contamination or other physical factors.

The key questions are: which of these levers is the main cause if a fault occurs, and how quickly can the fault be eliminated? They can only be answered intelligently if every detail of the production processes is known, because the statistics of the types and sources of defects are calculated on the basis of intensive process studies. In these process studies – the statistically based ones are known as SPC (Statistical Process Control) – the curves of process parameters and also product parameters are precisely recorded and analyzed over time. Top companies constantly strive to identify the various causes of process instabilities and machine breakdowns by this approach and to assess their relative importance, in order to further improve their process capability in production and assembly.

At many lower-quality companies, the only reason why systematic controls are not carried out consistently is that machine operators, maintenance staff or management think they know exactly what the problem is: 'typical wear and tear effect', 'classical maintenance problem, it's always been like that', 'we've been battling with this problem for a long time, in the last few years we have made dramatic improvements', and so on. Of course, one or other of the arguments will be valid, but very often the real causes of process instabilities, machine breakdowns, and down times are simply unknown.

This was the case at one manufacturer of plastic films which regularly had high reject rates on a specific machine. The reason: as a rule it took about 18 minutes for the machine operator to set the pressures, machine spacing, temperatures, and other parameters correctly, and during the whole of this start-up time rejects were being produced. Over the years, this had been accepted as inevitable. But a detailed analysis of the start-up procedure showed that it was not inevitable at all: all parameters actually reached their target values within 7 minutes; only temperature took about 18 minutes. However, even this delay was not a physical necessity – the temperature rose above its target value after only 8 minutes – it was the result of fine-tuning by the machine operators: it was set high to start with to get to full temperature as quickly as possible; the temperature therefore exceeded its target and had to be reduced again, and finally had to be increased again.

The solution lay in installing an improved temperature control which no longer allowed manual readjustments and did not require them, either. The target temperature is now reached in about 8 minutes, and the rejects from the machine have been reduced by more than half because of the machine's shorter start-up time. The prerequisite for the improvement was a precise understanding of the individual processes and how the individual parameters could be influenced. This precise diagnosis allowed considerable savings with minimal expenditure.

SPC

The strategy of stable processes sometimes makes real quantum leaps in quality possible. One company managed to reduce the rejects in the production of a certain mechanical component by almost 60 per cent within three years by increasing the share of processes with SPC from 53 to 86 per cent. This measure was supported by the introduction of quality circles which constantly developed further improvements on the basis of SPC analyses – the combination of 'Statistical Process Control' (SPC) with 'Systematic Problem Solving' (SPS) was the actual reason for the success (see Chapter 5, 'Japan, Europe and the US').

Once again, then, the 'human factor' is at the centre of things: intelligent and determined investigation of machine faults to get right to the source and not to cure symptoms. Here, especially, management must adopt a supportive and advisory position: who should carry out the SPC, at what level of detail, and above all who should analyze it? What problem-solving techniques should be used for the analysis, what know-how must be available in the workforce so that the true causes of defects can be identified quickly?

Of course, statistical process control needs computer support to ensure full data capture. However, many of the quality companies take a deliberate decision not to use extensive technology in the initial phase at least: the employees should, as much as possible, identify personally with the quality results. Workers who fill out SPC cards by hand feel as though they are 'master of the process' and not 'managed from the outside'. In addition, it is important for the staff – troubleshooters, engineers or the machine operating team themselves – to develop a good 'nose' for the causes of disturbances, so as to be able to go straight to the actual source of the fault wherever possible.

Training must be given in using problem-solving techniques – what to look for, who to consult, what order should things be done in? Part of this, for example, is always to ask first when a problem arises: 'What is actually *not* the problem?', 'Which member of the workforce or team checks the possible causes and in what order?', 'At what point should a superior or an expert be called in?'

Companies in the chemical and paper industries take a different approach here from many machine and component manufacturers. Their demanding process engineering calls for the employment of specially trained process engineers whose task it is to optimize the running times and speeds of the machines and, at the same time, to maximize the yield of quality products. These process engineers work hand in hand with the TPM (see below) and TQM trained teams on site. The process engineers help to decide on the optimum maintenance intervals and support the teams in trouble-shooting. They fine-tune complicated machinery and its processes to achieve maximum performance.

TPM

Comprehensive or preventive maintenance of the production equipment in accordance with the 'TPM' concept (Total Productive Maintenance or Total Preventive Maintenance) also helps to stabilize production processes. This approach improves productivity as well as quality. The core of the idea lies in optimizing machine availability and the technical state of machinery and plant by determining the optimum servicing intervals and keeping to them (similar to the A/B/C checks of varying content in passenger aircraft). As this usually means an extension of the servicing tasks, not only the maintenance function but also the employees have to be trained in and entrusted with these tasks. In the long term, the maintenance department can even be reduced to only a few experts, for example electronic engineers.

One French manufacturer of mechanical drive components went even further. He got rid of maintenance as an independent department. Servicing and repair were carried out by the employees, and experts, available within the hour, were called in to deal with tricky problems. The TPM tasks to be carried out were precisely set forth in standard operating procedures at all machines, stating times and responsibilities and using colour illustrations. Frequently required tools were kept on hand at the machines and the others were centrally stored.

To draw up TPM plans, the production processes and machine down times have to be systematically analyzed to discover the causes and the so-called 'break points' for quality. A manufacturer of body parts, for example, found out for each of his presses the number of traverses after which certain checks and services were to be carried out.

The TPM concept has been put in place in about 80 per cent of all high-quality companies, but only in 45 per cent of lower-quality players. The annual maintenance costs are only 1.8 per cent of sales at quality companies, almost 50 per cent lower. A striking feature is that quality companies subcontract almost twice as many maintenance tasks.

MAXIMUM QUALITY IN EXTERNAL RELATIONS

Top companies, with their process-oriented organization, do not see their production process as beginning and ending within their own organizational boundaries. They set standards in production quality in the same way as in R&D, which can only be fulfilled by targeted building of qualified suppliers. And, at the other end of the value chain, their own quality performance is not limited to the product; logistics and service are geared to the customers' quality requirements.

Targeted Development of Suppliers

Quality companies require their suppliers to match their own performance and what they offer the OEM: for example, stable processes, a high share of self-checking by employees, intensive use of quality circles. The performance of the sub-suppliers therefore varies according to the quality of their customers: quality companies are usually served by suppliers whose ppm rate is approximately 2,000; poorer companies accept levels of approximately 9,500 ppm. This means that there is still an enormous need for improvement for both groups.

As we saw in Chapter 3, the foundations are laid in product development, where the supplier is involved in development work as early and as intensively as possible. In addition, quality leaders invest just as heavily in the production of the sub-suppliers' current series, and they keep a close eye on their production quality. As in the product development process, some of the quality leaders' methods are to be encountered in the production process or current series in all good companies, above all permanent quality control and quality investment in the form of supplier training and joint teams.

Permanent quality control
The good suppliers in the automotive industry know and precisely measure how effective and progressive their own sub-suppliers' quality management is. This does not only mean measuring the defect rates of parts or components supplied. They also require sub-suppliers to use SPC, product audits, statistically planned experiments, or quality circles in the production process. These are demands on tools and concepts which go very much further than at companies of lower quality. The ultimate goal is to eliminate incoming goods inspection at their own company completely.

Quality investment in the form of training and joint teams
To reach their demanding quality objectives, quality companies invest a considerable amount in their sub-suppliers. Between 1988 and 1991, for example, about 19 man months per US$100 million of the annual purchasing volume were spent on joint quality improvement projects in the current production process (this compares with only four man months at weaker companies). A further 5.3 man months went into training sub-suppliers' personnel in the application of quality tools (at companies of lower quality: two man months). In addition, many companies have built up a team for supplier quality assurance which is often not located in the quality assurance function but directly in purchasing. These employees, with QA, production and technical know-how, train suppliers, introduce progressive

quality methods and tools at their companies, perform regular supplier audits, but also help in trouble-shooting when acute quality problems occur.

These efforts are reflected in much greater success in quality and rationalization. In the period mentioned, top companies, in collaboration with their sub-suppliers, achieved annual savings of an average of 8.5 per cent of manufacturing costs; at companies of lower quality the figure was only 3.5 per cent, i.e., less than half that amount. Here, quality companies stress the importance of having both partners participate in the resulting success: from their (considerably higher) saving on manufacturing costs, they passed on approximately 40 per cent to the sub-suppliers. The lower quality companies, on the other hand, only gave their sub-suppliers a 20 per cent share of the savings (Figure 4.8).

This kind of value-adding partnership between customer and supplier benefits both parties in the long term and in many cases leads to single sourcing and to a shared orientation toward optimum quality at minimum manufacturing cost. A further, more important, effect becomes apparent: the share of suppliers who deliver directly to the production line without incoming goods inspection is almost 60 per cent at quality companies, which is almost three times as high as at companies of lower quality. The suppliers undertake to draw up emergency plans so as to be able to meet delivery obligations under all circumstances. Conversely, the customer makes every effort to pass on reliable production forecasts and orders in good time.

The long-term development of the supplier means building trust and continually working together to achieve the lowest costs and highest quality for both parties.

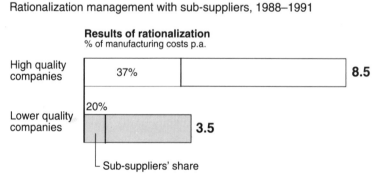

Fig. 4.8   *Sub-suppliers' share in results of rationalization*

Customer-Oriented Logistics and Service Quality

The defect rate of the product and the audit values during and at the end of the production process are now common quality indicators in most companies. Top companies take this one step further: for them the marks of quality do not stop at the functionality, appearance and packaging of the product, but also the speed and punctuality of delivery to the customers (Figure 4.9).

In logistics, efforts are not, therefore, only directed toward internal parameters such as days' stock, storage or transport costs. The logistics performance and logistics quality perceived by the customer take priority. Top companies painstakingly monitor every failure to meet a delivery deadline or comply with any other logistics parameter (Correct product delivered? Correct volume? At the right time? To the right place?), but also other quality factors such as readiness to provide information when customers inquire about order status. This is the only conceivable way to reach the quality objective – because it is the external, not the internal ppm rate that is required. The prerequisites for this are close cooperation with the customer in adhering to delivery deadlines and precise knowledge of every process step, from receipt of the order through the manufactured product at the end of the supplier's own assembly line to the first point of use in the customer's factory.

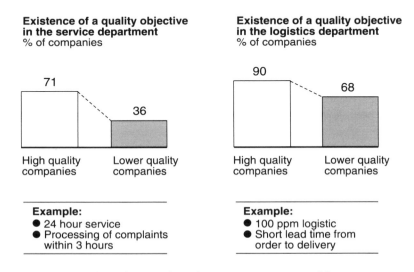

Fig. 4.9 *Clear quality objectives in service and logistics*

Very few customers systematically measure throughput times in their own companies and in their own value-adding processes. Quality companies do, and they also involve their customers. Logistics quality does not stop at the moment of dispatch, but in the incoming goods warehouse or upon delivery of the part for use at the customer's assembly point.

The same applies to *service*. Twenty-four- or twelve-hour service is not just a slogan in successful companies, it is practical reality, or at least a serious objective. Some companies even go so far as to record the actual processing times for complaints on an hourly basis; they record exactly what has been dealt with after three, six or twelve hours.

Successful service also means recognizing problems and defects in the company's own product in a fast and targeted manner when they first come to light in the OEM's factory, and putting a permanent stop to them. About eight out of ten quality companies (but only 35 per cent of lower-quality companies) have set up teams geared to rectifying these defects at the OEM. Trained in standardized problem-solving methods, they can quickly detect and deal with even difficult and unusual sources of faults. It is obvious just how important this know-how can be when a disruption occurs during ongoing production.

One company in our long-term study provides an excellent example of such customer-oriented service. There, contact with the OEM is not undertaken by a service department but by a service team made up of experts from purchasing, research and development, production, quality assurance, and sales. The customer receives a service file containing names and responsibilities – sometimes even with résumés – and above all the hotline telephone numbers. The customer knows exactly whom he should call for what problem; he will reach for the telephone more often and less reluctantly – and will build up a special relationship with his supplier (Figure 4.10).

Summary

As the second core process alongside R&D, production at leading quality companies is also oriented totally toward top quality. And even in the case of defect rates which, at about 70 ppm, are already lower than the foreseeable demands of customers, the level IV companies – the very best – are continuing to improve, aiming for

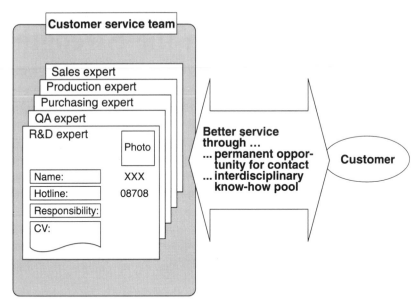

EXAMPLE OF ITALIAN SUPPLIER

Fig. 4.10   *High level of service through interfunctional customer team*

'zero defects'. For the poorer companies – the majority, and mostly based in Europe – it is perhaps here that the most demanding challenge in quality competition lies. With defect rates of about 4,800 ppm at level I and of about 900 at level II, it is vital for their survival to improve all quality dimensions simultaneously, just as the top companies do (only more so):

- Self-checking by employees and short feedback loops have to facilitate fast recognition and repair of employee errors, and foster a zero defects mentality.
- Minimizing machine defects calls for more than constant controls, fine-tuning and systematic, sustained elimination of the defect causes; the optimum fit of process capabilities with design tolerances must also play a part.
- To minimize defects in the materials, targeted development of supplier competence in quality concepts, tools, and processes is needed.
- Delivery and service weaknesses are also quality faults which have to be measured systematically and eliminated root and branch, preferably in cross-functional service and problem-solving teams.

5 Japan, Europe and the US: Learning from the Strengths of Others

Statistically speaking, 'quality' is synonymous with 'Japanese': more automotive suppliers approach the ideal of the quality company in Japan than anywhere else. But three out of every ten European, and four out of every ten American competitors are quality leaders. A comparison of regional strengths and weaknesses is more informative: different regions set their sights on different quality goals. They all have a lot to learn from each other. In fact, they have no option but to do so; Japanese companies, because the particular strengths of their Western competitors, are gaining tremendous importance even in the Japanese environment; the Europeans and Americans, because the Japanese lead in many areas has reached life-threatening proportions for the West – and because the Japanese have become world leaders in the most vital discipline of all, that of continuous improvement.

On the whole, the Japanese quality lead is confirmed by the McKinsey long-term study: 85 per cent of the Japanese automotive suppliers analyzed earned a place on level IV ('Perfection') or level III ('Prevention') compared with a mere 31 per cent of their European counterparts and 44 per cent of American companies. That is to say, they are close to 'total' quality company status by today's standards. The typical European or American company, on the other hand, conforms to the level II profile, settling for quality assurance (Figure 5.1).

If we then go on to distinguish between process and design quality, in accordance with the definitions of the long-term study, a differentiated pattern of regional strengths and weaknesses in quality performance emerges: Japanese companies have a clear lead in process quality, but their Western competitors show significant strengths in some areas of design quality.

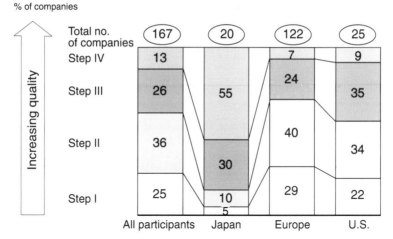

Fig. 5.1 *Regional comparison of quality performance in the Triad*

The clear strength of the Japanese companies is near-flawless production to specifications. It is thanks to this high level of process quality that Japanese companies can boast figures for rework and rejects just one-half to one-third of those achieved by European and American companies, combined with infinitesimal rates for returned goods and complaints from OEMs (so called '0-km rate') (Figure 5.2).

Europeans in particular like to attribute this to the fact that Japanese OEMs often set more generous specifications – i.e., they permit wider tolerances and therefore set less rigorous standards. Our experience, however, has shown us that in many manufacturing sectors this is just not the case, and in any case it still would not explain such huge disparities. On the contrary: why do British automotive manufacturers tend to have the fewest complaints about defective components on delivery of any Europe-based car makers? It is probably largely due to the presence in Britain of Japanese OEMs, their quality standards, and back-up support. British suppliers lead the way with 512 ppm, followed by the French with 780 ppm, and the Italians with approximately 800 ppm; German firms represent the European average for process quality with approximately 1,050 ppm (see Appendix B, 'Quality Profiles by Country').

An important indicator of the Japanese companies' secure mastery of process quality is the fact that they bring new products to the market much faster. It takes them on average a mere 17 weeks from the freeze on specifications to the start of series production, as against

Comparison of process quality indicators in the Triad, 1991

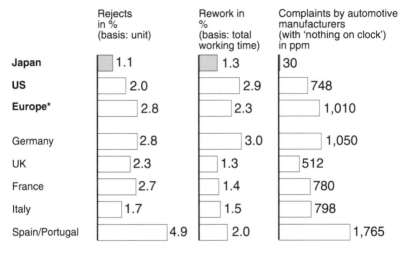

	Rejects in % (basis: unit)	Rework in % (basis: total working time)	Complaints by automotive manufacturers (with 'nothing on clock') in ppm
Japan	1.1	1.3	30
US	2.0	2.9	748
Europe*	2.8	2.3	1,010
Germany	2.8	3.0	1,050
UK	2.3	1.3	512
France	2.7	1.4	780
Italy	1.7	1.5	798
Spain/Portugal	4.9	2.0	1,765

* Weighted average

Fig. 5.2 *Japanese companies lead the way in process quality*

46 weeks in Germany, for example. In Japan, process quality is secured as early as the development phase, through targeted and synchronized product and process design.

Strengths and weaknesses in design quality tell a different story: around 29 per cent of the sales of Japanese manufacturers comes from products offering outstanding value to end customers and OEMs, a figure far exceeded by German manufacturers in particular, who can point to 42 per cent (the rest of Europe lies between 12 per cent and 30 per cent, see Figure 5.3). German companies, for example, spent around 5 per cent of their sales on average 'exploring' end customers, often independently of the OEM, and on developing products with superior value.

The American companies investigated in the study are also gaining ground. Around 32 per cent of their products are characterized by high value to the customer – a clear indication of the increasing technological competence of US manufacturers and also of the fact that they are taking a now highly independent approach to targeting the needs of end customers. Instead of continuing to rely on the specifications and R&D activities of the big three manufacturers (GM, Ford, Chrysler), between 1988 and 1991 they increased their own R&D expenditure from around 2.5 per cent of sales to around

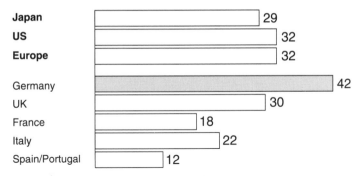

Share of sales of superior products by countries
% of total sales

Japan	29
US	32
Europe	32
Germany	42
UK	30
France	18
Italy	22
Spain/Portugal	12

Fig. 5.3 *Germany has product leadership*

5.0 per cent. Although 1994 saw a consolidation following this furious catch-up race, with expenditure dropping back to 3.6 per cent, American companies are already planning an R&D share of approximately 4 to 4.5 per cent for 1997.

The corresponding spend in Japanese companies was still high, at 3.8 per cent of sales, but these funds were targeted more towards OEMs than end customers.

This much can be concluded from the regional comparison: the Japanese participants in the study owe their flourishing level IV position above all to their outstanding process quality; the European level IV companies, on the other hand – and the German companies in particular – draw their strength mainly from their superior design quality, with a marked focus on the end customer.

This means that Japanese, Europeans, and Americans can all learn from each other. To do so, they need to understand how the different quality focuses have been and are shaped by specific regional industry conditions, and to recognize which quality management levers they should apply at corporate level to make a decisive contribution to their own particular lead:

- The different *relationships between OEM and supplier* play a decisive role in the individual regions as part of the *industry environment*.
- *The strengths and weaknesses in corporate level quality management* which today may decide a company's international competitive position have developed from the scope of action allowed the suppliers and the demands they have to meet.

For the most part, there is no reason why successful quality methods cannot be transferred, even if they were initially of regional origin. There are advantages to be gained on all sides in this learning process. However, the gap the Europeans and Americans have to close is not only bigger but also more urgent, as Japanese companies are already working very hard to eliminate their weaknesses.

SHAPING INDUSTRY CONDITIONS: THE OEM–SUPPLIER RELATIONSHIP

Of the three Triad regions, Japan has by far the biggest number of suppliers (not counting one-man businesses), currently 15,000. The average 'third-tier' supplier in Japan, however, only employs around ten workers. Most of the big suppliers are based in Europe, where 130 large companies employ some 450,000 workers, around half of them in the 20 largest firms.

Of far greater importance than such statistical comparisons, however, are the different competitive structures and the relationships between the automotive and supply industries in the individual regions (Figure 5.4). These are vital factors in the European, and increasingly, American concentration on design quality and the Japanese focus on process quality:

- In *Japan*, the '*Keiretsus*' determine the landscape – these are cooperatives, or at least very close links, between automotive manufacturers and their first-tier suppliers. These suppliers are for the most part bound by capital participation and by law to an OEM, which is their sole customer and with which they work in close partnership, in questions of both day-to-day business and long-term management. The traditional factor for success behind these suppliers has been not so much direct competition in the marketplace, but meeting the demands of their OEMs for products which enabled the maximum degree of process quality downstream; the end customer was the concern of the automotive manufacturer alone. In the face of global price and competitive pressure, this constellation is on the decline.
- In *Europe*, the structure is based on nationalities. The dominant large suppliers are mostly divisions of larger companies or private mid-sized companies, operating in free markets. Their customer

11 Japanese OEMs	18 European and 4 Japanese OEMs*	3 American und 7 Japanese OEMs
approx. 13 million vehicles	approx. 14 million vehicles	approx. 11 million vehicles

	Number of suppliers**	Employees (000)		Number of suppliers	Employees (000)		Number of suppliers	Employees (000)
"1st tier"	~ 500	~ 300	Large (>1,000 workers)	~130	450	Large (>100)	~ 50	160
"2nd tier"	~ 5,000	~ 200	Mid-sized	~1,120	410	Mid-sized	850	190
"3rd tier"	~10,000	~ 100	Small (<100 workers	~ 1,950	90	Small (<100 workers)	~ 1,800	~ 100
Total	**~15,500**	**~ 600**	**Total**	**~ 3,200**	**~950**	**Total**	**~ 2,700**	**~ 450**

* With annual production >30,000 vehicles
** Many additional 'one-man' workshops

Source: statistics from the different countries.

Fig. 5.4 *Structure of the automotive industry in the Triad*

base consists of six to 15 OEMs as a rule. Wooing and winning these OEMs means offering the end customer superior product value.

- In the United States, the relationship between OEM and supplier always used to be determined by an OEM policy of 'squeezing out the very last drop' and changing suppliers continuously. The oligopoly of automobile manufacturers, combined with their high level of vertical integration, means that there is even less continuity and partnership in supplier relationships than in Europe. For many years, short-term optimization has been the decisive factor. But particularly in the last few years, with the reduction of vertical integration at the OEMs and also increasingly slim in-house R&D, the offering of value to the (end) customer has also been growing in importance.

Japan: The Decline in the Influence of the Keiretsu System

The Japanese supplier system, with its rigid first, second, and third tier hierarchy and close ties with car manufacturers, is often cited as

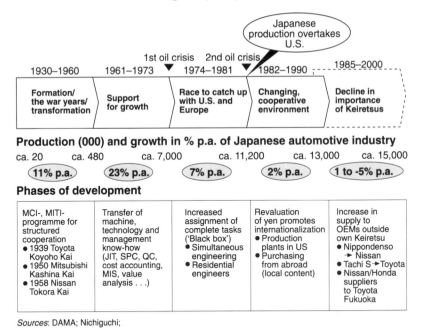

Production (000) and growth in % p.a. of Japanese automotive industry

ca. 20	ca. 480	ca. 7,000	ca. 11,200	ca. 13,000	ca. 15,000
11% p.a.	23% p.a.	7% p.a.	2% p.a.	1 to -5% p.a.

Phases of development

MCI-, MITI-programme for structured cooperation • 1939 Toyota Koyoho Kai • 1950 Mitsubishi Kashina Kai • 1958 Nissan Tokora Kai	Transfer of machine, technology and management know-how (JIT, SPC, QC, cost accounting, MIS, value analysis . . .)	Increased assignment of complete tasks ('Black box') • Simultaneous engineering • Residential engineers	Revaluation of yen promotes internationalization • Production plants in US • Purchasing from abroad (local content)	Increase in supply to OEMs outside own Keiretsu • Nippondenso → Nissan • Tachi S → Toyota • Nissan/Honda suppliers to Toyota Fukuoka

Sources: DAMA; Nichiguchi;

Fig. 5.5 *Development of the Keiretsus in Japan*

the driving force behind the efficiency of the Japanese automotive industry as a whole. However, the long-term study also made clear that the growing pressure to restructure and rationalize, largely a consequence of faltering growth, will not leave the *Keiretsus* untouched. Japan, too, can expect sweeping restructuring of the supply industry. A radical reduction of the number of suppliers and freer competition is likely to result; the surviving suppliers will be forced to develop new elements of competitive differentiation, using, among other elements, value to the (end) customer.

A historical overview of the development of the *Keiretsus*, which can roughly be divided into five phases, may help illustrate the fundamental changes taking place in this area (Figure 5.5):

1. Origins/the war years/transformation (1930–60)
The *Keiretsus* date back to a government program[1] to establish vertical, structured cooperation in order to satisfy military demand. This produced the Toyota *Keiretsu* (Toyota Koyoho-Kai) of 1939,

---

[1] Originating in the MITI (Ministry of International Trade and Industry) and MCI (Ministry of Commerce and Industry).

whose main task was to allocate rationed materials. Building on this pioneering role, the Mitsubishi Kashina-Kai was then founded in 1950 and the Nissan Tokaora-Kai in 1958.

In this period, car production expanded at a rate of 11 per cent per year from 20,000 to 480,000 vehicles.

2. Support for growth (1961–73)

The second phase, which lasted until the first oil crisis, saw the most vigorous growth of the Japanese car industry. Production rose from 480,000 to around 7 million cars – an average growth rate of 23 per cent per year. The driver of this growth was *Keiretsu* collaboration. Machine technology and management know-how were passed on to the suppliers. 'Just-in-time' (JIT), tool change and statistical quality control, value analysis, cost accounting and systematic, all-covering *Kaizen* activities (see below) were at the heart of this upskilling offensive.

3. The race to catch up with the US and Europe (1974–81)

This period was shaped by a technological catch-up race with the US and Europe, and extremely fierce competition on the domestic market. Cooperation in the *Keiretsus* intensified further, to the extent that more entire blocks of work were transferred to leading suppliers (or 'black-box suppliers').

Cooperation became particularly close in the area of R&D through Simultaneous Engineering and Residential Engineers (engineers from the supplier working permanently in the OEM's product development function).

In this period between the first and second oil crises, production increased again from 7 million to 11.2 million vehicles – an average of 7 per cent per year.

4. The changing cooperative environment (1982–90)

The revaluation of the yen in 1985 prompted Japanese industry to branch out overseas. OEM factories were relocated to the US and suppliers were required to follow. By the end of the decade, 128 supplier firms had also set up factories in the USA. The Keiretsu structure came under pressure in this period as the 'transplants' had to buy components abroad for reasons of local content regulations, but also because of shortening product life-cycles.

The rapid pace of product development demanded more use of technology by the suppliers (simulation techniques, CAD/CAM, telecommunications) and led to suppliers without R&D know-how dropping out of the market, and to the evolution of even more clear-cut sub-divisions into main and subsidiary suppliers.

Production increased in this phase by 2 per cent per annum, with the number of vehicles growing moderately from 11.2 to around 13 million.

5. The decline in the importance of the Keiretsus (1985–2000)
Since 1985, and more markedly in the 1990s, a tendency toward a decline in the importance of the *Keiretsus* has been observed. Suppliers have to deliver to more than one OEMs to pay back their fixed costs and R&D expenditure and to compensate for stagnating or shrinking sales volumes at their main customer.

For example, Nippondenso supplies Nissan with fuel injection pumps and Tachi S provides seats for Toyota. Local Nissan and Honda suppliers are the main providers to the new Toyota factory in Fukuoka, and since the reorganization of the Nissan *Keiretsu* (Nissho-Kai) in 1991 it has generally been open to suppliers who meet certain quality criteria. Similarly, Calsonic, the manufacturer of air-conditioning systems, coolers and exhaust systems, actively supplies to Mitsubishi and Mazda.

Typically of the Japanese mentality, the topic of restructuring is not willingly addressed openly. Those interviewed in the study, however, confirmed that it is happening. According to them, further concentration of the supply industry in Japan can be expected particularly in those component sectors which are currently highly populated, where major economies of scale can be achieved, and where there is a marked trend toward further modularization. For example, it is likely that out of 17 seat producers, 16 wheel makers, 13 manufacturers in each of the areas of steering columns, automatic gears and shock absorbers or eleven manufacturers of air-conditioning systems, a considerable proportion will be affected by restructuring (Figure 5.6).

EUROPE: RESTRUCTURING IN PROGRESS

In Europe, outsourced products account for about half the manufacturing cost of a car. The supply industry is correspondingly important to what is possibly today's most vital concern for

Production structure for important components and influences on
restructuring in Japan, 1993–94

	Production structure				Influences		
	OEMS	Japanese suppliers	EU/US suppliers	Total	Scale effects in development/ production	Modularization	Competition from EU/US
Seats	1	16	–	17	++	++	0
Wheels	3	13	–	16	++	0	+
Steering columns	2	10	1	13	++	++	+
Automatic gears	7	3	3	13	++	++	0
Sound proofing	1	12	–	13	++	++	+
Air conditioning units	3	8	–	11	++	++	0

++ = Strong
 + = Medium
 0 = Weak

Fig. 5.6 *Concentration of the supplier industry is to be expected in Japan as well*

European car manufacturers: to restore competitiveness to automotive production along the entire value chain on a global scale. That means making up a cost disadvantage of 30 to 50 per cent compared to Japanese and American competitors.

Up to now, car manufacturers have reacted to the perceived need for action mainly by drastically increasing the pricing pressure on suppliers. Initial successes in rationalization have been achieved by both sides, but the potential in this area seems to be more or less exhausted. From now on further – urgently needed – optimization will have to seek other dimensions: in R&D input from suppliers who will receive greater degrees of freedom in product development, and in the assembly contribution of suppliers who will increase their assembly level from single parts to components and modules (see Chapter 1, 'Introduction').

If this potential is exploited, there will be a marked fall in the complexity costs of suppliers and OEMs, better and more rational manufacturability will be attained in design (specifications), leading to a reduced need for coordination. Costs can be cut by 30 per cent or more.

A cost structure advantage also comes into play where value added is transferred from manufacturer to supplier: compared to OEMs, the suppliers are for the most part smaller and therefore less complex and

Supplier structure and personnel costs in the European automotive
industry
Index (1992)

	Hours worked hours/year	Costs/ worker/ year	Total costs
Automotive manufacturers	100	100	100
Large suppliers	110	80	70
Mid-sized/small suppliers	120	70	60
Low wage economies (former Eastern bloc)	130	10-20	7-15

Source: IKB industry reports.

Fig. 5.7 *Differences in personnel costs of up to 90 per cent*

'leaner' in their structure; their labour costs are not way in excess of
the basic rate like those of the OEMs, and the annual net working
hours are longer (excluding vacation, days in lieu, average sick leave,
and break allowances). This can result in differences in costs per hour
of 30 per cent in Germany, for example – or up to 90 per cent where
individual stages of manufacture are carried out in the low-wage
economies of Eastern Europe, such as the sewing of seat covers in the
Czech Republic or the manufacture of cable harnesses in Poland
(Figure 5.7).

As a result of the trend toward outsourcing modules or systems,
about a third of all European automotive industry suppliers, i.e.,
around 1,000 companies, can be expected to be taken over or pull out
of the market in the course of the next few years, and vanish due to
their failure to meet the technological and financial requirements
(Figure 5.8). In the German supply industry, for example, considerable changes of this type can already be observed, but not every
structural change is necessarily a pioneering development. An analysis of 300 major mergers and acquisitions involving German companies between 1989 and 1992 shows that the majority of transactions
made no significant contribution to concrete optimization of the
value added structure.

The activities of large conglomerates building or extending their
share of the automotive industry through acquisition ·or significant
investments are most in the spotlight. Around one in every five

Number and size of manufacturers

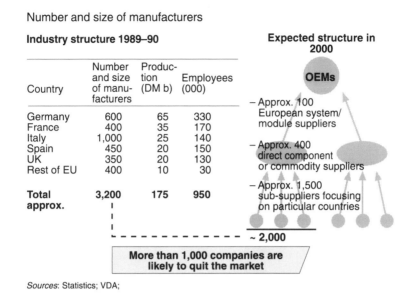

	Number and size of manufacturers	Production (DM b)	Employees (000)
Industry structure 1989–90			
Country			
Germany	600	65	330
France	400	35	170
Italy	1,000	25	140
Spain	450	20	150
UK	350	20	130
Rest of EU	400	10	30
Total approx.	**3,200**	**175**	**950**

Expected structure in 2000

OEMs

– Approx. 100 European system/ module suppliers

– Approx. 400 direct component or commodity suppliers

– Approx. 1,500 sub-suppliers focusing on particular countries

~ 2,000

More than 1,000 companies are likely to quit the market

Sources: Statistics; VDA;

Fig. 5.8 *European supply industry on the verge of dramatic restructuring*

transactions in the period studied fell into this category. About one-third of the acquisitions were aimed at gaining access to markets (over half of these were in the former GDR), and another fifth to achieving critical mass. Further activities served to optimize the product range or vertical integration. There appears to be no clear motive for some transactions, e.g., the entry of investment companies, or taking of equity stakes. Remarkably few activities were aimed at acquiring new technology or at improving the cost structure by moving into low-wage countries.

If we classify these mergers and acquisitions roughly according to their contribution to the optimization of the participants' value chain (Figure 5.9), only around a fifth of them can be classed unreservedly as useful because they are mainly about improving cost and technology structures. Around three in ten mergers and acquisitions appear 'partially useful' but cause considerable integration problems, for example. The remainder, around 50 per cent – even giving due consideration to possible future 'integration wins' – can be rated as dubious or mistaken in terms of results.

Overall, the driving force behind restructuring in Europe seems to be the fact that many suppliers are striving to become or remain direct suppliers to the automotive manufacturers. However, this is

Classification of mergers and acquisitions in the automotive supply
industry with German participation, 1989–1992

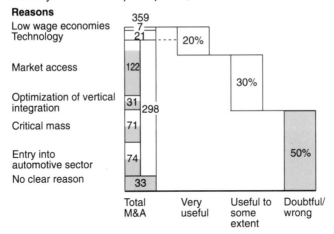

Sources: Amdata and Lotus databases; SAC; EIU; annual reports; press clippings.

Fig. 5.9 *Previous restructuring has sometimes been of doubtful value*

barely feasible in the sense of an optimum value chain and supply
structure, nor is it necessarily an attractive option for the supplier,
since high returns are attainable in every supply sector (see Chapter 1,
'Introduction').

The movement toward the module/system supply segment that we
are witnessing in the automotive supply industry – i.e., toward the
north-eastern corner of the R&D contribution/assembly contribution
matrix – will, indeed, continue (see Chapter 1). But 'north-east' will
not be the right course for every company in the industry to steer.
Many companies will find it impossible to leap-frog several quadrants
to enter a supposedly more attractive segment on the basis of their
existing capabilities and resources, particularly in the area of quality
management in the development and production processes. For
example, a glance at the patent statistics shows that one key requirement, technology know-how, is concentrated in a small number of
companies in Germany, and indeed in Europe as a whole (Figure
5.10).

It would make more sense to build and further develop capabilities
step by step via quadrants close to home, in order to be able to handle
later on the demands made on design quality in the module/system
supply sector, in the sense of value to the customer. In any case, it is

Share of patents of the 20 leading suppliers*, 1992
% of all patents

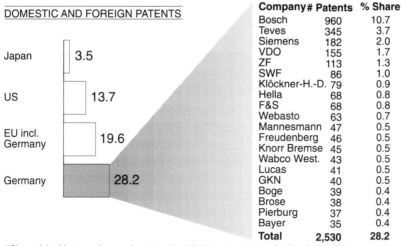

DOMESTIC AND FOREIGN PATENTS		Company	# Patents	% Share
		Bosch	960	10.7
		Teves	345	3.7
		Siemens	182	2.0
Japan	3.5	VDO	155	1.7
		ZF	113	1.3
		SWF	86	1.0
		Klöckner-H.-D.	79	0.9
US	13.7	Hella	68	0.8
		F&S	68	0.8
		Webasto	63	0.7
EU incl.	19.6	Mannesmann	47	0.5
Germany		Freudenberg	46	0.5
		Knorr Bremse	45	0.5
		Wabco West.	43	0.5
		Lucas	41	0.5
Germany	28.2	GKN	40	0.5
		Boge	39	0.4
		Brose	38	0.4
		Pierburg	37	0.4
		Bayer	35	0.4
		Total	**2,530**	**28.2**

* Share of the 20 automotive supply companies with the most patent applications in the industry
in their region.
Sources: Ifo Institute;

Fig. 5.10   *European know-how concentrated in a small number of companies*

safe to say that a sustainable competitive advantage can only be attained through genuine differentiation in R&D contribution (northerly course), but not by blithely traveling 'due east', i.e., expanding the assembly contribution.

US: The Increase in Productivity and Technological Expertise

The American automotive industry suppliers in our study increased their value added per employee by an average of 10 to 11 per cent per annum between 1988 and 1991. This means that their productivity grew significantly faster than that of their competitors in Japan (plus 6 to 7 per cent per annum) and Europe (plus 3 to 4 per cent) (Figure 5.11). The main trigger for this soaring efficiency was the entry of Japanese car manufacturers and suppliers into the US market from 1985 onwards. It sent shock waves through the traditional relationship between the oligopoly of the big three automobile manufacturers and their approximately 2,700 suppliers, which was characterized by extremely short-term cooperation and poor to, at best, average performance.

Value added* per employee in US$000

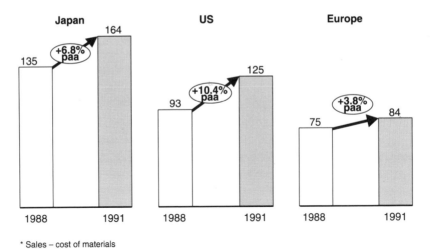

* Sales – cost of materials

Fig. 5.11   *Best productivity boosters are US companies*

Marked improvements were seen not only in the productivity of the suppliers, but above all in their R&D and quality position. This is revealed in the long-term study by a new generation of suppliers who came close to matching European figures with their volume of R&D (for their own products), for which they had independent responsibility. The popular European prejudice against technologically inferior American manufacturers is a thing of the past.

The increase in R&D expenditure mentioned above is one indication of this new strength, another is the growing number of people working in Research and Development in the US auto industry (Figure 5.12). Whilst the total number of people working in the car industry dropped from around 1 million to 800,000 between 1973 and 1990, in R&D departments the number rose from 30,000 to 50,000 in the same period. The share of R&D employees rose from 3 to around 6 per cent of the total workforce. And the investment has paid off on the supplier side as well, not least in the form of a share of sales of 32 per cent earned by the surveyed companies with competitively superior products.

As in Europe, a large number of sub-divisions in the supply structure and a trend toward module and system suppliers are emerging in the American supply market.

Development of workforce

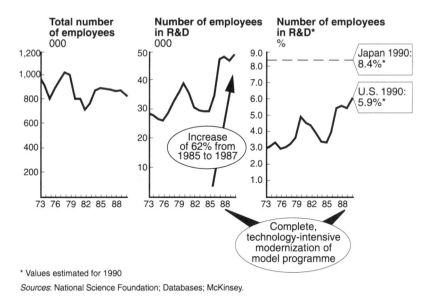

* Values estimated for 1990

Sources: National Science Foundation; Databases; McKinsey.

Fig. 5.12 *Growth of R&D departments in US automotive companies*

This development, too, was discussed in the 1980s as a reaction to the Japanese transplants and the suppliers they brought with them. America's 'Big Three' appear to have realized that their Japanese competitors had a far more solid supplier base, and therefore became anxious to forge similarly constructive links with their suppliers – links which suppliers were also interested in having forged. Despite this, there were few changes in the nature of cooperation to start with over the following years. The restructuring of the supply industry in the US did not pick up again until the beginning of the 1990s.

A productivity comparison by the McKinsey Global Institute and the interviews conducted during the long-term study can explain this delay. Under existing agreements between OEMs and their trade unions it was difficult to lay off staff on the basis of outsourcing decisions, over and above the already necessary measures to promote productivity. Added to this was the collapse in sales and profits in Detroit, which turned out to be much more drastic than expected and which turned the OEMs' attention toward short-term unit costs rather than closer cooperation.

And finally, system delivery was mainly seen as the supplier simply taking over assembly. However, unless complexity, specifications, and processes are optimized in the design phase over and above this no real added value emerges for the OEMs – and none whatsoever in the eyes of the end customer. Accordingly, OEMs were reluctant to reward the new performance levels. As a result, returns in the components business were for the most part considerably more attractive than in the loosely defined system business, which explains the small number of suppliers that took to it.

However, this period now seems to have passed, and, as in Europe, the supplier structure can be distinguished increasingly in terms of the R&D and assembly contributions of the players. Emerging from this development are module and system, component and parts suppliers with different roles and varying degrees of closeness to the OEMs. It can therefore also be expected in the USA that many of the current 2,700 supplier companies will disappear into mergers or acquisitions, or will quit the market.

THE LEARNING PROCESS AT CORPORATE LEVEL: REGIONAL DIFFERENCES IN THE NEED TO CHANGE

The traditional close working relationship with one OEM as the main customer is reflected in the quality management of Japanese suppliers. It has undoubtedly facilitated the integrated optimization process, since first-tier suppliers enjoy considerable development freedom in engineering their tasks and concepts. However, at the same time this one-to-one relationship also detracts attention from the end customer: a supplier with no need to compete for the orders of various different OEMs has little incentive to differentiate through superior end customer value.

European automotive suppliers show the other side of the coin. Their competitive situation has forced them to develop an experience and know-how lead in this dimension of design quality. Yet process quality has often fallen by the wayside in favour of product and innovation competence. Much the same applies to American suppliers: they have also pursued differentiation through design quality and caught up greatly in this area, mainly as a result of having to compete for orders from US OEMs and also from demanding foreign car manufacturers.

In the face of global competition, traditional, one-sided strengths in quality management will soon be inadequate. The learning objectives for every region's companies will be decided by what their competitors at the other corners of the Triad are doing better.

- Japan will have to build end customer competence.
- Europe and the USA will have to improve process quality.

Japanese Companies: Learning to Develop More End-Customer Competence

With the decline of the *Keiretsu* system, Japanese suppliers have been forced to redouble their efforts to expand. However, they cannot win enough customers outside the *Keiretsus* without independent development of value to the end customer. And that is an expensive game – the leading quality companies in Europe planned to increase R&D expenditure by some 20 per cent between 1991 and 1994, mainly to keep on building technology competence and design quality. Japanese participants in the long-term study were actually planning a 40 per cent increase. In view of dwindling returns on sales, this will be hard to finance (Figure 5.13).

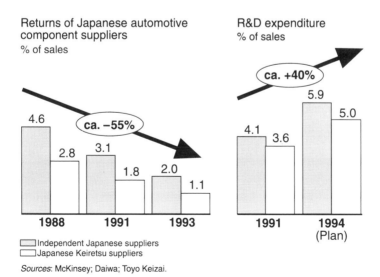

Fig. 5.13 *Increasing difficulties in financing R&D expenditure*

Japanese companies are likely to turn increasingly to European and Pacific Rim markets, with their attractive growth potential and relatively low level of penetration, in order to strengthen their financial base. There is a good deal of evidence to suggest that the need for further action has been recognized and practical steps taken: companies are trying to gain a better understanding of end customer requirements and are exploiting every potential for rationalization, which is most obvious where the hierarchy is most marked and self-determination at the operative shop-floor level is least developed.

Researching end customer requirements
Epic efforts are under way to make up the deficit in this area; the fact that Japanese suppliers are practising more QFD oriented to the end customer is clear evidence. A higher share of upstream development in total R&D will be the next step – today, the figure is around 11 per cent, measured by the number of employees (compared with the European average of 15 per cent, 19 per cent in Germany, and 17 per cent in the US). Suppliers will only be able to survive in OEM concept competitions if their upstream development function can identify important end customer and technology trends and translate them into suitable technical concepts for subsequent series development.

The experience of European quality companies shows the right direction and accessible routes, for example:

- End customer surveys of quality problems with the relevant supply components in their present cars, features they felt to be lacking after purchase, and future expectations.
- Dealer surveys, for example of dealers in the local area, investigating recurring quality problems and customer complaints.
- Product tests by end customers, possibly together with the OEM, the results of which are taken into account in ongoing development (depending on the type of product supplied).

These kinds of end customer contacts have resulted in products such as air-conditioning systems with individual cooling units for driver and passenger, glass sliding roofs (more daylight even in the rain), or high-frequency vibrating, heated wing mirrors (anti-rain and frost).

Dismantling hierarchies

None of the Japanese companies included in the long-term study had fewer than seven levels of hierarchy (Figure 5.14), whereas the leading European companies and average American companies of comparable size had five levels on average (see Chapter 2, 'Strategy and Organization'). Japanese structures were well over-inflated particularly in middle management (*kacho, kakaricho*) and in lower management (*shokucho, hancho*).

Surprisingly, the same was true of the size of quality assurance departments: whereas in Europe and the US 4 to 4.5 per cent of the workforce in the more successful companies were employed in QA, Japanese suppliers had around 8 per cent – almost 2 per cent more even than lower-quality European companies. The main reasons for this are the high level of planning and scheduling activities in Japanese quality assurance functions. In addition, inspection procedures (final inspection) in these companies are to some extent still performed by the quality assurance function, even though workers

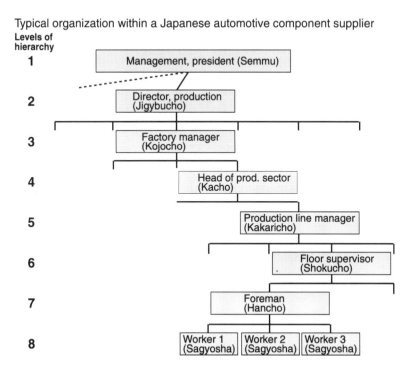

Typical organization within a Japanese automotive component supplier

Fig. 5.14 *Inflated structures must be slimmed down*

are largely responsible for checking their own work. The thought that quality assurance is being used as a kind of 'organizational parking lot' cannot be completely ruled out.

The most radical cutbacks are likely to be in the area of administration. There are historical reasons for its 'inflatedness': during the phase of steady growth the regular increases in productivity could be translated into additional volumes of output. In those days it was easy to adhere to Japanese principles of corporate management, for example, the guarantee of a 'job for life' for overhead and production functions. This generated a higher level of motivation among employees, which in turn benefited the continuous improvement process.

However, the job-for-life principle has only ever applied to part of the workforce, and our long-term study showed that almost all Japanese factories employed 15 to 35 per cent temporary employees. The first reaction to the painful falls in sales after 1990 was a reduction in this variable cost factor – a short-term adjustment in the workforce which would have been unthinkable in Europe and barely acceptable even in the US. But even after these cutbacks, underutilized fixed cost factors remained in overhead areas such as quality assurance which, because of the prevailing 'social principles', nobody dared tackle for a long time. The first reports of compulsory leaves of absence, redundancies, and factory closures – measures shaking the very foundations of Japanese life – indicate that these principles are no longer unconditionally respected. A wave of rationalization has finally started in the Japanese supply industry.

Creating entrepreneurship at shop-floor level
In addition to the end customer focus which can be learned from the Europeans and Americans and their lean administration methods, Japanese suppliers can now turn their attention to the entrepreneurship of the Americans at shop-floor level as the next area for improvement. The Americans are the Triad's world champions when it comes to working in self-managing teams with a broad range of tasks and decision-making powers.

These self-managing teams should not be confused with the Japanese *Kaizen* teams, which concentrate on improvements in quality and productivity and are not a formal component of the organization for the day-to-day running of the business. Self-managing teams (see Chapter 4, 'The Production Process') perform day-on-day production tasks, organize the internal assignment of tasks, and are responsible for machine setup, their own materials logistics, quality assurance, service, repair, and maintenance, as well as planning and control tasks in their own working area. Naturally enough, their responsibilities also include continuous improvement in their own processes and tasks.

First and foremost, this range of activities demands highly trained employees. This is why American quality companies invest US$500 per head in further training. It also demands extensive delegation of decision-making powers from the shop-floor supervisor or foreman levels to the level of the employee teams. The Americans lead the way in this field as well. In no other country were employees given so much responsibility: from stopping the production line, initiating fault-elimination measures, and stopping customer deliveries to rejecting incoming components which failed to meet specifications.

Eight out of ten American companies confer these responsibilities on their employees. Similarly, decisions on hiring a new team member or on job-rotation moves for existing team members are taken by the team itself. The teams also take joint decisions on minor investments, usually within a yearly budget of around US$5,000 to $10,000 granted to them by the plant management – one of the most conclusive proofs of the trust management places in its employees and of the will to mobilize and change.

The study found self-managing teams in operation in more than three-quarters of the American companies surveyed. On the one hand, they allow companies to tap rationalization potential, particularly by eliminating separate capacities for indirect activities and extra levels of hierarchy in the organization. But quality also improves when employees can use key quality assurance methods after suitable training and when motivation is significantly improved due to mobilization of personal initiative. In time, the employee becomes a little entrepreneur or manager in his field. In quite a few companies this is no longer a mere vision of the future, it is fast becoming reality.

There is usually a team leader in charge, who performs the same duties as his colleagues for the same pay, but also carries out some administrative tasks. There may also be a rotation system within the team for the position of team leader, depending on the qualifications of the members. This is, however, rare in the introductory phase of the team concept. In some American and European companies, the team leader is elected by his fellow members rather than being chosen by management. The majority of these firms have abolished the hourly-wage system, and with it the distinction between 'white-collar'

Assessment of performance and worker involvement

Work assessment
● Top 5 targets
● Degree of achievability
● Improvement measures

Specification of targets
● Parallel development of targets
● Measurement and discussion of degree of achievability of target

Personal assessment
● Knowledge (specific to work place and general)
● Planning and problem-solving skills
● Pleasure in decision making
● Work capacity
● Social competence (leadership and communication qualities)
● Cost consciousness

Improvement of environment
● Discussion of organizational environment
● Manner of leadership of superiors

Future perspectives
● Consciousness of responsibility
● Possibilities of promotion
● Qualification measures

Improvement in execution of work
● Assessment of workplace by workers
● Proposals for improvement measures

Criteria for the assessment of a worker by the team leader or manager ('top-down assessment')

Criteria for the participation of workers ('bottom-up assessment')

Fig. 5.15 *Systematic personal development on the work level as well*

and 'blue-collar' employees. A good example is at Rover in the United Kingdom, where 'employees' are now known as 'associates', i.e., partners – a sign of management's esteem.

Almost all American companies perform formal skill evaluation at the operative level to carry out systematic personnel development in this area, too (Figure 5.15).

In Japan, activities such as quality assurance, setup, and maintenance are likewise carried out by employees today, but these employees tend to be organized into 'working groups', which take instructions from supervisors and/or foremen, i.e., from an additional hierarchical level. They do not enjoy the same decision-making freedom as those in the self-managing teams, nor do they perform planning and control tasks in their own areas (Figure 5.16).

The study in Japan found 'extensive' team concepts in place in only one company, the subsidiary of an American supplier group. However, all the other participating companies were in the process of examining such concepts. They freely admitted that they were first made aware of such mobilization concepts, or began to pay more attention to them, while setting up their transplants in the US. If it means improving their own performance, learning from the strengths

Feature	Self-managing teams: 'Entrepreneur'	Kaizen team: 'problem-solver'	Working group: 'skilled worker'
Origin:	US (partly Europe)	Japan	Japan (and Europe)
Objective:	• Meeting performance targets in the relevant work area (costs, quality, throughput time, etc.)	• Finding sustainable solutions to day-to-day problems (elimination of 'waste')	• Meeting precisely defined performance targets (unit production, quality) for individual workers
Tasks:	• Carrying out and taking responsibility for daily routine • Integrated range of tasks (direct and indirect tasks, including problem-solving) • Staffing decisions taken by the team itself	• Problem-solving for improvement in quality and productivity • Analytical and creative tasks • Staffing decisions taken by superior	• Carrying out the daily routine • Taking on indirect tasks (e.g., setup, maintenance) depending on skill level; no planning control • Staffing decision taken by superior
Organization and management:	• Preferably organization of production into manufacturing or assembly cells (otherwise practical segmentation of flow production) • Allocation to workplaces by the team workers themselves • Democratic decisions within the team • Team managed by a leader chosen by the team • Reporting to product manager	• Independent of the chosen form of organization • Allocation of tasks by superior • Decisions taken and instructions issued by superior • Reporting to floor supervisor or production line manager	• Independent of the chosen form of organization • Allocation of tasks by superior • Decisions taken and instructions issued by superior • Reporting to floor supervisor or production line manager • Normally piecework pay or volume-based bonuses for individual workers
Skills:	• Multi-skilled (technical, problem solving, and entrepreneurial skills)	• Problem-solving/analytical skills	• Mainly manual skill, partly technical skill
Motivation:	• Through individual initiative (self management) • By group pressure	• By superiors • By group pressure	• By superiors
Team-composition:	• 6–10 workers (incl. team leader) and specialists if needed	• 6–8	• 10–20 workers form groups (not team work), no team leader or spokesperson

Fig. 5.16 *Comparison of self-managing teams, Kaizen teams and working groups*

of others seems the most natural thing in the world to these companies.

European and American Suppliers: Learning to Improve Process Quality

European suppliers in particular will soon start to feel the effects of the increased Japanese expansion drive in the form of increased competitive pressure. At the same time, they will find car manufacturers demanding a higher level of process quality: most are demanding a maximum reject quota of 100 ppm in 1995/96 – not least because they are planning a radical extension of warranty periods and are no longer prepared to be the sole bearers of most of the consequential cost of faults.

In addition to having to bear the immediate quality costs of component replacement, suppliers will also in future have to consider the car dealer's removal and re-installation costs, as quite a few OEMs are planning to pass these handling costs on to them. As a rule, these are around 5 to 10 times higher than the costs of the parts themselves. Hypothetically, if the quality costs of replacement components lie at 1 per cent, the additional costs of removal and installation could easily swallow up or exceed the year's entire profits.

Far more crucial, however, is the end result of this 'chain of consequential costs'; if the OEM alienates or loses customers as a result of poor quality, this will have a directly depressing effect on the supplier's order book.

In this respect, European and American suppliers can and must adopt the successful Japanese methods of maximizing process quality, especially since the Japanese are still setting a breakneck pace of improvement in this area – between 1986 and 1991 they managed to cut back the average reject rate alone by 14.5 per cent per year. Starting from a weaker position, European companies only managed an average annual improvement of 6.7 per cent in the same period. Only the European quality companies could almost keep pace with the Japanese, with an annual reduction rate of 11.1 per cent (similar to the Americans with 11.6 per cent) (Figure 5.17).

The first rule of learning from the best is to study their recipes for success before adopting them either 'one to one' or tailoring them to one's own requirements. The strengths of the Americans and Europeans in end-customer-oriented design and employee mobilization

Development of internal reject rate
%

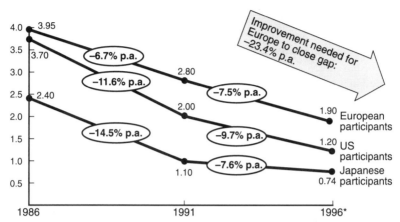

* Forecast (increased trend in Europe, slower trend in Japan due to Kaizen issues and in the US because of level).

Fig. 5.17 *Rapid improvement required*

and the most important Japanese formulas for success are all basically transferable. Although there are undoubtedly practices in Japan which are only feasible in that culture, such as detailed regulations on personal hygiene within the factory or public comparisons of absenteeism for individual employees, these are unlikely to have a serious impact on quality.

For a long time now, Japanese transplants in Europe and the US have been successfully practising typical Japanese methods of optimizing process quality with local employees, and almost always with local managers as well. The most important of these methods contribute directly to the performance gap in this dimension of quality between Japanese and European manufacturers. They can be briefly summed up as follows (Figure 5.18):

- *Kaizen* as a process of continuous improvement in production, which according to the results of the long-term study is the reason for almost 50 per cent of the Japanese lead in process quality.
- *Involvement of customers and suppliers,* accounting for around 25 per cent of the gap
- *Preventive quality management in R&D,* responsible for a further 35 per cent of the Japanese lead.

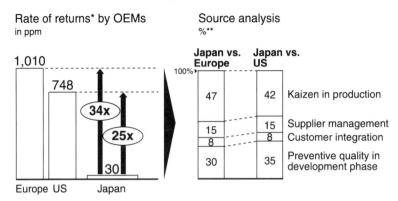

Rate of returns* by OEMs
in ppm

Source analysis
%**

*Products from automotive supplier rejected or classified as faulty by car manufacturers
** Contribution of management approaches to explaining discrepancies between Europe/US and Japan

Fig. 5.18   *Four main sources of process quality divide between Japan and Europe/US*

A regional comparison in representative product segments carried out by the long-term study proved that European companies are also capable of achieving top quality. In the areas of batteries, cable harnesses, and electro-mechanical components the reject and rework rates of the top European supplier were better than those of the top Japanese participant in the study (Figure 5.19).

Japanese companies tend to use the right methods in a more intensive and targeted manner. The most striking factor in their

Rework plus cumulative rejects in %

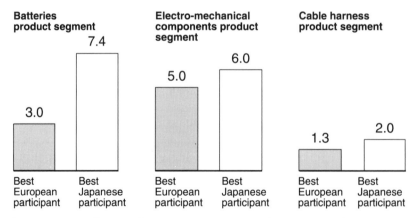

Fig. 5.19   *Excellent performance in process quality also possible in Europe*

success, however, is the consistent and uniform use of the entire 'tool-kit'. They get less bogged down in formalities, such as blow-by-blow instructions for applying tools in quality handbooks, for example. Far more emphasis is placed on practical training and systematic application on site. (This also explains Japanese fears that the Europeans could use the new ISO 9000 standard as a protectionist weapon; most Japanese firms do not have sufficiently detailed quality handbooks for the largely document-based certification process.)

Kaizen in the production process

Kaizen means constantly challenging existing performance levels and seeking better solutions – the process of continuous improvement, which is initiated by employees and has made a vital contribution to Japan's leading position in industry. The current adoption of the Western system of self-managing teams is not infringing on this achievement. On the contrary, the additional one-off saving of cutting back on superfluous hierarchical levels and some overhead areas, as well as the acceleration of procedures, is improving the basis for the continuous process of *Kaizen*.

The organizational seed of *Kaizen* activities lies in the quality circles (see Appendix A, 'Top Quality Tools') which have been in use in Japan since the mid-1950s. Quality circles in Japan take a different approach from those in Europe, where quality circles are also now widely used, though mainly as a psychological tool for improving motivation and enjoyment of work, giving the employee a high level of 'creative freedom' in the choice of topic and the way it is addressed.

Japanese companies use quality circles as a 'hard' management tool to improve quality and productivity. In concrete terms, this finds expression in the open communication of precise and ambitious targets and achievements (Figure 5.20).

- *More precise and ambitious performance targets*: As a rule, subject matter, targets, individual tasks, and methods are specified by superiors. Sub-objectives (for products, production areas, production lines, etc.), defined in terms of indicators of quality, cost, and time, are derived from ambitious overriding objectives. Such operationalization of targets is a characteristic strength of Japanese companies. Sometimes they even specify how many actionable suggestions (!) every single employee has to implement.

Chart displayed in the factory – quality circle activities

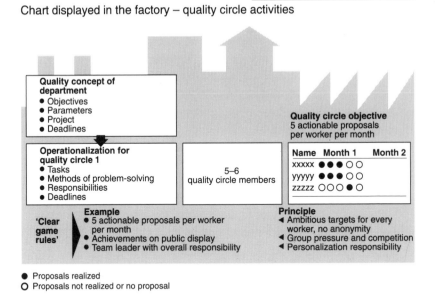

● Proposals realized
○ Proposals not realized or no proposal

Fig. 5.20 *Open communication of objectives and achievements*

- *Personified responsibility:* In addition to taking responsibility for defining the performance targets, the plant management team, i.e., the manager, group leaders, and supervisors/foremen, is itself assessed on the basis of the quality circles' results. The management's interest in success is correspondingly higher – in contrast to Europe, where some managers would fear a sacrifice in their own positions if their employees did well. Teams in Japan are given considerably more conceptual supervision and support in solving problems by managers who act as coaches on the spot and are in constant close contact with 'their' circles.

- *Institutionalized competition:* The publication of the activities of each quality circle on factory noticeboards encourages competition between *Kaizen* groups or quality circles as well as within each group. This in turn gives an extra boost to productivity. But institutionalized competition lives well beyond the confines of *Kaizen* groups. Take the example of a Japanese transplant in England, where large boards hanging from the factory ceiling exhort its employees to 'Beat Japan' – that is, to outclass the Japanese parent company in quality, costs, and delivery time.

- *Encouragement and acknowledgement*: To keep up the momentum, even minor suggestions are admitted and acknowledged. In the eyes of employees this counts as a positive reaction and proof of acceptance by management, which then encourages further suggestions. This is one of the major shortcomings of European companies, which miss out on the opportunity of creating an atmosphere of continuous improvement by offering their employees constant encouragement and acknowledgment. This recognition of success must be of an informal rather than a tangible nature. For example, the plant manager might have the best results presented to him fortnightly by employees (!), attend a chosen quality circle meeting every week as an active participant (not merely to keep an eye on what is going on!), talk to employees about current quality circle topics in the course of his daily tour of the factory, and ideally know all his staff by name.
- *Clear focus on implementation*: This point became crystal clear to us when we asked a Japanese plant manager what share of suggestions were actually implemented and he responded with a smile: suggestions are only put forward if their realization lies within the capabilities of those concerned or those participating. And in performance evaluations of individual employees, only the number of suggestions implemented is counted. It is therefore important for middle and top management to constantly monitor progress and, if necessary, to apply the appropriate pressure by visiting the place of work, to ensure that proposals are being followed through.

Even though the 'harder' Japanese approach appears to place less emphasis on the job satisfaction and motivation through creative freedom which European companies expressly and quite legitimately boost in their quality circles, this difference is only apparent. Indeed, in Japan, 72 per cent of employees surveyed said that they enjoyed the esteem of their managers, in contrast to a mere 30 per cent in Europe. Eighty-six per cent of Japanese workers felt that they were amply supplied with information at work, in contrast to only 43 per cent of their European counterparts. In the light of these statistics it will come as no surprise that twice as many Japanese as European production employees gave positive reports on job satisfaction, shared values and objectives, and their intensive involvement in problem solving. The personal commitment of the employees is

Quality circle and Kaizen activities

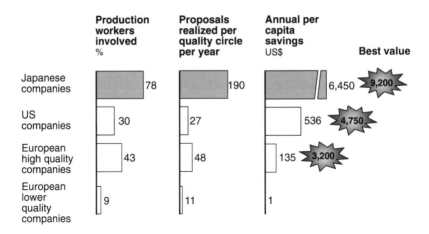

Fig. 5.21   *Broader worker motivation and more success in Japan*

correspondingly high, with members of quality circles meeting out-side working hours if necessary.

Japanese companies not only use quality circles to different ends but also more intensively and to greater effect (Figure 5.21). In the companies surveyed, almost 80 per cent of production employees were active members, whereas in Europe even the top-quality com-panies could only manage around 43 per cent participation (and at the low-quality end of the scale a mere 8 per cent). The Americans were also a long way behind the Japanese, with around 30 per cent.

A Japanese quality circle 'produces' around 190 suggestions a year, resulting in annual savings of US$6,450 per member of the total workforce. As an illustration, let us take a hypothetical company with 500 employees and sales of around US$100 million. Employees' suggestions on improvements will save their company US$3.2 million per annum – or 3 per cent of sales.

Even European quality companies, by contrast, produce only 48 proposals per quality circle and hence per capita savings amounting to all of US$135. It must be said in their favour that they achieve most of their rationalization goals using 'top down' measures in indirect areas (production planning, operations scheduling, industrial engineering, process development). Yet the Japanese also use these opportunities – and achieve success comparable to 'bottom up' approaches with *Kaizen*.

American companies were able to produce around 27 proposals per quality circle per year and save US$536 per employee. This places them well above the European average, but still some way behind that of Japan.

Ultimately, the success of the *Kaizen* system as a whole is based on a different conception of labour as a resource. Until a few years ago, employees in Europe were still regarded as helpers and operatives who could not be entrusted with problem-solving activities – which is particularly surprising in Germany, given the high level of training amongst skilled employees. In the mid-1950s, however, a time when Japanese products carried little clout on the world market due to poor quality, the Japanese had already come to the conclusion that production staff were actually in the best position to identify problems on the shop floor and search for solutions. Employees were kitted out for their tasks within the *Kaizen* groups with basic statistical and problem-solving tools (such as Pareto analysis and cause-and-effect diagrams) as well as need-based training in the application of the techniques.

Most European companies have now recognized this deficit and are working intensively on catching up. The Americans are a little further ahead than the European companies with their *Kaizen* activities – spurred on by the invasion of the US by Japanese car manufacturers and suppliers in the 1980s. As a result of the business links forged between these and American companies, partly driven by local content requirements, *Kaizen* know-how and the philosophy behind it have become widespread.

That *Kaizen* tactics can be used to considerable effect outside Japan is proved by the top European company surveyed (an English subsidiary of a German supplier): in this case, the quality circle produced per capita savings of around US$3,200. The top American company managed as much as US$4,750.

What typically happens in a *Kaizen* process? Here is an example from a Japanese cable harness manufacturer (Figure 5.22):

- The first three steps seek out the 'root of the problem' – the basic prerequisite for permanently eliminating a defect. If, for example, a screw always comes loose, the solution is not simply to screw it tighter (increasing the torque) but rather to improve the design of the thread.
- The fourth step then looks for concrete solutions. In this step of the process, Japanese companies place a great deal of faith in

Poka-Yoke measures (see Appendix A, 'Top Quality Tools'). These Poka-Yoke solutions, which are designed to prevent employees' mistakes, are common wisdom in Japan. For example, manually installed parts which are easy to confuse are marked with different colours; or assembly rigs are designed in such a way that parts can only be installed in one – i.e., the right – direction.

● In step 5, the effectiveness of the measure is tracked, and its precise value is quantified in step 6.

Setting the *Kaizen* process in motion and, more important, keeping it going are regarded as two of the most important tasks of management. It is basically a task of information and communication: continually giving production employees convincing answers to five explicit or implicit questions: What is the problem and why am I involved? What is the concrete objective? What contribution can I

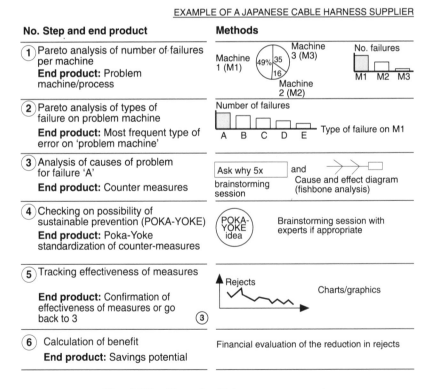

Fig. 5.22 *How the Kaizen process works*

make and how will management support my contribution? What was the effect of my contribution? Was my contribution significant from management's point of view?

Only when this process of communication becomes a credible and accepted institution – and a dialogue – can as many production employees as possible become committed and permanently involved in the process of continuous improvement.

Closer involvement of suppliers

Another decisive difference in approaches to quality management between Japanese car and their American and European counterparts lies in the training and supervision they offer their suppliers. The situation described in Chapters 3 and 4 is accepted practice in Japanese companies: they work with on average 30 per cent fewer suppliers and engage in targeted supplier development in joint projects with the most important ones.

Their extreme consistency and system in this practice again differentiates them from European and American manufacturers:

- *Selection by know-how*: Whilst there is still a strong bias toward 'blueprint specifications' in Europe and the US, and the choice of suppliers is based largely on price competition, Japanese suppliers pursue a targeted search for 'black-box suppliers'. Even before the product concept stage, those suppliers with a considerable impact on subsequent product quality are chosen on the basis of their product and process know-how; the question of costs is addressed later on in the development process by early target costing and joint value analysis.
- *Buyers as 'all-round managers'*: The different process for choosing and supporting suppliers inevitably affects the profile of the buyer as well. The modern buyer at Japanese quality suppliers is no longer a simple 'price negotiator' – he must simultaneously keep an eye on the costs, quality, R&D capabilities, and delivery capabilities of his own suppliers, and is selected for his technical and management know-how.
- *Joint project planning*: Detailed project plans are drawn up for core suppliers. These contain long- and short-term objectives, core working areas, and details of what manpower resources are to be supplied by the company and the supplier respectively. Workshops are often held to define and solve problems.

Resources for joint projects with suppliers
Working days per core sub-supplier, 1991

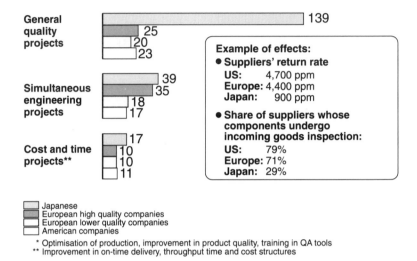

General quality projects

- 139
- 25
- 20
- 23

Example of effects:
- Suppliers' return rate
  US: 4,700 ppm
  Europe: 4,400 ppm
  Japan: 900 ppm

Simultaneous engineering projects

- 39
- 35
- 18
- 17

- Share of suppliers whose components undergo incoming goods inspection:
  US: 79%
  Europe: 71%
  Japan: 29%

Cost and time projects**

- 17
- 10
- 10
- 11

☐ Japanese
▓ European high quality companies
☐ European lower quality companies
☐ American companies

* Optimisation of production, improvement in product quality, training in QA tools
** Improvement in on-time delivery, throughput time and cost structures

Fig. 5.23   *Investments in sub-supplier development*

- *Investment of more resources*: The Japanese invest on average 139 working days a year per key supplier in joint quality-improvement projects for the production process; the top European companies invest only 25 working days and the Americans only 23. Somewhat less was invested in cost and time projects, but the Japanese were still the clear leaders. The same was true of the involvement of suppliers in the development process: Japanese companies invested on average 39 working days a year per supplier in simultaneous engineering projects with their suppliers (Figure 5.23).
- *Top management involvement*: It is not unusual for board members – and even the CEO – to participate in supplier workshops. This demonstrates the importance of the themes being discussed and is the main driver behind rapid and sustainable improvement at the suppliers. Only two European companies included in the study practised this style of top management support.

In order to mobilize sub-suppliers on a broader basis, many Japanese automotive suppliers hold competitions inviting suggestions on cost, quality, and innovation issues. 'Supplier clubs', as they are known, also help to improve quality standards. Their main purpose is the systematic exchange of know-how between suppliers and sub-suppliers and, most importantly, between individual sub-suppliers, in themed workshops lasting several days. The aim of these meetings is not to 'get together and party' but to define concrete objectives, which are to be attained by systematic preparation and implementation. Here, too, the attendance of top management highlights the importance of such workshops.

This all goes to show that Japanese suppliers conduct a fair but 'tough' partnership with their sub-suppliers. If they have a know-how basis which can be upgraded they offer them support and upskilling, but in these cases they plan for long-term relationships. If it turns out that they made a mistake in their careful selection process, they will stop working with the company concerned. As the supplier structure in the Japanese automotive industry consolidates further, these game rules will become tougher still. The real challenge will lie in transferring supplier management practices to non-*Keiretsu* companies.

The statistics show just how successful the Japanese approach has been: in our study, figures for complaints by suppliers to sub-suppliers stood at 900 ppm in Japan, 4,400 in Europe, and 4,700 in America. This higher quality allows Japanese companies to dispense with incoming quality controls altogether for more than 70 per cent of their sub-suppliers (29 per cent in Europe and 21 per cent in the US).

Targeted cooperation with OEMs
In view of the *Keiretsu* system, it is hardly surprising that not only the sub-suppliers, but also the OEMs as customers are much more closely integrated with suppliers than is the case elsewhere. But even independent suppliers, which deliver to four or more car manufacturers, collaborate much more intensively with OEMs than do their European or American counterparts. The Japanese invest an average of 205 working days a year in simultaneous engineering projects at their customers, whereas the top European companies invest 100 working days, the less successful ones around 65 days, and the Americans around 74 days on average (Figure 5.24).

Fostered by the widespread single-customer relationships, a completely different concept of simultaneous engineering between manufacturers and suppliers has emerged in Japan. The large number of organizational and technical interfaces (particularly for products like

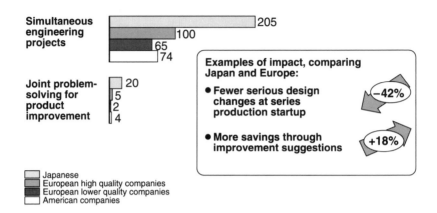

Joint projects in customer's factory
man days per customer, 1991

Fig. 5.24 *Cooperation with customers in the development phase*

air-conditioning systems and gears) demands close cooperation to start with; in addition, the OEM considers it extremely important to make the best use of the supplier's know-how.

One sign of close cooperation is mutual participation in design reviews. The 'residential engineer' arrangement is another: the supplier's design engineer is based permanently in the customer's development department and forms an integral part of the design team. He thus guarantees the flow of information from supplier to OEM and acts as an on-the-spot representative of the supplier's position. In Europe, the movement toward such openness in the use of supplier know-how has been a very slow process so far, partly because of the traditionally high level of in-house development at European OEMs and partly as a result of the still-prevalent 'not invented here' syndrome.

Some suppliers, too, have reservations about such 'trust-based' cooperative arrangements as jointly developed proposals for unit cost reductions. Some European suppliers have fundamentally challenged the validity of these activities, on the grounds that (a) it is difficult to get their ideas accepted by the OEMs' R&D organization, and (b) they would be actively reducing their own sales. However, these suppliers are overlooking one important factor: a long-term partnership and cooperation on tapping improvement potentials will eventually transform this short-term 'sales slump' into a medium-term increase, as a result of improved products and/or reduced costs. And both parties profit from that.

The potential benefits of this style of simultaneous engineering are illustrated, for example, by the number of significant design changes at and after the start of series production: the study showed a figure 42 per cent smaller in Japanese companies than in European companies in the same product segments.

The condition for and consequence of close cooperation with the OEM is an organization structured by customers in the R&D function of all independent Japanese suppliers. It is important that such a structure is achieved within overriding, homogeneous product groups, in order to enable technical synergies and essential special skills to be exploited. To ensure the exchange of know-how within the development function and to prevent 'reinventing the wheel', special units – such as 'Product innovation' – are also created for cross-customer upstream development and experience gathering, as far as confidentiality agreements allow.

Even after series production has begun, the Japanese invest more in joint product improvement with their customers than Europeans and Americans (see Figure 5.24).

These activities can be compared to those of quality circles in production, with the one difference that employees from design engineering, production, and quality assurance are also involved here. The effectiveness of these joint problem-solving ventures is reflected in the fact that savings in product unit costs in Japan are 18 per cent higher than in Europe.

A common argument among European suppliers is that close cooperation with car manufacturers is far easier to achieve in Japan than in Europe. They claim that the Japanese 'saw the writing on the wall' much earlier and were therefore more open to corresponding proposals. This may have been largely true in the past, but in the meantime Europe is also undergoing a major sea change, led by a handful of OEMs that are following declarations of intent with action. In view of the potential cost and value advantages, we can expect cooperation between manufacturers and suppliers to develop on a broad front over the next few years.

Preventive quality assurance in R&D
The use of preventive quality assurance tools represents another major difference (Figure 5.25). All Japanese suppliers use product and process FMEA (failure mode and effects analysis), error tree

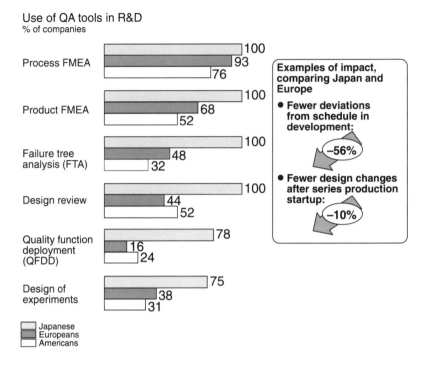

Use of QA tools in R&D
% of companies

Process FMEA: 100, 93, 76
Product FMEA: 100, 68, 52
Failure tree analysis (FTA): 100, 48, 32
Design review: 100, 44, 52
Quality function deployment (QFDD): 78, 16, 24
Design of experiments: 75, 38, 31

Japanese
Europeans
Americans

Examples of impact, comparing Japan and Europe
• Fewer deviations from schedule in development: −56%
• Fewer design changes after series production startup: −10%

Fig. 5.25 *Better product development through preventive QA tools*

analysis, and design reviews. Seventy-eight per cent use quality function deployment, which not only serves to identify customer requirements, but also supports their translation into smooth processes (see Appendix A, 'Top Quality Tools'). Originally, Japanese suppliers' use of QFD was oriented to the OEM as the customer, but a stronger focus on the end customer has begun. Seventy-five per cent use statistically planned experiments. In almost all of these areas, Europe and America lag far behind Japan.

The use of quality assurance tools is complicated, and must be sharply focused to achieve the necessary depth of penetration. That is why Japanese companies are very selective – restricting product FMEA, for example, to parts which are critical to product performance. Likewise, quality function deployment is not used routinely for every new model or application product, but only in those areas where customer requirements have not yet been clearly identified or are continually changing. Also, the Japanese do not restrict the use of QFD to products that have directly obvious end customer relevance, such as seats; it is also used by battery manufacturers, for example.

This, too, shows the recently increasing effort to improve design quality by establishing a clearer understanding of end customer needs.

The greatest difference between European/American and Japanese quality management in the R&D function lies in the importance placed on process capability in the development of a product. Japanese product developers are not only responsible for the functioning of a product, but also for its manufacturability at the lowest possible cost of defects. Accordingly, 90 per cent of Japanese companies surveyed supplied their R&D departments with concrete indicators of process capability (C_{pk} values) and ensured that they were adhered to by taking measurements during test and pilot production series. Only 32 per cent of European and 25 per cent of American companies carried out such measures.

We were particularly impressed by the example of how one Japanese company ensured manufacturability and ease of assembly. It had newly developed prototypes of mechanical steering components assembled by blindfolded employees, with the design engineers looking on – the ultimate test of manufacturability. Afterwards, engineers and employees got together in several workshops to improve ease of assembly in joint discussion.

Japanese product developers are generally much closer to production than their counterparts in other countries. Almost all of them begin their careers in the production function, where they typically spend a whole year. Here they manage the series startup of new products, where gaps in quality are most strikingly obvious; they improve ongoing production processes; they supervise quality circles; and they also take managerial responsibility for production lines and departments. It is not unusual for them to return to production jobs later on in their careers, in the context of systematic job rotation, for instance.

Another aspect of manufacturability is the smoothest possible fit between product and process. Japanese suppliers take this area so seriously that they will adapt the specification of a product to suit production machinery which cannot produce the originally specified dimensions with the necessary process stability. In other words, product tolerance does not always take priority. Instead, Japanese companies examine in detail what tolerance is needed for perfect functioning, and any remaining scope for altering the product is used to ensure process stability. That is 'integrated product/process development' in practice.

Efforts to make products as simple as possible are also of benefit to the product/process fit. Standardization is not restricted to the product portfolio; all the Japanese companies we visited told us that they planned to improve their cost and quality positions with standard parts, multiple-product assembly groups, and a smaller number of variants. One manufacturer of air-conditioning systems has even included its aim to reduce the number of end product variants and parts used by more than half in its short- and medium-term corporate planning.

In other words, ensuring process quality begins in the product development stage, with standardization and complexity reduction, for example, and Japanese companies consider this an issue of strategic importance. This is the only explanation for the Japanese lead in process quality.

Summary

The gap in quality levels between automotive industry suppliers within the Japan–US–Europe Triad proves that higher quality does not have to be bought at higher cost. Most quality leaders are also cost leaders. And they are all based in Japan. But regional conditions are becoming increasingly uniform, while quality is becoming an increasingly vital competitive factor. For every supplier in every region, survival depends on identifying and addressing weaknesses in its quality profile and learning from the strengths of others. Europeans, Americans, and Japanese are all role models in different quality disciplines in this learning process.

- *Japanese companies* offer outstanding *process quality* – the 'zero defects culture' in manufacturing – with extremely low rates of rework, rejects, and complaints. But as their supply relationships extend beyond their *Keiretsu* alliances, they need to improve their end customer capabilities – an area that has traditionally been the preserve of their American and European competitors. They will only find the resources to build these capabilities by slimming down hierarchies and mobilizing workers. They are already hard at work on this, taking lessons from the West.
- *European and American automotive industry suppliers* lead the way in *design quality*. They can boast the highest share of products with outstanding customer value, for OEMs as well as for end

customers. However, their Achilles' heel is a deficit in process quality. Faced with the high demands of automobile manufacturers – a maximum reject rate of 100 ppm, for example, coupled with correspondingly high penalties – their chances of survival depend on improving their performance in this area. A process of continuous improvement in production, as perfected by the Japanese in their *Kaizen* system, will be just as important as close involvement of suppliers and customers in development and production, and the expansion of preventive quality assurance in the development process.

6 The Road to Quality

Suppliers of systems have a glowing future. There is plenty of evidence to support such an assertion, as manufacturers move increasingly to subcontract entire value-added stages and concentrate their purchasing volume. Nevertheless, in the automotive supply industry, where this restructuring is in full swing, the future will still hold suppliers of parts who are more successful than many suppliers of systems. But only if they have a superior quality level, because increasing global competitive pressure means that the quality gap is much more serious than any 'system gap'. The road to quality can take a company in any segment and in any location to its goal. Success here is equally vital to suppliers of parts, components, and systems.

There is no such thing as the perfect quality company. The top companies at level IV, which have been discussed in preceding chapters, make up 13 per cent of the participants in the McKinsey long-term study. Collectively, they fulfil all the criteria for top quality; individually, each one comes only more or less close to the ideal. And yet, a glance at the best of them shows how powerful the quality lever can be. The 'top 5' European companies, which come very close to the level IV ideal, earn profits towering above those trailing at levels I and II, with return on sales six-and-a-half times higher and five times the sales growth (Figure 6.1).

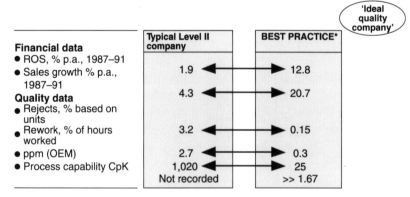

* Average figures for top 5 European companies

Fig. 6.1 *Ahead in all performance indicators*

154

The top companies are most aware of the connection between quality and performance. They are the least inclined to rest on their laurels, and continually work toward further improvement in every dimension of quality. The path to becoming a quality company is and remains a demanding change programme for the entire organization. Depending on where the company is starting from, it requires a more or less sweeping change in corporate culture:

- From 'inspecting in' quality to developing and manufacturing quality
- From a cost focus to a focus on growth and returns
- From compromises between functions to cross-functional group- and process-oriented objectives/philosophies
- From an exclusive focus on the OEM to an intensive end-customer focus
- From the all-powerful quality department to self-managing teams
- From goods inward inspection to development of suppliers
- From internal to external quality management, across company borders.

Unless companies are ready to tread these completely new paths, even the best initiatives soon get fouled up among the old rules, and the sceptics and heel-draggers again win the upper hand. Wherever your starting point may be on the path between 'inspection' and 'perfection', the most important thing is to begin and maintain a process which ensures constant renewal and learning in the company. The entire corporate culture must become geared to high performance.

This means that a quality programme should not confine itself to the 'hard' elements of the organization such as structures, systems, or pure numbers. It must also permanently influence the 'soft' elements such as employee skills, personal interaction, corporate style, and the underlying system of shared values.

It is not easy to create such a culture from scratch, or even to develop it further once it is in place. After all, the entire value-added chain and all levels – from the supplier to the customer and from top management to the employee on the factory floor – have to be involved, and the culture must foster both direction-setting leadership and decentralized responsibility. Using tools and simple structures efficiently, it must also produce the highest standards of value to the customer with zero defects – world-class quality. Our experiences in international consultancy work, as well as industry analyses and benchmarking studies with the world's best companies, have shown that it is possible. Fortunately, the necessary concrete steps are now accurately known and the theoretical tools well developed.

Companies that have made the change successfully were, as a rule, reacting to pressure from two quarters: internal pressure from corporate management and external pressure from the market/competition. Both are generally needed to get the process of change off the ground: with visionary leadership but no pressure from the market, the company might have moved in the right direction, but mostly in a gradual, slowly evolving process. With pressure from the market but no leadership, the situation might have often been controlled with ad-hoc measures, but only in the short term, because the visionary thinking needed for a sustainable higher level of performance would have been lacking. But the two elements together – market pressure and leadership pressure – can bring about a real quantum leap in quality culture within a short space of time.

In today's automotive supply industry, market pressure is a fact of life. What is needed now is strong and visionary leadership. Top managers must map out and live this new culture, they must fundamentally challenge and redesign many corporate features and give employees the scope they need to make their own decisions.

- Whatever the company's point of departure, the *role model* should be nothing less than the ideal quality company.
- The *agenda* will depend on this actual point of departure between quality levels I and IV; what should actually happen and in what order.
- To provide stimulus and encouragement (or even warning) en route, it is important to observe other companies' experiences. Two *case studies* are presented at the end of the chapter.

THE ROLE MODEL: THE IDEAL QUALITY COMPANY

As we conceded above, the ideal quality company is yet to be found. The following profile therefore describes a combination of all known 'best practices' in quality management. It is a picture of the ideal company which, like a successful decathlete, is superior in all disciplines – in this case, it has to succeed in all those areas where total quality programmes so often fail:

- *Lack of vision/objectives*
  'Who actually has to achieve what?'
  'We are pretty good anyway, let's just wait and see.'
  'Our customers are dreaming the impossible dream again.'
  'The conditions aren't right.'
- *Wrong structures/processes*
  'How are we supposed to produce quality when our parts manufacturing department and the suppliers just deliver rubbish?'
  'Process stability depends on our fully integrated "quality information system".'
  'With this process design, process stability is nothing but a dream.'
- *Poor mobilization*
  'Yet another staff exercise.'
  'After some initial wins, the movement collapsed.'
  'Nobody ever asked us, we only work here.'

By contrast, these problems define the yardstick for any company that has ambitions to achieve world-class quality: it must have an ambitious vision and objectives, excellent core processes, 'design to quality' and 'zero-defects production', as well as sweeping and sustained mobilization of the workforce.

Ambitious Vision and Objectives

Quality companies can expect to achieve excellent results. Take the systems segment, for example. Here, the quality company achieves average growth of about 20 per cent per year with likewise higher-than-average returns of about 12 per cent. In its core segment, it strives for a market share of 35 to 40 per cent. More than half of its products should be clearly superior to those of the competition in terms of value to the customer and resistance to failure. And concentration on core products, customers, and suppliers – together with lean production processes – should create an excellent cost position.

Capital intensity is appropriately high, as attractive returns allow forward-looking investment in new technologies. Labour productivity is around DM250,000 of value added per employee.

Only two objectives are good enough for a quality strategy: reaching world-class benchmarks and matching the performance of the most demanding customers. The strategy is developed by top management and implemented along the entire extended value-added chain, from the supplier to the customer. Concrete objectives are derived for all areas, principally production, development, and purchasing, of course, but also sales and marketing. The results expected are clearly defined for every hierarchical level.

Excellent Core Process: 'Design to Quality'

The development department must have perfect mastery of 'design to customer value'. With its eye firmly fixed on the needs of the car driver as the end customer, it designs superior products in intensive contact with the car makers as the direct customers. In particular, it carries out joint projects and design reviews together with the OEMs' design departments; sometimes employees even have a permanent place in the customer's development department.

At the same time, the development department also uses optimized product/process fit to achieve stable processes (Cpk above 2.0), in which reject and rework rates stay below 0.8 per cent. To this end, it uses tools such as product and process FMEA and fault tree analyses and manages quality in conjunction with suppliers: numerous joint projects, right through to training the suppliers' staff in the application of quality tools, ensure that parts purchased from outside already fulfil the required high-quality standards. This means that, in later series production, no incoming goods inspection is needed at all.

The best suppliers apply quality tools in the development stage as needed and, most importantly, at the right time: design reviews are carried out throughout the product development process but focus on the design engineering phase; quality function deployment (QFD) is used mainly in the concept and design phase; process FMEA comes into play in the design and test phase. Process capability even before production start-up is considered the main indicator of subsequent process stability, so last-minute design changes are often made just before start-up to optimize this process stability.

Excellent Core Process: 'Zero-Defects Production'

Production in our quality company is generally carried out on dedicated production lines; 'mass production' and 'exotic variants' are kept clearly separate from each other. Vertical integration is determined strictly by whether long-term benefits are to be gained by outsourcing systems or modules or buying from low-wage economies. The materials flow is simple, and based on the optimization of throughput times. Production staff have mastered the tools to ensure process stability and check and improve their own quality.

Three-quarters of the entire labour force are included in a process of continuous improvement, ensured through quality circles or self-managing teams. Ninety per cent of ideas generated are rapidly translated into practice, on average within two weeks.

Statistical process control and fault elimination are carried out by the operative units, the Cpk value is known and – at over 2.0 – extremely high. If problems crop up or, a more likely scenario, customer requirements change, the sales and marketing departments are informed immediately because of their personal relationships with customers, and the problems can be solved using fast-moving, standardized processes.

Comprehensive Mobilization of the Workforce

Two elements must come together for the committed involvement of the individual employee on all levels: skill and will. The quality company has developed both to the highest standard. Along the entire value-added chain, employees have the necessary competence to produce 'zero-defects' quality, since an average of five days' quality training per year for each employee is standard practice. In addition, regular and frequent job rotation, especially within and between development and production, ensures an exchange of know-how in the company.

The hierarchy is flat: about 80 per cent of employees are organized into small, self-managing units. Most of the responsibility for quality is delegated to the shop-floor employees; if quality problems occur, they are empowered to stop the assembly or production line and immediately take whatever actions are necessary to eliminate the causes of the problems, or to prevent delivery of faulty goods to customers. The quality assurance department itself is relatively small (about 2 per cent of the entire workforce) and has strategic, consultancy, and training roles. There is only a limited separate company suggestion scheme outside the teams and quality circles, mainly to glean brilliant individual ideas.

Finally, motivation and skills are promoted by an incentive scheme which penalizes poor quality and considers high quality the norm. Outstanding quality is not rewarded by a 'quality bonus' but by better career opportunities and a fulfilling social position in the workplace because of the recognition of colleagues and superiors.

All these characteristics are typical of the quality company. But perhaps the most important of all is that it never rests on its laurels: the quality culture is characterized by constant learning; targets are always being set a little bit higher. The quality company is a continuously and rapidly learning organization.

THE AGENDA: FROM INSPECTION TO PERFECTION

Like every new beginning, the quality offensive should start with a full and complete diagnosis of the current situation. By determining which quality levers it is currently using (see Appendix B, 'Quality Profiles by Country'), a company can quickly assess how far along the path to top quality it has reached.

Typically, a company will not have arrived at the same level with all the features; the profile is likely to show certain strengths and weaknesses. This will allow the company to target the weaknesses specifically and so take the most effective route. However, in our experience every overall profile can generally still be assigned to one of the levels (Figure 6.2).

Once its quality level has been established, what step can and should a level II company, for example, take first, and what step next? Which processes can run in parallel? Clearly, not all the features of a quality company can be created at once; robust design, for instance, is hardly possible if the process parameters and capabilities are unknown. Nevertheless, it would be disastrous not to aim for high quality and a Cpk value of > 1.33 right from the start.

As shown in Figure 6.3, some features are gradually added during the improvement process and are characteristic of individual levels, for example the improvement of process stability at level II. Other features such as investigation of value to the end customer can be introduced at any time, no matter where the improvement process

Profile of a typical Level II company

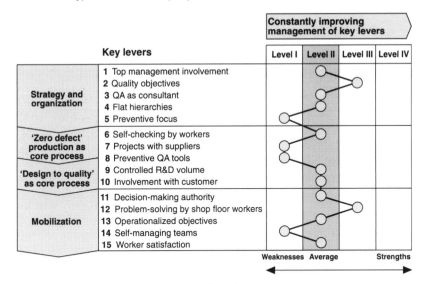

Fig. 6.2 *Levers of quality management*

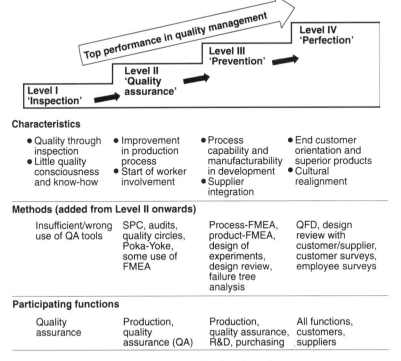

Fig. 6.3 *Four levels of quality*

begins. There are also methods and patterns of behaviour which perhaps still play an important improvement role at level I, but are superseded by more effective tools such as product FMEA at later levels.

The following pages provide a typical profile for each level and show where further development should start.

Becoming a quality company does not have to take forever, as an analysis of several hundred improvement programmes shows. The best companies progressed from level II to level IV in two or three years; five to seven years seems about 'normal'. A true quality company never stops striving for perfection. From today's point of view, level IV companies have reached the top, but they are already trying to imagining what tomorrow's ideal quality company will look like. For this reason, the (current) level of 'perfection' is also included among the following improvement agendas.

Level I: From Inspection to Quality Assurance

At quality management level I, companies have their products checked by the quality assurance department before dispatch. There is no corporate quality concept, world-class objectives are not known, let alone attributed to individual functions and levels of hierarchy. At best there are specific quality targets for production, but only for reject and rework rates. These targets are not aimed at rivalling competitors, but are mostly formulated as percentage improvements on the company's own poor performance (ppm rates up to about 4,800; reject rate 5.5 per cent; rework rate 3.1 per cent). As a rule, top management is not involved in the quality process and only steps in to deal with complaints from important customers. The company directors do not usually know the ppm rates achieved or the measure of process stability.

The quality assurance department is very large, employing about 6 to 8 per cent of the total staff, and is usually centrally managed. Only about half of all quality inspection is undertaken by production staff; final testing is carried out by quality assurance. Limited preventive measures are employed (a mere 13 per cent of quality costs), one or other preventive quality tool is applied occasionally on an experimental basis.

Joint projects with suppliers or customers are unknown at level I. Product differentiation and additional value to the end customer are correspondingly low, particularly as no supra-functional 'cross-ferti-lization' occurs through 'internal' customers and suppliers. Production usually follows the customer's blueprints, and the company's own development know-how is limited. The share of products sold which are superior to the competition is less than 20 per cent of sales.

There is little systematic staff development to be seen. On average, less than one day and DM300 are invested in formal training per employee per annum. There is no job rotation and communication between functions is kept to the absolute minimum.

Labour productivity, at less than DM120,000 per employee, is relatively low, and the workforce is poorly motivated; each employee makes less than one improvement idea per year (only about one-third of them are implemented, after an average of eight months – the decision path alone takes a good three months!).

Finally, it is also apparent that these companies have far higher complexity to manage than quality companies: adjusted to comparable sales and purchasing volumes, they have about two-and-a-half times as many products and variants, three-and-a-half times as many customers and about twice as many suppliers. This is demonstrated by the lot sizes, which are only 25 per cent of the optimum in parts production and only 20 per cent in assembly. So it is not surprising that a level I company grows more slowly than the industry average, at 5.4 per cent per year, and, even in the boom years of 1987 to 1991, hardly earned any money (return on sales: 0.6 per cent).

Where next?

Where should you start when the situation is so unsatisfactory on all fronts? The most important step is to consolidate competitiveness by restructuring production as a 'zero-defects process' from the supplier to the customer. In the short term, this means aiming for a ppm rate of well under 1,000. This has implications in practice, principally for target-setting and employee mobilization (Figure 6.4).

- *Set concrete quality objectives.* Top management, in partnership with the quality assurance and production departments, defines clear, quality-oriented targets, defined in detail for individual stages in the value chain (e.g., goods inward) and for production stages and processes. The development function is also involved, in order to heighten its understanding of the production parameters and to encourage a process-oriented approach.

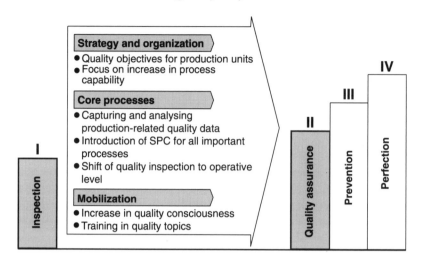

Fig. 6.4　*Moving from level I 'inspection' to level II 'quality assurance'*

- *Increase self-checking.* As processes are better understood and mastered in the transition from level I to level II, quality inspection is shifted more and more to employees on the shop floor. It is not too much to expect about 60 per cent of controls to be carried out 'in process' by the employees themselves.
- *Train employees in quality.* It is important to drastically improve employees' understanding of their own production – process parameters, the main sources of faults, etc. The workforce must also learn to apply the basic quality tools and problem-solving techniques, especially SPC, process FMEA, Pareto and trend analyses, cause and effect diagnostics, etc. (see Appendix A, 'Top Quality Tools'). Ideally, this learning should take place on the job (i.e., in teams which include representatives from production, quality assurance, and development) and over the entire value chain. The company can also begin targeted job rotation at this stage.

Level II: From Quality Assurance to Prevention

At level II, quality assurance is in place throughout a company's own production process, but generally in the form of eliminating faults after they have occurred. There is a clear quality concept for incoming goods, production, and sometimes dispatch, although targets are often not very demanding.

The quality assurance function is usually centrally managed and works closely with production. The development function is still little involved in this process, and production is often still based on the customer's blueprints. SPC and process FMEA are generally used as quality tools. There are joint projects with suppliers from time to time, mostly directed at solving acute quality problems. Quality circles and problem-solving groups are set up but are not a permanent part of the corporate culture, and, when used, are not nearly as effective as at levels III and IV. Quality problems are still mostly solved by experts (in quality assurance). Job rotation and targeted staff development are almost unknown as systematic tools.

Level II companies face complexity similar to that at level I. However, process stability is much better: the ppm rate is about 900, the reject rate about 3.1 per cent and the rework rate about 2.7 per cent.

The next step on the road to quality leads from correction to prevention. Probably the most important strength that needs to be built here is good process capability as early as the pilot series, a major precondition for later high quality in series production. If this is to be achieved, however, the product concept must be made as clear as possible in the preliminary phase. And the organization must be in a position to manage a lot of last-minute alterations quickly and competently before series production starts, not only to improve the product, but above all to increase process stability. This can only be achieved if the supplier has full responsibility for the product or collaborates closely with the OEM's development department. In addition, close cooperation between the development team, the production department, and the most important suppliers is essential for an optimum product/process fit.

Where next?

The most important steps in growing out of level II can be summarized as follows (Figure 6.5):

- *Raise objectives to world-class level.* The top management team itself must show clear commitment. In close collaboration with the relevant functions and the quality assurance department, they set ambitious targets, including goals for development and purchasing. These targets are derived from the benchmarks of the

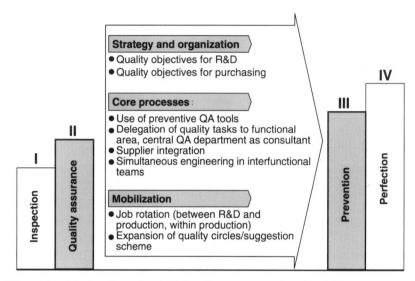

Fig. 6.5   *Moving from level II 'quality assurance' to level III 'prevention'*

world's best companies and the standards of the most demanding existing or target customer.

- *Introduce 'simultaneous engineering'.* The managers of the purchasing, quality assurance, production, development, and sales functions seek a form of collaboration which will make it possible to achieve the targets. The best approach in our experience is simultaneous engineering. Interfunctional teams drawn from the five areas agree on the objective of stable production processes, and then determine the product specifications and design to manufacture accordingly. FMEA and fault tree analysis (and sometimes also QFD) are used as the main quality tools. The development department should lead the teams until the target process stability is reached, at which stage leadership should pass to production. This is the only way to make integrated and/or simultaneous development of products and production procedures possible.

- *Transfer most responsibility for quality to the shop floor.* At this stage, at the very latest, the role of the quality department shifts towards one of quality strategist, consultant, know-how supplier, and trainer, and the department will shrink to about half its original size (based on the approximately 5 per cent share of quality assurance staff at level II). After appropriate training in problem-solving techniques and with intensive on the job training, shop floor staff (supervisors and employees) can perform 80 per cent of the necessary checks themselves. In this phase, it is also imperative to introduce the concept of 'internal' customer/supplier relationships and to give the corresponding cost and profit centres a great deal of responsibility, not only for quality, but also for human resources issues. The managers of these units should be developed into entrepreneurs.

- *Use more preventive quality tools.* It is essential to increase the use of tools such as QFD, product and process FMEA, and design reviews (in some cases QFD is also already in use) if products are to attain high process capability as early as possible (see Appendix A, 'Top Quality Tools').
- *Involve suppliers.* Collaboration with suppliers becomes much more intensive. Above all, joint teams work on concrete tasks to do with quality assurance or productivity increases.
- *Job rotation and quality circles.* At least 40 per cent of employees at the operative level are members of quality circles. Job rotation becomes a matter of course, particularly for group leaders and the levels above. This also helps to reinforce the principle of the 'internal customer'.

It is here, between levels II and III, that the leap from the worse to the better half of the quality scale occurs. To make this leap it is essential to reduce internal complexity. Studies have shown that level III companies are two to four times 'simpler' than those at levels I and II. Above all, superfluous levels of hierarchy are removed. Level III companies have at most half as many suppliers, end products, or variants to manage (relative to comparable purchasing and sales volumes), so that their lot sizes in parts production and assembly are at least twice as large. Experience shows that it is only by managing its own complexity that a company can aim for – and quickly achieve – the quality standards needed for level III.

Level III: From Prevention to Perfection

Much that still seems 'pie in the sky' to a company at level II is achieved by companies at level III. In close collaboration with the quality department, production, development, and purchasing have set themselves clear 'world-class' objectives. A major share of the development spend now goes on preventive measures. Preventive quality tools such as design reviews and product and process FMEA are mastered and applied selectively. The quality department is decentralized and over 80 per cent of tests are performed at shop-floor level.

Internal customer/supplier relationships are part of the shared values, and projects are carried out selectively with external customers. Job rotation and training – systematic staff development in general – are considered important and take place regularly. Clear focal points and flat hierarchies curb complexity, and process quality – with a ppm rate of 300, a reject rate of about 1.5 per cent and rework rate of 1.7 per cent – has already reached an impressive level.

Where next?

The improvements continue. After the more gradual development since level I, the leap from level III to level IV is in itself another cultural revolution, characterized by the will to achieve absolute perfection, an organization shaped by team-work and the process mentality, a marked external orientation (customers and suppliers are 'part of the process') and a culture of continuous improvement (Figure 6.6).

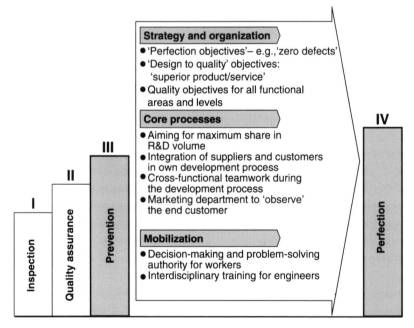

Fig. 6.6 *Moving from level III 'prevention' to level IV 'perfection'*

- *Make absolute perfection everyone's objective.* Top management formulates extremely demanding objectives, even for the sales, marketing, and administrative departments. Within these departments, these targets are specified for each hierarchical level in such as way that, if they are fully achieved, products will have zero defects and superior features. The share of quality costs spent on prevention now rises to over 30 per cent. Statistical process control is applied in a targeted manner to critical and not yet fully mastered processes. 'Zero-defects design' is perfectly mastered, so that high stability is achieved for most processes. In-process quality control is transferred almost entirely to shop-floor employees, and traditional final inspection can be dropped.
- *Concentrate and integrate suppliers more closely.* The share of single sourcing rises to 80 per cent, and careful evaluation leads to a strong concentration of the remaining suppliers, which are then more closely integrated. The company carries out projects serving its own process stability with every key supplier, ranging from joint product development to supplier quality training.
- *Collaborate closely with customers.* This step is particularly important in the transition from level III to level IV. It causes several sweeping changes:
  - The development function begins to carry out joint projects with key customers. These projects include joint design reviews, intensive end-customer surveys, and analyses of the type and frequency of product use, providing information about where additional benefits can be created. It is best to select the most demanding customer for a pilot project, which is carried out by a highly qualified joint team in order to then transfer the experiences gained to other customers and teams.
  - A detailed understanding of the customer is built actively throughout the organization. For example, some engineers work directly in the customer's service department; faults arising are analyzed in detail and eliminated in collaboration on site.
  - As soon as possible, a central function to collect, structure, evaluate, and store customer and competitor information is also formed. Successful companies dedicate up to 1,000 person days per year to this kind of customer information.
  - Intensive training and the use of special quality methods (see Appendix A, 'Top Quality Tools') round off the understanding of the customer.

- *Make team structure the decisive element.* About 70 to 80 per cent of all employees in all areas are organized in teams which are responsible for their own quality results. This objective is realized by a kind of snowball system: problem solving teams are established in production at level II and gradually incorporate other functional areas during the transition to level III. In the transition to level IV, as many of the operative employees as possible and many from development and sales also become involved; with special projects, customer employees also participate. The chief executive officer is actively involved, even to the extent of participating in quality circles and production team meetings: quality is now indelibly written on top management's agenda.
- *Create a culture of continuous improvement.* The extension of team organization in itself causes the quality orientation to be passed from one employee to another. This effect is reinforced by a customized incentive system comprising primarily intangible components, a sophisticated staff development system, and job rotation (30 to 40 per cent of employees have more than a year's experience in other functions). In addition, employees' skill and satisfaction levels are regularly surveyed and corresponding improvements made. Constant challenge to the status quo is the driving force and main feature of this high-performance and perfection culture.

This transformation into a problem-solving organization is best demonstrated by the number of improvement suggestions submitted and implemented. At level I, there is just over one suggestion per employee per year; at level III the average is 8 to 10, which should rise to 20 during the leap to level IV. (If this seems extreme, world-class Japanese companies achieve suggestion levels of 50 to 70 per employee.) The impact of the suggestions reinforces the point just as clearly: top companies decide on whether or not to implement the ideas in a matter of days, and the decision is almost always positive, while poorer companies have a decision process of three months or more, and half the suggestions are rejected.

Level IV: Perfection: A Moving Target

In the best of all possible worlds, the 'ideal quality company' described above would be realized at level IV. Yet this level of perfection has never to our knowledge been fully achieved. However, here are a few striking features observed in four real examples:

- To make sure that customer-oriented targets are set, one company also takes over all marketing responsibility for its components on behalf of its OEM customers, including customer surveys, market research, and marketing plans. Its impact thus extends right through to the end customer.
- To strengthen integration with suppliers and customers and tighten core processes, three of the company's development engineers are seconded to the customer's development department at any given time. Teams work alternately in their own company or at the customer as required. They make up an informal part of the customer's organization.
- All product-related design reviews are carried out jointly with suppliers and customers.
- Every manager's performance includes an upward evaluation by the employees to document joint responsibility and strengthen employee commitment.

Yet another feature was common to all the quality companies in our long-term study. At or close to level IV, they had all taken a leap forward in terms of 'simplicity'. Compared with level I companies, they earned comparable sales with only 30 per cent of the products and variants. This means that lot sizes in parts production and assembly are three to four times larger. Mainly because of 80 per cent single sourcing, the total number of suppliers is two-thirds smaller than at level I. There are only four levels of hierarchy; the company is very decentralized, highly flexible, and free of functional borders – either internal or external.

What is there left to do?

The level IV company is still not completely satisfied with its outstanding performance. Its immediate objective is to reach perfection in every quality dimension simultaneously. Moreover, the most visionary quality leaders are aiming still higher. For example, they no longer think of their product range in terms of systems, but in terms of application functions.

Take the brake manufacturer mentioned in Chapter 2, for example. The driver only perceives the brakes as performing 'well' if his head bobs downwards slightly during braking. Visionary quality leaders, therefore, are more concerned with the 'function of braking' than with the actual brake system. And we know that this subjective perception is influenced not only by the braking system itself but, for instance, to a great extent by the seat. The design of the seat determines how much or how little the driver will be 'pressed' into it during braking. The visionary quality leader, therefore, will also think about including the seat manufacturer in the development of a new product generation in order to meet this requirement.

The visionary quality leader also plans his labour policy according to expected future technology developments. The manufacturer of electronic products, for instance, knows that, as the year 2000 approaches, his products will increasingly become undifferentiated commodity-type articles and that the decisive competitive know-how advantage will then be in the system software. For this reason, the share of software development engineers will have to be more than doubled. To effect this change, the supplier has to work out a detailed staff development concept.

EXAMPLES: DIFFERENT ROADS LEAD TO QUALITY

The road to quality can and will be different in each individual case. However, the basic features of the development from level to level will be more or less as described above.

Companies who travel this road successfully can expect significant improvements. One aggregate manufacturer raised his return on sales from 3 per cent to 10 per cent within four years, for example. The foundation for this success was ultimately a quality offensive where the management raised process stability to a C_{pk} value over 2.0, causing the ppm rate to plummet from about 1,500 to less than 100. Machine availability rose from an unsatisfactory 75 per cent to 96 per cent and the reject rate fell by 60 per cent.

The company achieved all this by 1993 from a not very promising starting point in 1989. At that time, quality awareness in the work-force was underdeveloped, quality objectives were defined only in production (but not throughout), and production processes were characterized by long throughput times and low stability. The company could not differentiate its products from those of its main competitors, as development know-how was lacking and was scattered over too many projects.

The systematic approach which led to this success covered all areas of quality management. The company took the following key steps:

- It realigned the entire business system to core processes with the superordinate goal of raising quality.
- It expanded in-house research step by step and concentrated on the core business.
- It slimmed down its vertical integration and outsourced entire modules or sub-systems.
- It doubled the effort invested in joint projects with suppliers and customers.
- It established an all-embracing team concept with short feedback loops, team incentive systems, and intensive training. This led ultimately to the introduction of cells with 100 per cent self-checking by the workers and full line responsibility.

Similar success patterns are to be found in principle in all level IV companies, because they all make full use of every improvement opportunity. However, as the following two recent examples demonstrate, a company's situation will make a difference to the route it takes. Both these automotive industry suppliers manufacture the same product (electric switches for lights, electric windows, rear window heating, etc.) and both are at level IV today. They are both part of the same international corporation (TRW), but one – TRW Fahrzeugelektrik in Radolfzell – operates in Germany, the classic high wage economy, and the other – TRW Electronics in Sunderland – in a depressed area of England.[1]

The German company was granted a contract in 1989 to develop and produce the controls for a new generation of models for a Japanese customer in Great Britain. In the same year, the company built a new factory on a greenfield site. So begins the story of the English level IV company – and the rise of both companies from the level II quality situation typical of the time (ppm value 1,200–1,500, reject rate 2.5–3.0 per cent, rework rate 2.5–3.0 per cent) to a position of excellence in terms of quality and profit (Figure 6.7).

---

[1] TRW has kindly agreed to allow us to deviate here from the principle of anonymous examples only.

Quality and financial indicators over time

Level IV company from England

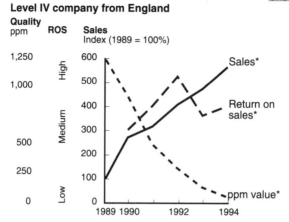

Level IV company from Germany

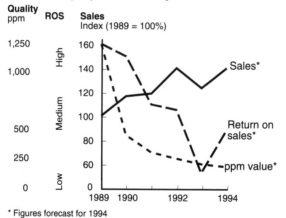

* Figures forecast for 1994

Fig. 6.7 *Improving financial performance on the way to becoming a quality company*

- The English company was a success in terms of its quality and financial ratios. By reducing the most important measure of quality – the ppm rate – to the Japanese level (60 ppm in 1994), it doubled its sales between 1990 and 1994, combined with growth in return on sales to an impressive level during 1993, a crisis year for the car industry.

- But the German company's achievements were also significant. Between 1989 and 1994, the ppm rate was lowered from an unsatisfactory 1,250 to 200 ppm, and sales grew by about 40 per cent. Return on sales hit rock bottom in 1993 because of the recession, before rising to a satisfactory level again in 1994.

Two equally impressive achievements under different operating conditions. The following glance at a few selected steps shows how the routes differed.

In England: Focus on Mobilization and Supplier Integration

In the German company, the existing manual assembly lines were being more and more radically automated. The trend culminated in a fully automatic assembly line on which five different product types could be produced and which had an output of around one million units per annum. The investment in a plant of this kind is around DM1 million to DM1.5 million.

The English company took a different path. It started by moving an assembly line from Germany to England, thus establishing the focus of the quest for quality: the aim was to achieve a stable production process on the basis of the existing manual assembly system.

Because of significantly lower labour costs and lack of process technology know-how, it was decided to optimize the simpler manual assembly lines, which only require an investment of about DM15,000 per line at an output of 30,000 units per year. Right from the outset, all employees were deliberately involved in the improvement process. Process and team orientation became the philosophy of the company. A recruitment procedure was rapidly developed which was concerned as much with team capabilities as with analytical skills (e.g., simple arithmetic). Team leaders conduct the deciding interview to recruit a new assembly employee for their own groups.

Right from the start, all the assembly lines were organized into self-managing teams, each responsible for the quality of its own products. At the same time, every employee has two tasks: to produce high quality and perfect products, and to continually improve his or her own work process. To this end, three-quarters of the workers are organized into quality circles which were set up as soon as the team structure had been secured. The result of constantly involving employees in this way was the highest saving per employee per year achieved with these kind of measures in Europe – equivalent to US$3,200.

But it is a logical consequence of employee involvement that employees and teams should be assessed according to their results, for example on the basis of the ppm values of individual production lines or the number and quality of improvement suggestions. The contribution of each individual group, even of each individual employee, is known to all, as these ratios for each group are displayed on a noticeboard by every assembly line, where they are also visible to other groups.

If you believe that such pressure to perform lowers job satisfaction among the employees, think again! Figures and personal impressions prove the opposite. For example, one assembly employee who conducted us around the production department described the individual production stages as well as the employee evaluation scheme, and told us enthusiastically that one of their self-appointed goals for the following year was to reduce absenteeism from 3.0 per cent to 2.5 per cent. (While many German companies are also considering how to reduce the absentee rate, this only concerns the management, and the rate is usually nearer 8 per cent.) The mobilization of employees permeates every area of the English quality company and is definitely the driving force behind the improvement process.

All this was achieved within four years of starting operations. It took about a year and a half to secure the self-managing teams in the production organization (Figure 6.8) – a typical period of change for top companies, according to our study. This core idea was extended step by step, adding elements such as a target system for production, a training concept, quality circles for continuous improvement, a selection procedure for new employees, and a system of employee evaluation and compensation. It was only the combination of all these measures that enabled the company to achieve top-quality performance.

The company also tried at a very early stage to extend its own team philosophy to its collaboration with suppliers. Instead of simply continuing with the existing supplier base from Germany, the company decided to work only with suppliers which expressly accepted its own values and targets. Critics claimed that this created unnecessary complexity in the purchasing department and, moreover, went against the idea of global sourcing. But the results speak for

Sequence of focus on individual areas

Areas

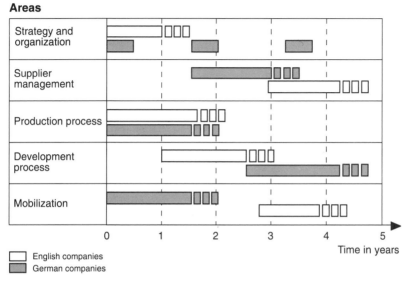

English companies
German companies

Fig. 6.8 *Different routes to the same goal*

themselves: even compared to the German top-quality companies, the English company has 25 per cent fewer core suppliers and needs only one-third of the staff in purchasing. In 1992, the German company was also further away than the English company from realizing global sourcing; only 10 per cent of its suppliers were located abroad, compared with 40 per cent for the English company.

These were the leitmotifs of the English company:

- Our own results are only as good as those of our weakest supplier.
- Our suppliers are an extension of our own processes.
- Prevention begins with analyzing supplier quality.

Not only did these improve quality decisively, but goals such as having a 'lean supplier base' and a greater proportion of 'global sourcing' were also achieved at the same time, almost as a by-product.

As with employee participation in the improvement process, close supplier involvement also depends on a delegation of responsibility. But this delegation does not occur until the supplier can fulfil a number of demanding criteria: its ppm rate has been less than the benchmark set for twelve months; supplies have been subject to no significant complaints for the past twelve months; the system to introduce improvement measures in the case of quality problems is working properly; the supplier wishes to and is capable of collaborating with the company and in quality improvement programmes.

Adherence to these conditions is constantly reviewed. This review process might take place, for example, at the monthly joint meetings of the goods inward department and supplier development function, where the ten worst-performing suppliers 'on the day' are ascertained. These suppliers are then required to draw up an improvement programme, whose implementation is normally the task of a project team comprising employees of both companies. This interplay of stringent quality targets with delegation of responsibility and support for the implementation of improvement concepts is highly effective. Our English top-quality company masters it with flair.

Redesign of the 'purchasing department' into 'supplier management' is associated with sweeping changes. Our top-quality company embarked on this transformation when its own quality philosophy had reached the implementation phase (see Figure 6.8). No other approach is possible: how can you possibly communicate a quality orientation to your supplier if you do not already have one in your own company? We did not find any companies with excellent supplier management which had not yet sorted out their own direction.

The English company needed a total of about a year and a half to establish the most important elements of its supplier management: developing new evaluation benchmarks for suppliers; building/consolidating the supplier base; developing an improvement programme for suppliers; and training its own employees in the tools of this improvement programme. This time-scale was also one of the best.

In Germany: Focus on Value to the Customer in the Development Process

At the beginning of the 1960s, the German company (then still at quality level II) was giving careful consideration to possible growth strategies. Of the three decisive factors affecting its own sales – number of cars produced, vehicle features, and its own product's market share – it was obviously able to directly influence only market share. Trying to increase market share by a price war seemed neither sensible in terms of returns nor desirable in the interests of a productive supplier/manufacturer relationship. The company reached the inevitable conclusion that the only option was to achieve superiority through a significant quality lead, and quality here meant value to the customer.

Superior customer value in its own product had to encompass value both to the end customer, i.e., directly perceptible to the car driver, and to the direct customer, the car manufacturer. By extending its understanding of the customer in this way, the company was entering unknown territory. It began its end-customer offensive with a questionnaire to find out what the customer wanted of the following features of the switches offered: position in the vehicle, appearance, type of activation (toggle switch, rotary switch, press switch), and function.

The company looked specifically for differences in the preferences of different buyer segments (lower, middle, upper classes, niche segments) and regions (comparison of the Triad regions Europe/US/Asia and within Europe). The survey findings provided not only valuable suggestions for the development of new products but also, at the same time, selling points to use in negotiations with OEMs. Thanks to its quantitative survey, the company became a much more competent negotiating partner for these direct customers, in terms of both market knowledge and the development and production process.

The second dimension of customer value in the automotive supply industry – added value to the direct customer – was also expressly defined as an objective by the German company. Its proposition was also to help the car manufacturer to reduce complexity. By practising simultaneous engineering with certain core customers, the company moved in the direction of quality level IV in this aspect as well.

As one lever, the company chose reduction of complexity in the manufacturer's production (and, at the same time, its own). The many electric switches visible inside the car (for the lights, rear window heating, electric windows etc.) have traditionally had different wiring schemes – even the circuitry for a light switch often varies from model to model in a manufacturer's range. This complexity in contact systems, in voltage, and in current, usually caused by technical reasons connected with differences in the available space, could be seen in the 250 end products the company offered. It was a variety of no benefit either to the automotive manufacturer or the end customer.

The emergent quality company took as its starting point the following consideration: today's miniaturization in the electronics industry made it possible for different wiring systems to be installed on the same circuit board. It followed that only one circuit board per OEM customer should be enough; the switches for the lights, rear window heating, and all the other electrically operated accessories would only vary between a manufacturer's different models in terms of the operating control. This would reduce variety by a factor of 7 to 10. For the direct customer, this reduction of variety would all occur behind the scenes of the visible switch. A brilliantly simple idea for a simply brilliant product.

Of course, ideas of this kind cannot be realized without close cooperation with the car manufacturer in question. Contact systems have to be standardized, and there must be sufficient space for the switch behind each operating control – in other words, interfaces have to be precisely defined. A simultaneous engineering team comprising development engineers from both companies worked on this problem for nine months, alternately at the supplier's and at the direct customer's.

Once the interfaces have been defined, the automotive manufacturer must leave development and engineering design to the supplier. Constant attempts to influence design, such as are often to be observed, stem from a false understanding of simultaneous engineering. Our quality company went through a learning process with its core customer and, despite all the obstacles, production of the standard switch for all the manufacturer's models started in January 1994.

Commonalities in the Fast Lane

A five-year review of their improvement programmes reveals that both the English and the German company have achieved similar results and are now both world-class in terms of process and design quality. Their respective paths to this goal differed more in terms of the sequence of events than in their actual content.

This sequence depended above all on which strengths were most highly developed in each company and could thus serve as the basis for an improvement in competitive position. The German company's strength was its development know-how. The first objective, therefore, was to redesign the development department, away from traditional quality concepts to an uncompromising (end) customer orientation with stringent and demanding targets.

The outstanding strength of the English company, no doubt partly as a result of a new beginning on a greenfield site, was its employees' readiness to undertake a cultural revolution. The company's great achievement was to build on this strength and, through the measures outlined above, to set and keep in motion a continuous learning programme. To achieve this, it had to concentrate initially on its own production process, then on developing suppliers and, only after that, on the development process.

Summary

As we have seen, in the Europe of the mid-1990s there are at least two more quality automotive industry suppliers than there were at the beginning of the decade. On the way to this position, the two have learned the same thing as other companies in other regions and industries: reorientation to total quality entails a strategic and organizational redesign, one that leads from central, functional structures to decentralized structures that are oriented toward core competencies and processes. Much more than this, it is a cultural revolution, leading from hierarchical top-down processes to a more pronounced external emphasis on the end customer, to a combination of top-down and bottom-up levers, to more teamwork as well as the development of know-how and the ability at all levels to analyze and eliminate problems independently and to take on more responsibility.

Finally, a self-learning organization is also created, which is constantly setting new, more aggressive targets and is in a position to achieve them or to adapt if business conditions change.

In the foregoing chapters, we have tried to illustrate the actions in strategy and organization, development and production that contribute to this change, and what can be learned from regional specifics. But one thing seems, in our opinion, to be more important than anything else: the development of the 'cultural' skills that are distilled into the value system, the capabilities, and behaviour of employees. These are the driving and long-term sustaining forces of this process, much more so than the 'structural elements' (Figure 6.9).

With this 'cultural edge', a company gains a sustainable competitive advantage which cannot be imitated, at least in the short term. It can only be built – or caught up with – by a massive, systematic, and

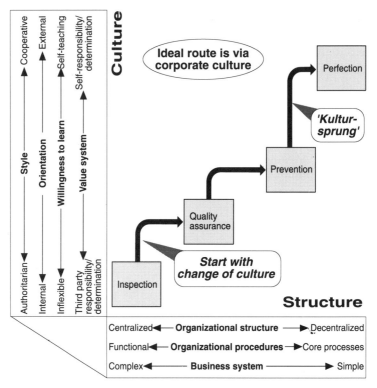

Fig. 6.9 *Becoming a quality company needs a new corporate culture*

mobilizing action programme. This takes three years at best, but five to seven is a more usual time-span.

Eight rules seem to determine progress on the quality path:

1. Development of a quality culture only succeeds if *top management* is actively involved and plays a hands-on role in this culture.
2. The only *vision* good enough to aim for is '*world-class*', derived from the standards of the most demanding customer, but also going beyond that as a moving target.
3. Successful quality programmes begin by setting *clear quality, cost, and time objectives* – translated into concrete *output-oriented targets* for each individual function and level.
4. Only an unbiased *situation assessment*, made in the light of the main quality levers, provides knowledge of the *quality gap* and the *principal improvement opportunities*.

5. The organization needs to have a product-oriented structure along the *core processes* of '*zero-defects production*' and '*development for quality*'.

6. Without regular and open *information and communication* across hierarchical and functional borders, there can be no continuous improvement process.

7. *Formal training and informal incentives* have to accompany the development from 'command and control management' to 'personal responsibility' and have to be tailored to the employees' real needs.

8. The *entire value chain* to be mobilized extends beyond the company itself to include *suppliers and customers*.

And last but not least, the whole thing is a *dynamic process*. Today's level IV will be tomorrow's level III as the competition and its demands continue to grow. No company – not even the best – can afford to rest on its laurels.

Appendix A: Top Quality Tools

It takes more than a baton to make a great conductor. The outstanding quality that helps companies achieve top rates of growth and return is, as we have seen in the preceding chapters, a management and leadership task. It entails setting, communicating, and operationalizing ambitious objectives, redesigning businesses along the core processes, integrating customers and suppliers, and above all mobilizing the workforce. It is not easy to do these things well, but some sophisticated quality tools can help. Managers ignore or abuse them at their peril.

This appendix will introduce you to the most important of these tools. Not in the manner of a detailed text book – a number of reference works, some of them excellent, have already served this purpose.[1] Our intention is, rather, to use the information gleaned from our consultancy practice and the empirical study to show what can be achieved by using modern quality tools and how management can ensure – or obstruct – their most effective application.

After outlining the main features of each method in brief, we will illustrate which industries/product segments/manufacturing processes they benefit, how and by whom they should be used and how progress should be monitored, what conditions have to be established – or what mistakes avoided – for successful implementation and what improvements these tools can produce. We have selected for this overview nine tools which we consider to be particularly useful for quality planning and assurance:

- Quality function deployment (QFD)
- Failure mode and effects analysis (FMEA), subdivided into product, process, and interface FMEA
- Fault tree analysis (FTA)
- Design of experiments, also known as statistically planned experiments (Taguchi being the best-known method in this family)
- Design review
- Statistical process control
- Quality circles
- Poka-Yoke
- Quality audits for products and systems.

---

[1] For example, W. Masing (ed.), *Handbuch Qualitätsmanagement*, 3 vols, 3rd edition, Munich/Vienna, 1994.

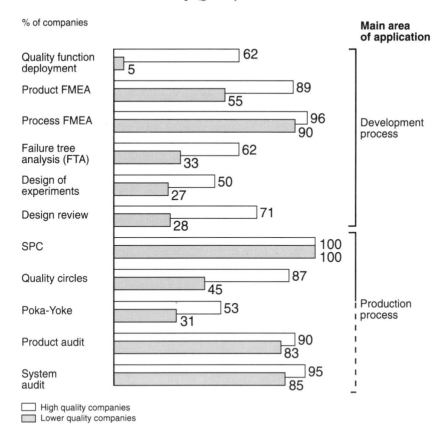

Fig. A.1 *Intensive use of QA tools in the development process*

The first five of these methods are used in the development process, the other three mainly in production.[2] However, quality companies use Poka-Yoke and SPC in the development process as well. Quality audits are not restricted to any one stage, even though the two main forms, product and system audits, initially arose in production. One interesting fact emerging from the study was that quality companies used QA tools more intensively in the development phase than other companies do (Figure A.1).

---

[2] For the quality assurance methods used in the development process, see Hans-Werner Kaas' dissertation 'Integriertes Qualitätsmanagement in der Produkt- und Prozessentwicklung' (PhD thesis in preparation, planned to be published in 1997).

QUALITY FUNCTION DEPLOYMENT (QFD)

The Method

In line with the quality objective of 'total customer satisfaction,' QFD provides guidelines for a customer-oriented working and management style. It bundles the knowledge, skill, and will of the entire workforce in order to translate customer demands into products, services, and processes.

QFD starts from the latent or explicit requirements of a target segment which is jointly defined by sales/marketing, customer service, and R&D. These customer requirements will either be available in the form of more or less systematically organized data, or will have to be ascertained by market research. The resulting requirements on products and processes then have to be quantified or described to such a level of detail that the end product will correspond to the original requirement as accurately as possible and will, at the same time, prevent faults in manufacturing and use. Four steps are needed for this process, from deciding on design and engineering features to specifying manufacturing instructions.

The four steps (also known as matrices or 'houses') of the QFD process build on each other (see Figure A.2): at each level the questions of WHAT the customer needs (on the left beside the 'front door') and HOW the demand can be met (cross-beam over the front door) have to be resolved; the HOW of every step then becomes the WHAT of the next.

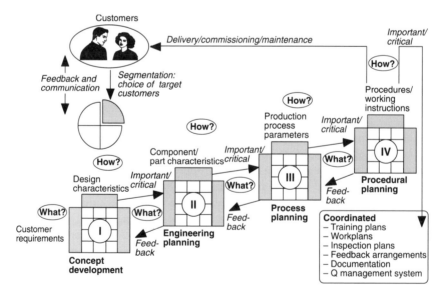

Fig. A.2 *Systematic development and implementation of customer requirements with the QFD (quality function deployment) method*

- *Step 1 – Concept development:* In the customer demand matrix, every customer demand (WHAT) is assigned to clearly defined design/engineering features (HOW). These quality traits are weighted according to their importance for the customer and set out in writing, as a list of specifications, for example. Because customer requirements and product traits can influence not only elements of the other category but also each other, tradeoff analyses are usually called for (the conjoint method, for example, provides information on the priority of different product features for the customer).
- *Step 2 – Component/design planning:* The most important of the HOW components developed in step 1 become requirements (WHAT criteria) in the step 2 matrix. Each of these quality features is then once more assigned a HOW, in the form of the necessary (measurable) features of the component/subassembly in question.
- *Step 3 – Process planning:* Taking these component and subassembly features (the new WHAT) as a starting point, a process plan is elaborated to determine the critical parameters in the production process (HOW). Checkpoints are also defined for each of these parameters.
- *Step 4 – Procedure planning:* Concrete procedural and working instructions (HOW) are then laid down to ensure that the most important parameters (WHAT) are observed.

The results of FMEA and design of experiments (see above) can contribute to steps 2 and 3 if need be.

When Should QFD be Used?

The use of QFD is not restricted to any specific manufacturing type or process. However, one rule of thumb does apply: the more complex the product or the more innovative the development assignment, the more appropriate is the use of QFD. This is because QFD makes transparent the relationships between complex or new requirements. It is therefore a good planning tool for manufacturers of systems and complex components in the automotive supply industry. It is also practically essential for car manufacturers, where it can be used for anything from entire cars to systems which the manufacturer develops and produces independently.

How Should QFD be Applied?

All functions participate in QFD, albeit in varying degrees at the different steps (Figure A.3). This means that QFD is ideal for introducing and establishing interdisciplinary and process-oriented thinking and action in

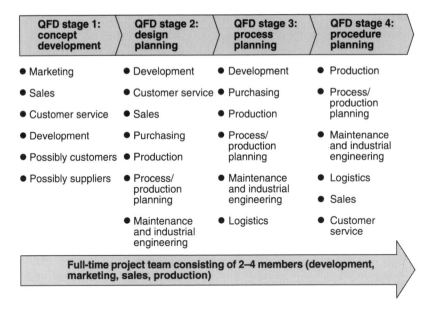

QFD stage 1: concept development	QFD stage 2: design planning	QFD stage 3: process planning	QFD stage 4: procedure planning
● Marketing	● Development	● Development	● Production
● Sales	● Customer service	● Purchasing	● Process/ production planning
● Customer service	● Sales	● Production	
● Development	● Purchasing	● Process/ production planning	● Maintenance and industrial engineering
● Possibly customers	● Production		
● Possibly suppliers	● Process/ production planning	● Maintenance and industrial engineering	● Logistics
			● Sales
	● Maintenance and industrial engineering	● Logistics	● Customer service

Full-time project team consisting of 2–4 members (development, marketing, sales, production)

Fig. A.3 *Functional areas with varying contributions*

an organization. However, its successful implementation naturally depends on the active involvement of top management in the process, including a strong top management role in implementation. This can take the form of the appropriate allocation of resources or participation in selected team meetings, for example.

The following steps are particularly important in using QFD:

- Introduction of top management and executives to the objectives and procedure of QFD
- Selection of two pilot projects in order to gain experience quickly. These projects should meet the following criteria:
  - They should be straightforward, but not trivial
  - They should have a clearly defined objective, in the form of a concrete product or product development assignment for the implementing company
  - They should attract wide interest within the company
  - They should be designed to meet a real customer need
  - Customer information should be at hand or obtainable:
- Appointment of the teams from different hierarchical levels and functions such as marketing/sales, customer service, development, purchasing, production, production planning, and logistics. Each team should consist of five to eight members (2 to 4 of them full-time), the skill profile

of each member (i.e., specialist knowledge, interdisciplinary knowledge, team skills) and their motivation (see Chapter 3, 'The Development Process') being of the utmost importance here. In the introductory phase, facilitation by external consultants has proved helpful. Once the project has got off to a successful start, the work can be handed over to the company's own staff.

● Training and upskilling of project participants in the form of on-the-job training. Initially, external QFD experts will be there to train team members – but, following the principle of training the trainers which applies to most QA tools, also to train the subsequent in-house trainers. This is the only way to ensure the dynamic dissemination of knowledge and of the customer-oriented philosophy within the organization. With training geared toward the immediate application of the newly acquired knowledge and methods, the latter remain fresh in the minds of the employees, thus sustaining the momentum of the QFD launch.

Project work should be controlled by regular reviews within the teams and in consultation with top management (see description of Design Review later in the chapter). During the project, the team members should be relieved of their usual line tasks, since otherwise an overload of hours could jeopardize the success of the project. The ideal organizational framework for a QFD is tight project organization with a truly entrepreneurial personality as a figurehead. This project manager should have far-reaching powers, particularly when it comes to making final decisions on the setup and staffing of the project organization, as well as the allocation of work within the teams.

When properly conducted, QFD is a complex and time-consuming exercise, so that companies sometimes limit themselves to those individual steps ('Houses') where they have the most pressing gaps. For example, a company may decide to concentrate on step 1 if it has previously encountered difficulties in translating customer requirements into design specifications.

What are the Do's and Don'ts?

A solid foundation in the form of reliable data and information on the market, customers, and competitors is needed for successful application of QFD. To prevent important information from going astray or being overlooked in the course of product development, it is vital to adhere closely to the QFD system. This is another reason why training during the project must not be neglected.

Another extremely important but often underrated condition for success is clear documentation, which ensures that data and experience can be passed on. It is also advisable to concentrate resources at step 1, because the weighting of customer demands and their translation into concrete proposals is the most challenging part of the process. In some companies, it has proved valuable to invite customers (from focus groups, for example, see Chapter 3) to participate in meetings at this level.

The success of a QFD project can be crippled by overly rigid functional and hierarchical structures which get – or keep – the upper hand over the project management. A good example of this situation is the observed case of one QFD team member, who was asked by his head of department to seek his approval on every important decision – an unacceptable situation, which in addition undermines the project team's basis of trust.

What are the Benefits of QFD?

Top quality companies cite the complete and precise fulfilment of customer demands as the main benefit of QFD. This benefit is hard to quantify, but sales growth is one gauge of success: companies using QFD experienced an average growth rate of around 15 per cent per year in the period under observation, the average of all the companies surveyed was around 8 per cent. The ratio of these companies' income and expenditure told the same tale: despite the high initial outlay, it was estimated at an average of 1:15.

Thanks to QFD, Toyota was able to reduce the budgeted introduction costs of one model by 61 per cent by avoiding ex-post alterations at product concept and glitches in production startup. One bearings manufacturer in our study saw a 30 per cent increase in the sales of its new product, a wheel-bearing with ABS sensors. The product concept was developed using QFD from its inception, making it possible to fulfil the OEM's demand for compactness. And that was not all: the startup quality at the beginning of series production improved in the space of six months to 150 ppm, with the additional bonus that the product was much more reliable than its predecessor. As if that were not reward enough, the manufacturer also managed to cut its costs for design changes by 10 per cent.

FMEA – FOR PRODUCTS, PROCESSES, AND INTERFACES

FMEA stands for Failure Mode and Effects Analysis. It is concerned, then, with pinpointing possible failures which may arise in a product, in the functional interfaces of a system, or in a process, and the effects they may have on quality.

The Method

FMEA is a qualitative process which taps in to the knowledge and creative potential of the corporate workforce in order to recognize and evaluate potential faults (risk analysis) and to prevent them or at least reduce their number with design changes.

All important functional elements and/or attributes of a product or process are analyzed in respect of their functional performance and failure modes. The aim of this is to predict every conceivable fault in both new and modification development, or in manufacturing and assembly processes (product and process FMEA). It is also used in complex systems to examine functional interdependencies at important interfaces, between hardware and software, for example. In other words, this interface FMEA is basically an integral part of a product or process FMEA.

The consequences of the failure are evaluated according to their seriousness (S), the probability of their occurrence (P), and the probability of their detection at the customer (D). A risk priority number (RPN = S × P × D) is then extrapolated from this data. Design improvements are then deduced for products or processes with high risk priority numbers, i.e., products with a high probability of serious failure modes. These measures prevent the source of the failure from arising.

FMEA involves the following steps:

1. Specifying the functions
2. Analyzing the functions
3. Pinpointing potential failure modes and their seriousness for the customer (S, P, D)
4. Identifying the weak points by calculating the risk priority RPN
5. Analyzing the causes of failure
6. Devising design improvements and a plan for their introduction (including responsibilities)
7. Updating the FMEA after improvements have been introduced.

The results are then carefully recorded on a special FMEA form (DIN 25448) (Figure A.4).

When Should FMEA be Used?

As with QFD, the more complex the product and/or process, the more appropriate is the use of FMEA. FMEA can also be used in any area and is applied widely in many different industries. In the automotive supply industry, where OEMs insist on its widespread – if not always effective – use, FMEA is particularly important for the manufacturers of components and systems. This is because they are selling 'functionality' on which the OEM – and, of course, the end customer – has to be able to rely completely.

S	= Seriousness of error
P	= Probability of occurrence
D	= Probability of detection
RPN	= Risk priority number = SxPxD
R	= Responsibility
T	= Deadline

<u>EXAMPLE</u>

Bosch			FMEA				Page:	1
Quality assurance	Product: Ignition system Article no.:						Department: FMEA-No.: Date:	27.08.93
Components	Function/ purpose	Mode of failure	Effect of failure	Causes of failure	Prevention of failure	Detection of failure	RPN = SxPxx	Measure R/T:
System FMEA								
Starter	Release torque	No torque release	No engine start No vehicle start	Interruption	—	Noise		
Design FMEA								
Lever armature shaft*	Transfer torque	Shaft broken	No torque release	Shaft-diameter too smalll	Radius calculated by computer program	Strain limit test	8x3x5 =120	
			No engine start	Indentation radius too small	Design according to design guide-lines	1. Strain limit test	8x6x4 =192	
			No vehicle start			2. Space vibration test	8x6x4 =192	FEM calculation V: K/EWG T: 03.94

Source: Bosch GmbH Stuttgart (Masing/Kersten, 1994).

Fig. A.4   *System and design FMEA*

FMEA is basically needed in the cases of:

- Safety-related systems, components, or product features
- Potential failure modes with serious or costly consequences
- Basic new developments
- New technologies, materials, and processes, especially if these have not been sufficiently 'secured' in upstream development
- Changes in concept or function
- Re-use of components which have caused problems in the past
- New/revised conditions of use for existing products.

The experience of developers, design engineers, and customer service engineers often proves extremely valuable in selecting the areas of application. QFD can also be used to define features which are important to meet customer demands (I) but difficult to realize (D). These features are positioned in an I&D diagram; difficult and/or important features are then singled out for priority FMEA treatment.

Product FMEA should be carried out in parallel to the design phase, i.e., before the first prototypes are constructed. The same applies to process FMEA. Functional reliability must be secured by process FMEA before process planning reaches the 'hardware phase'. The general rule is, therefore, to use FMEA as early and preventively as possible. However, many companies learn the hard way and find that they have to 'catch up' on FMEA in the production phase as a result of taking short cuts in development.

How Should FMEA be Used?

An FMEA is carried out by an interdisciplinary team. Although product development plays a leading role in a product FMEA, it is crucial to involve quality assurance, process development, production planning/operations scheduling, customer service, and sales as well. Some top-quality companies also invite their main customers to the FMEA workshops. A process FMEA must be led by process planning and production planning/operations scheduling, with quality assurance, maintenance, product development, and staff from the relevant production line/production department as permanent members of the team.

In view of the interdependence of product and process (the reliability of a product function depends on adherence to process parameters, for instance), it is important to integrate and synchronize the use of the two methods in the sense of integrated product and process development. There should therefore be a considerable overlap of personnel between the interdisciplinary teams for product and process FMEA. Figure A.5 illustrates the cause-and-effect relationship between the various types of FMEA.

	Type of FMEA	Component or process	Function purpose	Failure Effect ⟵ Mode ⟶ Cause		
Product FMEA	System FMEA	Ignition distributor	Distribute stress impulse	No ignition Vehicle does not move	Failure of pulse discriminator	Shaft broken
	Design FMEA	Distributor rotor	Press fit on camshaft	Failure of pulse discriminator	Shaft broken	Blow-hole
Process FMEA	Process	Distributor rotor-injection molding	Guarantee homogenous structure	Shaft broken	Blow-hole	Pressure too low

Discovery of 'root cause'

Source: Masing/Kersten, 1994.

Fig. A.5 *Interdependency of product and process FMEA*

The FMEA team meetings should be chaired by a specially trained facilitator. His or her facilitation skills will be a decisive factor in the effectiveness and efficiency of the FMEA projects, particularly in the introductory phase. FMEA facilitators should receive further training over time in their capacity as instructors, so that they themselves will be able to train FMEA facilitators, and dissemination of the procedure throughout the organization will be secured.

FMEA facilitators must meet the following criteria: (1) broad technical *knowledge* (education and training, for example), several years of experience in various different areas or inter-disciplinary know-how/understanding; (2) general *skills*, such as good analytical and abstract thinking, ability to work in teams, initiative, ability to motivate others; (3) *personal strengths* such as persuasiveness, self-confidence, and creativity. FMEA facilitators should not – as is often the case – be staff people; this additional function should be carried out by quality assurance or development employees, who can regularly contribute the experience and knowledge acquired from their day-to-day business as well as their broad knowledge of methodology.

An introductory plan for the FMEA might look like this:

1. External training of FMEA facilitators, at an appropriate trade association or other expert body.
2. Prioritizing of critical development projects (seriousness, scope, and urgency of possible quality problems).
3. Choice of two critical development projects for FMEA implementation.
4. Brief introduction to FMEA techniques for top management by external experts, top management then passes on information to the development function as a whole.
5. Formation of two or three FMEA teams per development project – facilitators and team members – by top management (unless the FMEA teams have already been formed as project teams under the leadership of the project leader).
6. Internal training of FMEA team members by in-house FMEA facilitators (with external support if necessary), with simultaneous FMEA workshops on both development projects to reduce the 'areas of risk' (see steps in the section on Method above).
7. Team debriefing: Exchange of experiences between the FMEA teams and training in company-specific FMEA techniques, optimization of organizational FMEA procedures, etc.
8. Rolling out FMEA techniques to further development projects with simultaneous parallel training.

It is important to implement FMEA immediately after or during training – the old 'practice makes perfect' rule also applies here.

What are the Do's and Don'ts?

A complete and thorough investigation of all serious failure modes and their causes and effects demands the utmost analytical precision. It is therefore vital to be critical and as objective as possible in assessing risks. This may not come easily to some developers when their own product or assembly unit is under scrutiny, since ultimately they are being asked to criticize their own work and results constructively. This is where the persuasive powers of management and FMEA facilitators must come into play; those concerned should be offered an 'amnesty' on previous errors of omission or commission in design or development. A high level of creativity is then needed when working out design remedies; creativity training might then be beneficial or even necessary.

Want of detail is one of the main recurrent problems. Many FMEAs only skim the surface, whether for lack of time, misguided use of energy, or insufficient know-how. The term 'Pseudo-FMEA' has become common currency. In addition to thorough training, this problem can be redressed by intensively targeting a few critical functions, which are then subjected to a rigorous FMEA.

When it comes to securing employee acceptance of the proposed FMEA techniques, open information supplied early on in the process is important, as are presentations about successes in other companies (by the external trainers, for example). Furthermore, top management support must remain an intrinsic part of the FMEA beyond the introductory stage; this can take the form of having presentations made to the managing board on the results of FMEA workshops for important development projects, for example.

What are the Benefits of FMEA?

Since FMEA helps to prevent failures, its main benefit comes in the form of reduced costs. But the benefits do not stop there; in the medium term it can vastly improve a company's quality image in the eyes of the customer: recurring failures are eliminated, bad product design is avoided, the risk of recalls is reduced, and warranty and ex gratia costs are cut.

The example of one supplier of a mechanical component shows how impressive the results can be. After the company had carried out three product and one process FMEAs for its new product generation, it succeeded in reducing internal rejects from 1.8 per cent to 0.9 per cent and rework from 1.4 per cent to 0.5 per cent. Warranty costs in the first two years then also fell by 68 per cent.

There are additional benefits which are less quantifiable, but definitely pay off in the medium term. The staff's quality consciousness is enhanced, the exchange of information and experience (particularly among departments and disciplines), is heightened, and the initial training of new employees improved. A full roll-out of FMEA will therefore bring a company several steps closer to achieving a zero-defects strategy – even a zero-defects culture.

FAULT TREE ANALYSIS

Fault tree analysis takes its name from the way its results are presented, with the logical links between functional failures at the level of parts, components, and systems set out in a pattern resembling a tree.

The Method

Like FMEA, fault tree analysis (FTA) belongs to the risk analysis family of quality tools. But while an FMEA identifies individual potential failures, their causes and effects, FTA starts with a specific fault – or 'undesirable outcome' – which is of particular inconvenience to the customer. It identifies the possible causes of the fault and examines their logical ramifications. Each method can make use of results of others; for example, if the probability that individual failures will occur – as calculated by FMEA – is known, Boolean algebra can then be used to work out the probability of the 'undesirable outcome'. The reliability and safety of a system can ultimately be assessed on this basis. FMEA, on the other hand, uses the results of FTA as input parameters to prioritize the risk, for which design measures have to be developed ('Risk Priority Numbers'; see FMEA above).

Fault tree analysis consists of the following steps:[3]

1. Detailed system analysis, covering not only system functions, environmental conditions, resources (such as sources of energy), and system structure, but also the interactions of components, reactions of the system to different environmental conditions (in particular, possible human intervention), and internal failures.
2. Identification of the 'undesirable outcome', which may affect either the reliability of the system or sub-function or its operating readiness, and the failure criteria.
3. Establishing reliability parameters which provide information about the frequency of failure and down times within a given period of time.
4. Ascertaining the failures in components and functional elements which may result from the 'undesirable outcome'.

---

[3] See also DIN 25 424.

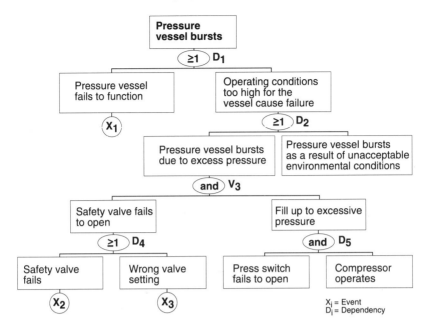

Source: DIN 25 424.

Fig. A.6 *Example of a fault tree: 'pressure vessel bursts'*

5. Drawing up the fault tree, starting with the 'undesirable outcome' (Figure A.6).
6. Compiling the input parameters which influence the 'branches' of the fault tree (conditions such as temperature, or outcomes such as failures); the probability of failure or down times, for example.
7. Analysis of the fault tree (often with the help of simulation techniques). Typical results of the analysis are:
   – fault combinations which can lead to an 'undesirable outcome'
   – probability of the fault combinations arising
   – probability of the 'undesirable outcome' arising
   – minimum probabilities of fault combinations leading to the 'undesirable outcome.'[4]
8. Interpretation of the results and their incorporation into the FMEA action plan.

---

[4] For further information on the mathematical and statistical basis, R. Arnold and C.-O. Bauer, *Qualität in der Entwicklung und Konstruktion*, Verlag TÜV Rheinland, Cologne, 1992, is recommended.

When Should FTA be Used?

As far as the area of application and use is concerned, the same principles apply to fault tree analysis as to FMEA. It is applied during the development process and its importance increases with the complexity of the product or production process, particularly in the case of safety-related systems and components, potentially serious consequences of failures, and basic new developments and new technologies.

How is FTA Used?

Because of the complex production of today's products, especially in automotive engineering, fault tree analysis is becoming an increasingly useful tool. With the multitude of technical interfaces and interdependencies comes a multitude of potential combinations of causes of faults which cannot be completely covered by FMEA. For this reason, FMEA should always be broadened and deepened by fault tree analysis in areas where high risks and interdependent causes of faults have been identified.

As with FMEA, this tool should also be used in an interdisciplinary team. Marketing/sales, or possibly product development, identify the most important 'undesirable outcomes'. Product and process development, supported by the statistical know-how of quality assurance, then generate the fault analysis tree. FMEA facilitators (see FMEA above) should conduct and monitor the team work. We recommend the eight-step plan described in the FMEA section as an introduction. The FMEA *and* fault tree analysis must be carried out simultaneously and in an integrated manner for every step. Considering how closely the two methods interlock, this last point is a vital requirement.

What are the Do's and Don'ts?

'Focus' is the key word for the successful implementation of a fault tree analysis. The method is sophisticated and time-consuming, and so the focus should be on a small number of extremely crucial 'undesirable outcomes', which should be subjected to the most thorough analysis possible. FTA must always begin with a thorough system analysis, even if the product concept is considered mature. This system analysis forms the basis for establishing the logical connections between their faults and causes. If it is carried out hastily or carelessly, important links may be overlooked and the results of the entire process may be distorted.

Fault tree analysis is another part of the 'brainwork' invested in the product concept. When the first prototypes or feasibility models are produced, the causes/faults identified or measures generated should be statistically tested. The up-front investment will pay off in every case.

What are the Benefits of FTA?

One of the companies surveyed in our study drew up a fault tree analysis for its new product design. As a result, the OEM's return rate (measured in ppm) fell by 71 per cent compared to the preceding product in the first year after market launch. This was without doubt an outstanding achievement – due in no small measure to the high skill level of the participants – when the average return-rate figure for all FTA users in the study was 30 per cent. If the consequential costs of return deliveries are considered, it soon becomes clear that such improvements can also lead to considerable savings. The most important factor, however, is the quality image a company builds vis-à-vis the customer with such dramatic increases in the level of quality.

DESIGN OF EXPERIMENTS

Design of experiments – or statistically planned experiments – is, as the name suggests, the planning of a series of experiments. The object of the exercise is to use statistical methods to identify the optimum settings for one or more product or process parameters.

The use of design of experiments is neither a precondition for the use of statistical process control (which will be described later) nor an alternative to other quality assurance tools. It is a special accessory in the quality management repertoire which is used when a breakthrough in product and process quality is required.

The Method

Design of experiments helps to answer quality questions such as 'How does quality feature A of the product change if we use material Y instead of material X?' or 'How does quality feature B of the product change if we raise process parameter Z (cutting speed, for example) by 10 per cent?' In short, design of experiments studies the effects of one or more factors of influence or input ('independent variables') on the target or output parameters ('dependent variables').

The first step involves isolating these factors of influence from those whose effect on the target parameters is not under scrutiny, but which cannot be kept constant over the course of the entire experiment. These latter are then arranged into blocks in the design of the experiment, in such a way that their effects can be measured ('block factors'). In addition, there are also factors which are not taken into account in the experiment; this may be because their effect on the target parameters is of no interest or to avoid overburdening the experiment. The target parameters – or output figures – are those quality features of the product which are assumed to be affected by the input parameters.

The procedure can be divided up into the following stages:

1. Formulation of problems and targets
2. Collecting the necessary data
3. Using brainstorming to ascertain the factors of influence and their interrelationships
4. Selecting factors of influence and other factors to be examined
5. Planning and specifying the experiment program
6. Carrying out the experiments
7. Evaluating and analyzing data[5]
8. Interpreting results and suggesting measures for product and/or process improvement (validating these proposals by means of a confirmatory experiment).

In the course of the experiment, the parameters should be set in such a way that, on the one hand, the desired mean value of a quality feature can be realized and, on the other hand, variance can be minimized. This is best done in a two step process: first, by optimizing the mean value and then the variance – or vice versa – using the appropriate combination of factors.

The best known form of design of experiments is the eponymous Taguchi method, developed by the Japanese quality guru. In the design of a product, Taguchi made it his objective to set his parameters or factors (material, for example) in such a way that the quality features of the product (its strength, for example) would be as insensitive or 'robust' as possible to the variable parameters of the process (temperature, for example). This 'parameter design' is preceded by 'system design', which defines a preliminary concrete configuration for the product concept (choice of material and components, etc.). The third and last step of the Taguchi method is 'tolerance design', in which the tolerances for the control parameters of the process are optimized.

In Chapter 3 we mentioned the example of the brick kiln: by altering the composition of the material (i.e., optimizing the design parameter), Taguchi succeeded in considerably reducing the sensitivity of the brick to variations in the temperature of the kiln (factor of influence); i.e., the quality feature 'strength' was rendered more 'robust' vis-à-vis this uncontrollable input factor.

---

[5] For the mathematical basis, implementation procedures and the designing of experiments, see Masing, pp. 494 ff (footnote 1 above).

Taguchi makes developers view their work from a completely new angle: away from the blinkered approach of only looking at exceeded tolerances, to quantifying ongoing losses in quality (and hence losses to the business) caused by deviations from target values. This Taguchi loss function generally forms a parabolic curve on a graph, whereby losses increase with the deviation from the target values.

A less well known approach is Shainin's method of determining factors of influence. After distinguishing between important and less important factors ('importance' in the sense of the strength of their influence) according to the Pareto principle, this method goes on to reduce the variance of the key process parameters and raise the tolerances of the unimportant ones in order to cut down on costs.

Where Should Design of Experiments be Used?

These statistical methods are used to acquire the most reliable information possible about interdependencies from as few experiments as possible. They are therefore useful wherever the results of a process depend on a large number of interactive factors and the dependencies between them are unclear or unknown. For example, a target parameter dependent on 15 factors of influence each with two characteristic features would theoretically require $2^{15} = 32,768$ experiments – a completely unfeasible number in practical terms. A certain Taguchi experiment plan (balanced orthogonal array) would require only 16 experiments and would have a high probability of coming very close to the desired target value. Besides its economy, there is a further advantage to the 'multi-factor method'; it can also help to determine the interactions between factors of influence.

Design of experiments can be applied to any branch of industry, product segment, or type of production. It should be used most intensively in product and process development in order to avoid subsequent complicated modifications and the quality 'losses' incurred up to that point (on steps 2 and 3 of QFD, for example, this method can provide useful information). It can also be used for ongoing processes, however, if an immediate solution is required for critical quality problems.

How Should Design of Experiments be Used?

In the light of the costs and know-how requirements of design of experiments, its application should clearly be selective and targeted. In the early stages, above all the identification of possible factors of influence and their interactions, it has proved worthwhile to involve a mixed team of workers from production, maintenance, quality assurance, product and process development. The subsequent conducting and analysis of the experiments, however, should be left to experts with the relevant training (mostly from quality assurance). The inter-disciplinary team re-forms to interpret the results and generate actions.

It is advisable in design of experiments to train a small corps of experts intensively, rather than having expertise 'snowball' throughout the workforce as recommended for QFD and FMEA. The participants from other divisions should receive instruction in the most important principles whilst the project is in progress. This provision of information must be taken seriously. It is particularly important for employees to keep successful examples from other companies in mind, as a process of this delicacy runs a particularly high risk of potential 'blockades'.

What are the Do's and Don'ts?

The critical step – the decisive one for the cost/benefit ratio – is setting out the experiment plan.

In particular the connections between influence factors and target values should be evaluated with the most minute attention to detail. There is no set formula. However, experience has shown that the best guarantees of success are the interaction of experienced employees from the different departments and precise analysis of the problematic manufacturing processes (identifying 'patterns of error' – i.e., which errors arise from which conditions?).

The greatest sources of error are inaccurate statistics, unknown constraints or factors of influence, and insufficient know-how. A solid theoretical foundation alone is thus not enough; over and above this, confirmatory experiments should be constantly conducted to validate the measures developed and avoid the pitfalls of statistical irrelevance. The companies surveyed gave the demanding know-how base required by the tool as its greatest weakness, and this weakness underlines the need for intensive training of the expert group.

What are the Benefits of Design of Experiments?

Results only come with time, as experience plays a particularly important role here. The fact that this tool is only used by 50 per cent of quality companies is an indication of the caution and selectiveness with which it should be approached. Those companies which work with it do have an average cost/benefit ratio of 1:10, however, due to a considerable reduction in experimentation and in the costs of errors.

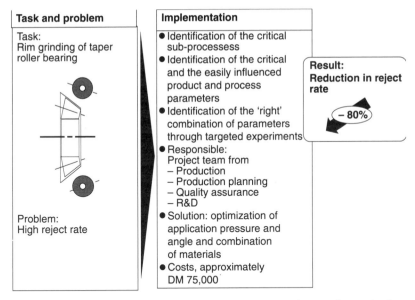

Fig. A.7 *Parameter optimization through use of Taguchi method*

One of the companies surveyed used the Taguchi method for rim grinding of taper roller bearings. By improving the combination of materials, the application pressure and angle, they succeeded in reducing the reject rate by 80 per cent (Figure A.7). With one-off costs of its execution coming to around DM75,000, this meant a cost/benefit ratio (based on one year) of around 1:11.

DESIGN REVIEW

As the name suggests, design review is a systematic examination (to be carried out at regular intervals) of development results, i.e., of design in the narrower sense, in terms of conformance with specific requirements.

The Method

From the point of view of the management scientist, design review is a classic controlling tool: planned and actual values for the most important product *and* process requirements are compared at regular intervals. The aim is to ensure that the customer requirements defined at the beginning of the development process are met. Not only cost and time parameters are tracked; design review also performs a very valuable function in monitoring quality specifications and features. This affects elements of customer value (such as important functions of the product required by the customer), subsequent process quality in the production process, and the product's manufacturability and/or ease of assembly. The importance of this tool becomes clear in the light of the impact of product development on the 'product quality' which is subsequently passed on the customer.

Design review is based on detailed project planning and definition of the target parameters to be tracked. First of all, the development process is sub-divided into phases (concept study, product development, prototype/test/ optimization, test series, pilot series, series startup) and sub-phases. For every phase and sub-phase, i.e., for every 'milestone', planned values are established for the target parameters and compared with the actual values when the milestone is reached. If discrepancies occur, actions must be developed with accountabilities and deadlines. The efficiency of these measures is then put to the test at the next design review, when the new set of planned and actual values are compared. (An example of a list of possible target parameters is shown in Figure 3.8.)

The results of the design reviews at every milestone are recorded on concise and detailed plan/actual forms with columns for the relevant actions (see Figure A.8). Even qualitative features and target parameters can be 'quantified' (with percentage fulfilment grades 0 per cent, 25 per cent, 50 per cent, 75 per cent, 100 per cent). Critical milestones should be treated with particular care.

EXAMPLE OF MECHANICAL MANUFACTURING

Project: ABC
Team: XYZ

	Plan	Actual	Comment
● Weight	18.0 kg	19.1 kg	Weight reduction round started
● Number of variants	4	4	
● Number of components	60	62	Accepted
● Share of material costs in components purchased	10%	13%	
● Production time	12 min.	11 min.	Further potential of 1 min. available
● Number of tools	100	103	Accepted

Fig. A.8 *Form for tracking strategic objectives*

When Should Design Review be Used?

Design review can be used regardless of the type of product or production process. However, its use is particularly recommended for complex products or large-scale new developments, as in these cases the number of target parameters to be controlled simultaneously is naturally very high. We found systematically conducted design reviews more often at component and systems manufacturers than at manufacturers of individual parts.

How Should it be Used?

As mentioned above, workers from various different functions are involved in design review. To guarantee optimum use of resources, however, their participation should vary according to the stage of the development project. For example, marketing, sales, and product development carry the main workload in the early concept and product development phases, whilst production and process development contribute only to certain areas in this stage.

In companies which practise consistent simultaneous engineering with project management, these team structures are already in place and form the organizational platform for design review. In addition, experts are consulted at individual milestones if necessary. It makes sense, for example, to include quality experts in the project if the results of a statistically planned experiment are being dealt with regularly.

The intervals between design reviews – at least, those by the 'standard team' should not be too long. If, for example, a review takes place only at the end of each downstream development stage, drastic deviation from a target parameter may not be recognized early enough, so that counter-measures take effect too late, or not at all. A four- to eight-week cycle may even be appropriate, particularly when design review is being introduced in a company for the first time. Ultimately, then, a company-specific tradeoff must be made between the scope and depth of the review and the time intervals.

Design review can even serve as a framework for the development plan; objectives, interim, and end results of the individual quality assurance tools (such as QFD and FMEA) are discussed in the review meetings and recorded in the review forms. One important class of target figures is the results of function checks or production experiments. Close attention to these often ensures that errors and sources of errors are detected early, so that countermeasures can be decided on in good time. In our experience, this group of parameters is culpably neglected by many companies, often with disastrous results for customer satisfaction and loyalty.

What are the Do's and Don'ts?

We have already stressed the importance in design reviews of really regular progress control in fairly short cycles, and of up-to-date, clear documentation. Accordingly, tight project management with formalized documentation and execution is an important factor for success.

The 'mix' of workers involved also has to be right; alongside those directly involved in the development project, 'neutral', experienced members of other projects, or from line management, should have a seat and a voice on the design review board. Top companies also form 'customer committees' consisting of in-house workers who represent the voice of the (external or internal) customer. In the case of particularly important milestones, the customers themselves are often invited to the design reviews, a sure way of avoiding any manipulation or undesirable 'good will' when checking whether objectives have been reached. It should go without saying that suppliers of key technologies or development units are regular participants in design reviews.

Errors mainly arise when the objectives for individual milestones are not formulated in actionable terms, and are therefore difficult to control. The philosophy (and practice) of operationalized objectives, permanent tracking and personalized responsibility may be revolutionary for many developers, but it is essential.

What are the Benefits of Design Review?

Design review makes a decisive contribution to the rigorous implementation of development concepts and to early recognition and elimination of errors, making it a core element of quality management. Realization of the concept, in so far as it lies within the 'target sphere' of the customer, allows the company to attain its target sales figures. The early elimination of faults ensures customer satisfaction and lower costs of quality.

One manufacturer of automotive electronics calculated the cost of errors discovered and eliminated in development at DM1,850 on average. For errors identified at the system test stage the company had to shell out DM5,500. But most costly of all were errors which went undetected until the customers themselves complained; these cost the company around DM14,800. The majority of companies surveyed which conducted regular design reviews mentioned their high preventive impact – above all because of the use of teamwork, improved exchange of information and the constant need to review progress.

Another important function of rigorous design reviews is that they make a major contribution to the culture change in product and process development, as the design engineers involved have to force themselves to examine the results of their work strictly from the point of view of value.

Complaints are occasionally heard about the 'huge amount of time' involved in design reviews. These critics must have got their arithmetic wrong, however: they have obviously forgotten to take into account the time taken up by corrective action meetings further down the track, long after the development stage is over.

STATISTICAL PROCESS CONTROL (SPC)

The use of statistical methods to monitor and control manufacturing processes is now standard practice. Quality-related product parameters (as the end products of one step in the manufacturing process, the diameter of a shaft, for example) or process parameters are measured and analyzed with the help of statistical methods (especially sampling techniques and Gaussian distribution). The comparison of these analytical results with target values decides whether and to what extent the parameters of a manufacturing process have to be adjusted. This analysis, control, and improvement of the process is commonly known as statistical process control (SPC).

The Method

The core of this method consists of an ongoing comparison between planned and actual conditions in a manufacturing process or between different product parameters resulting from the process. Its aim is to correct the process by adjusting important process parameters if need be (cutting speed in metal processing or pressure in chemical processes, for example). There is no point in such interventions unless actual values persistently deviate from plan. Systematic monitoring is carried out to provide a sound basis for decision-making in the form of statistically meaningful measurements.

SPC charts (Figure A.9) are used to record quality-related process or product parameters over time. Upper and lower tolerance limits for variances from planned values and a pre-calculated random scatter range are given, so as to determine whether deviating measurements relate only to individual samples or are systematic, i.e., persistently exceed the upper and lower random limits. Systematic variances of this kind can be recognized with varying levels of precision, depending on design of the SPC charts.

There are three steps to SPC: determining process controllability, specifying process capability, and tracking and improving the process over time on the basis of the ratios obtained.

1. Determining process controllability using statistical techniques
First, it must be ensured that every SPC card is in harmony with the actual process, i.e., the frequency and scope of the samples must cover the typical course of the process. Once these criteria are met, it must then be determined

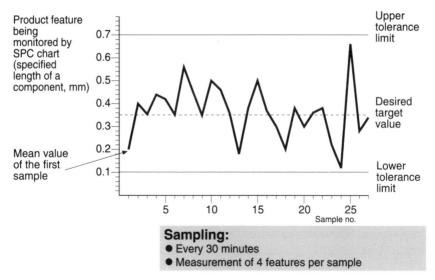

Fig. A.9 *Example of an SPC chart*

whether the process can be described by the Gaussian distribution model. This will entail scatter and mean value analyses of the parameters monitored. If these show that the parameters are only affected by random forces in no fixed order, i.e., that scatter and mean value are statistically stable, effective process monitoring and control using statistical techniques is possible.

2. Process evaluation on the basis of capability indices

The quality capability of manufacturing processes is described in terms of capability indices. These show how far the process is capable of error-free production.

Process capability is defined as the ratio of the prescribed tolerance (= upper tolerance limit − lower tolerance limit) to the process scatter (to be precise, the scatter of quality-related parameters). In this relationship, process scatter is a function of standard deviation, which, in the case of statistically controllable processes (see step 1), can be approximately calculated from the SPC charts. In a fault analysis which includes cases both above the upper tolerance limit (UT) and below the lower tolerance limit (LT), process scatter is taken as the standard deviation × 6.

So process capability, C_p, is:

$$C_p = \frac{\text{upper tolerance limit} - \text{lower tolerance limit}}{\text{Standard deviation} \times 6}$$

Example	Standard deviation σ (for upper and lower tolerance limits)	Tolerance range	Process capability C_p	Failure rate F (from chart showing standard distribution)
1	1.50 σ	3.00 σ	$C_p = \dfrac{3.00\,\sigma}{6.00\,\sigma} = 0.50$	13.3614% = 133,614 ppm
2	2.25 σ	4.50 σ	$C_p = \dfrac{4.50\,\sigma}{6.00\,\sigma} = 0.75$	2.4448% = 24,448 ppm
3	3.00 σ	6.00 σ	$C_p = \dfrac{6.00\,\sigma}{6.00\,\sigma} = 1.00$	0.2700% = 2,700 ppm
4	4.00 σ	8.00 σ	$C_p = \dfrac{8.00\,\sigma}{6.00\,\sigma} = 1.33$	0.0064% = 64 ppm

Fig. A.10 *Correlations between process capability C_p and failure rate*

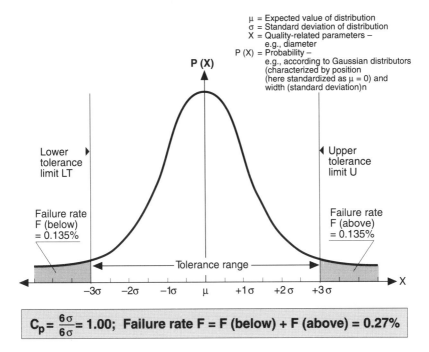

Fig. A.11 *Process capability C_p and failure rate F for centred process*

On the basis of the statistical regularity of the scatter, certain failure rates can thereby be approximately allocated to the various C_p values (Figures A.10 and A.11). We should distinguish between the following three cases:

$C_p < 1$: The process scatter or standard deviation exceeds the tolerance limits, resulting in high failure rates; a C_p value of 0.5 will represent a failure rate of 13.3614 per cent, for example.

$C_p = 1$: The process almost meets the specification limits; the failure rate will be around 0.27 per cent.

$C_p > 1$: As a rule, the process scatter lies within the tolerance limits. Under normal circumstances, there should be hardly any failures.

However, the capability index tells us only about the absolute process scatter. This means that the above applies only in cases where the process is 'centred' (i.e., where the mean value of the measurement corresponds exactly to the target or expected value). Otherwise, C_p indices greater than 1 *can* lead to failures. As a result, both centering and process scatter have to be controlled. The C_{pk} value takes this into account, and is consequently more meaningful in the long run.

To calculate the C_{pk} value, the two capability ratios C_{pu} and C_{pl}, which measure the 'one-sided' process scatter or capability at the upper and lower tolerance limits, must first be determined:

$$C_{pu} = \frac{\text{Upper tolerance limit (UT)} - \text{Process mean X}}{\text{Standard deviation} \times 3}$$

$$C_{pl} = \frac{\text{Process mean X} - \text{Lower tolerance limit (LT)}}{\text{Standard deviation} \times 3}$$

The smaller of the two values, which corresponds to higher deviations, is the C_{pk} (critical capability ratio – see Figure A.12). If the process is normally distributed and under statistical control or monitoring, the C_{pk} value can be used to estimate the failure rate.

3. Long-term tracking/improvement of the process on the basis of the capability index

Once the capability indices for a process have been initially calculated, they then have to be monitored continuously. The statistical data required to this end can be taken from the current entries in the SPC charts. To improve a process, specific causes must be identified and measures drawn up on the basis of the variance analysis. Structured problem-solving processes, carried out by quality circles (see below), for example, provide the framework for this. Design of experiments (see above) can also provide valuable support for targeted process improvement.

Incidentally, capability ratios are management information. Unfortunately, all too many managers still see them as expert know-how for quality

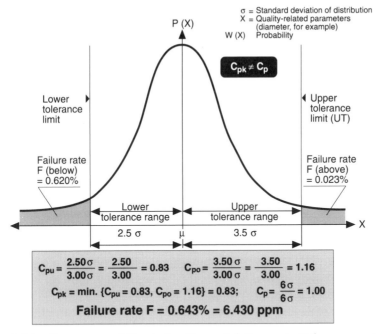

Fig. A.12 *Process capability index C_{pk} and failure rate F for non-centred process*

assurance and process engineers. They are, however, early indicators of a company's quality performance (measured in reject, rework, and return rates) and therefore belong on the production manager's desk, and ideally the R&D manager's as well.

When Should SPC Be Used?

In principle, SPC should be used for all manufacturing processes with quantitative features and/or parameters and a continuous character (constant features); the statistical discussion above applies to processes of this kind. Assembly, on the other hand, normally has discrete features such as 'assembled' or 'not assembled'. Discrete statistical distributions have to be used in order to make '0–1 processes' of this kind accessible to SPC.

In the case of one-off or small-scale production, the use of SPC is limited, because the information provided by small samples is not reliably meaningful. In other words, intervention and warning limits can only be set reliably after around 200 measurements. SPC's classical area of application is therefore mass production.

In the majority of companies, SPC is used in the production phase (which is undoubtedly where it is most useful). However, the more prevention-oriented top companies use SPC in the development stage. They apply it to test and pilot production to obtain the most reliable data possible on the quality capability of their critical production processes before start-up (see Chapter 3). If the results fall short of the target values, they can optimize their products and processes (in the sense of synchronized product and process) before series production ever starts.

Where Should SPC Be Used?

The most important principle for the application of SPC is that the shop-floor employee, not the quality assurance engineer, has to fill in the SPC charts. This integration into employee self-control plays a major role in increasing quality consciousness at the grass roots. Depending on the level of training of the employees involved, it can also be beneficial to entrust them with further tasks such as analyzing the results or designing process improvements. Unfortunately, in many companies these tasks are still left to quality assurance experts.

It is also advisable to record the measurements in the SPC charts manually at first; the resulting learning effect and enhanced awareness of process capability are of inestimable value. In the course of time, as familiarity with the methods grows and application is expanded throughout the company, computer-aided SPC is likely to be more efficient.

A key issue is the way in which SPC is introduced. 'On the job training' is more important for SPC than for any other quality tool. Unfortunately, companies in which employees barely understand the point of the technique (if they are involved in its application at all), despite extensive SPC training, are all too common. The problems are always the same: overly theoretical training with little relevance to practice and often long intervals between training and application. In a nutshell, SPC training belongs in the factory, at the machines, and with the manufacturing process concerned.

Consider one salient example. After initial pilot projects, a components manufacturer introduced SPC to mechanical production by bringing the classroom into the factory. Simulation stands (SPC charts, computer graphics, simulation software for manufacturing processes, etc.) were set up in all three areas of the factory, at which each employee in succession received several training sessions over a six-month period. Their foremen or team leaders, who had received intensive training beforehand, then accompanied the freshly trained workers to their newly upgraded SPC workplace, and provided practical instruction on the spot.

Alongside such successful 'introductory tricks', it is of paramount importance for management itself to be convinced of SPC. Until the production director grasps the significance of a C_{pk} value (he does not actually have to know how to calculate it), no extensive and successful use of SPC can really be expected in his company. In this sense SPC, unlike other tools, requires persuasion and encouragement from the 'bottom up'. The ideal setup, of course, has a management team that is convinced from the outset and backs the introduction, supplying resources and ensuring that the SPC philosophy filters down through all levels to the workforce.

What are the Do's and Don'ts?

The most important point has already been stated. SPC is part of the employees' job and should be taught as practically as possible. A further guarantee of success is careful analysis of the data, as changes will not come from SPC alone. Only the meticulous analysis of causes, structured problem-solving, and corrective action can lift the process capability ratios.

As in other areas, many companies fall into the trap of failing to focus. They pursue a plethora of apparently important parameters, instead of concentrating on those which are genuinely relevant to quality. Analysis of the weaknesses identified and the design of corrective measures then only receive perfunctory treatment. Top companies concentrate on specific areas; if the process is 'capable' (if its C_{pk} figure is higher than 2, for example) and remains so over a long period of time, they will turn their attention to less 'capable' processes (as long as there is no conflict with the explicit requirements of the OEM).

When random tests are being carried out, the minimum requirements must be kept in line with the statistical relevance (5 to 10 parts for individual samples, 50 parts altogether). In addition, the intervals between two random tests should be kept short: one hour at most, and always less than the life of the tool!

What are the Benefits of SPC?

What made quality companies stand out from the rest in our study was not SPC as such, but the consistent breadth of its application; quality companies achieved C_{pc} values of over 1.33 for 73 per cent of their (SPC-controllable) processes on average, lower quality companies achieved this figure for only 45 per cent of their processes.

Above average process capability means lower costs of rejects and rework, and that in turn is reflected in return on sales. We discovered an average return on sales of over 11 per cent for companies with C_{pk} values of over 1.67 in related product and process sectors. For the remaining companies surveyed, the figure was 4.4 per cent. One company managed to reduce its reject rate by 58 per cent in a period of three years by increasing the number of SPC-controlled processes from 52 per cent to 86 per cent and the number of processes with C_{pk} values of over 1.33 from 36 per cent to 68 per cent. Success stories such as these undoubtedly justify the introductory expense of SPC (introductory and on-the-job training, purchase of the necessary equipment). SPC can make a significant contribution to the realization of a zero-defects strategy, not only at production level, but also in R&D (particularly if production employees constantly pass on their 'process experience' to the development engineers). Developers should also be familiar with the principles and methodology to support this.

QUALITY CIRCLES

The concept of the quality circle originated in Japan at the end of the 1950s as part of broad-based drives to boost quality. Since then, it has become widely established (also under the name of quality control circles, problem-solving groups, small groups, or quality groups). In the past few years various different forms of this concept have emerged, all with the same objective: to solve quality-related problems on a voluntary basis[6] and to strive to improve the quality produced on the basis of combined staff efforts.

The Method

In actual fact a quality circle is not 'just' a method, but also an organizational approach. A group of workers comes together to help improve the quality produced or productivity by means of structured problem-solving processes.[7] Not only does this mean using the most valuable resource of the company – that is, the individual skills and experience of employees – it also involves making an important contribution to their self-actualization and to enhancing work satisfaction and motivation.

A quality circle usually consists of from 4 to 8 voluntary members. They meet on a regular basis during working hours,[8] to solve important shared quality problems, generally from their own working environment. The group chooses its subject matter itself or pursues suggestions from top management, and sets about analyzing and solving the problem using structured processes (Figure A.13). The subject matter is usually defined in such a way that improvements can be effected within the group's own responsibility.

---

[6] In Japan there are more forms of quality circles in which participation of employees is expected or ordered by superiors. In these cases, concrete output goals and the contributions of the individual employees are laid down in advance (see Chapter 5, 'Japan, Europe and the US').

[7] For a detailed description of quality circles with detailed instructions on how to conduct them and supply them with information, see Zink, K.J. and Schick, G., *Quality-Circle-Problemlösungsgruppen*, 2nd edition, Vienna, 1987.

[8] In Japan it is also common practice to meet outside working hours; the term 'official working hours' is defined somewhat more broadly in Japan.

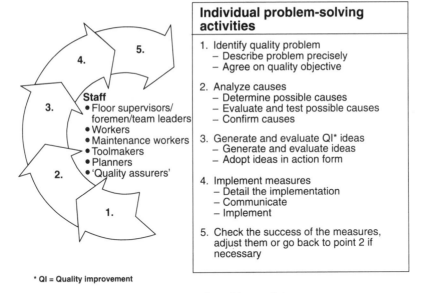

Staff
- Floor supervisors/foremen/team leaders
- Workers
- Maintenance workers
- Toolmakers
- Planners
- 'Quality assurers'

Individual problem-solving activities

1. Identify quality problem
   - Describe problem precisely
   - Agree on quality objective

2. Analyze causes
   - Determine possible causes
   - Evaluate and test possible causes
   - Confirm causes

3. Generate and evaluate QI* ideas
   - Generate and evaluate ideas
   - Adopt ideas in action form

4. Implement measures
   - Detail the implementation
   - Communicate
   - Implement

5. Check the success of the measures, adjust them or go back to point 2 if necessary

* QI = Quality improvement

Fig. A.13 *Structured problem-solving process*

It is essential that a clear quality objective is agreed upon and systematically pursued; it can be chosen by the team, but may also be set by management. This 'dedication' of the team to the desired result serves to channel all the group's efforts. The objective should be demanding but realistic, and above all it should be specified in quantitative parameters, to enable verification that the results have been achieved. For the same reason, a time limit should always be set. The results of the group work should be recorded in a concise and accurate form, clearly stating the formulation of the problem, the objective, the solution and the relevant actions (and possibly the first results). In top companies, the work of quality circles is also documented in the immediate vicinity of their place of work, or even throughout the department concerned: the illustration of conditions 'before' and 'after' (using photographs if necessary) offers conclusive proof of what has been achieved and acts as an incentive for other employees.

When Should Quality Circles be Used?

The answer is simple: all the time! They are not limited to specific corporate functions, nor to certain industries or product lines. They are currently concentrated in production, i.e., an area in which, for a long time, employees knowledge has been used only at a superficial level. In many cases, particularly fertile ground would also be found in administration, an area too readily 'forgotten' by such projects.

How Should They be Used?

Ideally, quality circles should, of course, concentrate on the most critical problems. One condition, however, is that employees – on whose voluntary initiatives such circles are based – should be constantly aware of such problems. This in turn requires a high level of motivation and interest in what is going on within their own working area, as well as readiness to commit themselves. This is where motivational actions and, above all, the provision of straightforward and open information by management come into play. Our study has also confirmed that the best-informed employees are also the most highly motivated. Another factor, of course, is confidence in the skills of the workforce, which can be expressed by assigning them decision-making responsibilities, for example.

If the problems being tackled arise in one particular area, the quality circle should be composed of employees from that area. These days, however, quality problems in manufacturing more and more often affect several other departments or even functions. As a result, the groups should be cross-functionally constituted accordingly.

A 'corset' of organizational structure supports and promotes the successful work of the quality circles. This should include a steering committee, a coordinator (for the initial phase at least), the members' superiors, QA experts, a facilitator, and a team leader or spokesman for the quality circle.

- The *steering committee*, composed of members of the top management team, promotes the work of the quality circles and, above all, ensures that such work is used as a tool for personnel management and development in all areas. Besides drawing up a concept for company-wide introduction (including provision of resources), their participation in quality circle meetings and final presentations sends credible signals.

  The presentation of their own results to the corporate management by members of the circle is a special winning experience which has a high motivational effect on employees. A common reply to the question posed by top management 'Why did we never do this before?' is 'Nobody asked me'. On the one hand this is characteristic of the dilemma of the past, on the other it is an indication of the still unexploited 'know-how potential'.

- The responsibilities of the position of *coordinator*, which can be taken on by an employee part-time, include advising management on the selection of facilitators and pilot areas, execution and support of informational activities, organization of presentations and exchange of know-how, etc.

- *Superiors* play a key role in the successful functioning of quality circles. First, they supply the organizational requirements (rooms and facilities), relieve employees of their normal duties to work in the circles, and help to implement actions – or to get the group through a sticky patch. They also forge contacts with technical specialists. Their participation at selected quality circle meetings signals the importance of the circles' work and acts as an incentive to further initiatives.

- *Experts* from a wide variety of departments in the company act as advisors to the circle on a case-by-case basis and provide support on methodology.
- The role of *facilitator* is taken either by direct superiors or a member of staff versed in problem-solving techniques (such as Pareto analysis, cause-and-effect diagrams, brainstorming, scatter diagrams, histograms, tally sheets, trend analyses); he or she may also be a member of the team.
- The responsibilities of the *circle spokesman* or *team leader* include organizing and moderating the group work, giving instruction in working methods, ensuring expert support, and preparing presentations.

It is essential that work done in quality circles should be given due acknowledgment. Alongside material rewards in the form of bonus payments, employees must receive less formal forms of acknowledgment: a meal together, a letter of thanks, praise from top management at a final presentation, or even the publication of results in the company newspaper or on the main noticeboard can pave the way for an undiminished stream of initiatives. However, honest feedback on failures is just as vital; undeserved praise never helped anyone.

In the introductory phase of a quality circle, it is advisable to adopt the following 'top-down' approach:

1. Consultation at top management level, formation of opinion, and the development of a company-specific concept.
2. Briefing of the works council by top management.
3. Finalization by top management of the company-specific concept and approach.
4. Formation of the steering committee, selection of coordinators, facilitators, etc. by top management.
5. Briefing of executives by the steering committee and trainers for the quality circles.
6. Briefing of employees by the appropriate executives.
7. Formation of the quality circles and specification of subject matter on a voluntary basis and/or at the suggestion of management, briefing and introductory talk for the first meetings by facilitators and quality circle leaders.

The circle members' superiors can and should be of great help when it comes to identifying problems. They do not necessarily have to force specific projects on the group, but can offer a shortlist of the most important topics, from which the team members can make their choice. This is, of course, less important when groups get together on their own initiative as a result of specific problems.

What are the Do's and Don'ts?

The driver of success in quality circles is independent initiative. The most important management task of superiors is to encourage this through open information, communication, interest, participation in meetings, etc. Stories are often heard about quality circles lapsing into lethargy, which is hardly surprising, considering the all too frequent waning of interest from 'above'. It is vital for management to realize the value of quality circle activities, not only in the sense of measurable output, but also the secondary effects in the form of higher job satisfaction and motivation.

Another common cause of failed initiatives is that members of quality circles develop improvements but are then not allowed to follow them through. Quality companies have a major lead in this area; almost half of them (compared to 19 per cent of poorer-quality companies) entrusted their employees with far-reaching responsibility for implementation. The most important factor is that these companies did not slacken off in their efforts, they acted as 'safety nets' for the 'trapeze artists' in the quality circles.

Inclusion of the works council at an early stage is essential, since it can give most initiatives decisive support. It is up to top management to convince the council of the value of this form of employee involvement.

What are the Benefits of Quality Circles?

In our study, quality circles showed a cost/benefit ratio of 1:10 to 1:20. Quality companies in Europe made savings of $135 per head, those in Japan achieved a remarkable per capita figure of $6,450. (The average saving for lower-quality companies in Europe was a mere $1 per head.)

One European company reported a reduction in its reject rate in production of 3.8 per cent to 1.2 per cent after two years of active quality circle work. At the same time, the new culture of quality which gradually developed cut customer returns (measured in ppm) by more than 40 per cent.

POKA-YOKE

Poka-Yoke is neither an innovation among quality assurance tools nor is it typically Japanese, despite its name. The term means no more than 'prevention of errors' (and is often translated in fun as 'fool-proofness'). The term 'source inspection' expresses the fact that the process for preventing errors is implemented at the actual source, i.e., where the relevant operation is performed.

The Method

The aim of Poka-Yoke is to avoid typical, inadvertent, human error in the production process by designing the workplace and work routine (or even the product itself) in such a way that such errors are prevented. For example:

- Marking components with certain colours, for example brake pads for different varieties of brakes, in order to reduce the possibility of confusion on assembly.
- Forms of holding devices that only allow components to be installed in one way (for the assembly of steering columns, for example).
- The use of sensors which indicate that a component has been forgotten in assembly, for example.
- Intelligent design of a product or sub-assembly which only allows a specific assembly sequence.

Poka-Yoke devices are often fitted with appropriate sensors or detectors, which indicate an 'abnormal' condition as quickly as possible (sensors can indicate the correct position for drilling holes, for example).

Poka-Yoke measures can be applied at three different points: (1) at the beginning of a work process, to prevent the start of the first process step if specifications are not met; (2) during the process, so that only correctly machined components are accepted; (3) at the end of the process, to prevent a defective component from reaching the next stage.

When Should Poka-Yoke be Used?

Poka-Yoke is applied mainly in manufacturing, but it can also be of value in administrative working procedures. It should basically be used for repetitive and monotonous tasks, because these jobs in particular can often lead to a loss of concentration and thus to inadvertent errors.

How Should it be Used?

Poka-Yoke can serve as an excellent supplement to process or product FMEA if the measures for prevention of potential failures are designed along Poka-Yoke lines. It should also be noted that even statistical process control on its own is no guarantee of completely error-free production; extra reliability can be achieved here through the appropriate design of attachments or routines. In any case: Poka-Yoke should be considered at the product and process development stage, and should not (as is the case in many companies) be put off until errors have already occurred.

However, comprehensively designing a process with Poka-Yoke measures is an extreme technical challenge, which can be met only by all those concerned working in cooperation: product and process engineers, tool and attachment makers, maintenance workers, operations planners, and, of course, employees themselves.

What are the Do's and Don'ts?

The successful implementation of Poka-Yoke requires the development engineer to get under the skin of the process (and its participants) as fully as possible. He should ask himself such questions as, 'What might go wrong?', 'Where might confusions or misunderstanding arise?'. To answer these questions reliably, product and process engineers not only need to have a good relationship with production, but also have to be well informed about the application of the product at the customer, a factor that is commonly neglected. Intelligent product design also safeguards against improper application or use, and therefore cannot be replaced by operating manuals, however good they may be.

As a rule, the most intelligent Poka-Yoke solutions are those developed by teams. Shop-floor employees and staff from the customer (OEM) can often contribute their own ideas and suggestions to joint discussions with product and process developers.

What are the Benefits of Poka-Yoke?

The benefits of Poka-Yoke solutions often significantly exceed the costs, as extremely simple and inexpensive measures are often enormously beneficial. One European company reported that simply by colour-coding components, which avoided all possibility of confusion, rework in one production line could be reduced by around 35 per cent. Our survey encountered endless examples in the same vein in quality companies that have championed Poka-Yoke.

QUALITY AUDIT

Quality audit has proven to be a useful tool for continuous quality and cost improvement, and is now an intrinsic part of the quality policy of many companies. Quality audit is defined by ISO 8402 as systematic and independent inspection, with the aim of ascertaining whether quality-related activities and their consequences correspond to the stated instructions, and whether these instructions are suited to achieving the objectives which have been set.

The Method

Quality audit examines the efficiency and effectiveness of a company's quality management. First, weaknesses are identified in a study and analysis of current performance. Subsequently, improvements are initiated and their effectiveness tracked in order to ensure both the desired level of quality and the cost-effectiveness of all quality assurance measures.

Quality audit is typically applied to the elements of the quality management system itself, i.e., to processes or products (including services), but it is not restricted to these areas. The various types of audit approach the target from different angles:

- The *systems audit* ascertains whether the quality management system includes the necessary components. It checks the skills and know-how of inspection, maintenance, and production staff and the condition of the individual elements of the system, such as important controlling and measuring systems, documentation, and the quality information and reporting systems.
- The *process audit* is concerned with the quality capability of processes and work routines, the basic appropriateness of certain processes and activities (work documents, operating supplies, inspection equipment, etc.), and whether they are being observed. It also generates improvement actions.
- The *product audit* examines a given number of end products, intermediate products, or parts to see whether they meet specifications and requirements, draws conclusions about the strengths or weaknesses in the quality management system, and develops improvements for key areas. Product audits should focus on drawing attention to key problems. For the most part they are not as statistically relevant as SPC, but do ensure that the minimum requirements correspond to the sample parameter (i.e., consumption of time and labor).
- The *service audit* assesses to what extent certain activities meet customer requirements.

The results of the audit can be condensed into a quality index with the help of point scores and weightings, making it possible to compare the quality management systems of different companies or to track the development of a company's quality management system over time. Quality audits can be carried out on a company's own initiative or at the instigation of a contractual partner or third party; accordingly there are 'internal' and 'external' audits (product audits are a purely internal affair). In the automotive industry, OEMs' audits of their suppliers have long been a part of 'quality relations'.

When Should Quality Audits be Used?

By definition, the audit has an unrestricted range of application. It can be implemented in all functions and for all processes, in short, for all elements and activities of quality management. An efficient quality management system can ensure high quality right up front, particularly in product and process development.

The quality system guidelines of the Ford Motor Company ('Ford Q-101') illustrate the potential breadth of the audit's scope: They go so far as to include the recruitment of top management.

How Should Quality Audits be Used?

Quality audits are conducted either at set intervals or under certain circumstances (for example, if complaints or quality costs increase). Regardless of the type of audit, introduction of the tool should comprise the following steps:

1. Audit design (objectives, area of analysis, scope, facts to be examined, questionnaires, plans of action, necessary technical and organizational documents).
2. Selection and training of auditors. Auditors should be familiar with the QA system, have an excellent technical, management, and quality-specific knowledge, have good interviewing skills, be well versed in analytical methods, and combine common sense with objective judgment.
3. Implementation planning (product- and system-specific details, times/deadlines).
4. Information session with the personnel in the area being audited.
5. Implementation of the quality audit.
6. Drawing up of the quality audit report and approval of actions.
7. Supervision and tracking of the actions implemented.

Quality auditors are usually selected from the quality assurance department, but staff from R&D or manufacturing may also be appointed if they fulfil the above criteria.

What are the Do's and Don'ts?

A detailed plan including a detailed questionnaire, tailored to the specifics of the area to be audited, is vital to the success of an audit. It is important to appoint auditors who are not professionally connected in any way with the department under scrutiny, to ensure that their approach is unbiased.

However, probably the most important success factor is ensuring that the departments being audited are informed and involved in good time; they have to be convinced that the audit is being conducted to support them. If they do not receive adequate assurance to this effect, a siege mentality may develop. Employees may interpret the audit as a form of control from outside or even as an attempt to blacken their reputation with top management.

What are the Benefits of a Quality Audit?

The majority of participating companies in our study reported positive experiences with quality audits. It should be stressed that the audit is primarily a tool for continuous improvement, so few companies reported major breakthroughs. The cost/benefit ratio lay between 1:6 and 1:3 for most companies. An important factor is probably that the areas being audited receive stimulus for continuous improvement from 'outside'.

Appendix B: Quality Profiles by Country

The McKinsey long-term study on 'Excellence in Quality Management' was not designed as a comparison of different regions. And as this book shows, it revealed common features in both the quality leaders and the quality stragglers which did not stop at international borders. However, if the 'quality companies' and 'lower- or average-quality companies' are grouped by their regions of origin, a clear divide appears within the three Triad regions of Japan, the US, and Europe. For Europeans, especially, it should also be interesting to see how these differences are perpetuated at the level of the individual countries of Europe (Figure B.1). The following pages give an overview of the most striking national quality management features.

Allocating the companies to the four quality levels gives a first impression of relative strengths and weaknesses in quality performance as a whole. For practical purposes, however, the need and opportunities for improvement have to be specified in greater detail. To this end, we have considered for every country which *main levers of quality management* are being applied, which *supplier segments* the companies belong to, and what strengths or weaknesses are expressed in the *figures for productivity and returns*.

- As *levers* of quality – whose use distinguishes successful from less successful quality management – we analyzed over 100 modes of behaviour and procedures. It emerged that corporate strategy and organization, the management of the two core processes 'zero-defects production' and 'design to quality', and mobilization of the workforce all had a clear and direct impact on process and design quality. There are 15 main levers in these areas which a company can use to influence its position in the quality ratings[1] (Figure B.2). As each level corresponds to a specific focus on individual levers, an analysis of this kind will help in determining the position of a company or country, and thus the point of departure for a quality program (see Chapter 6, 'The Road to Quality').

---

[1] See the dissertation by Hans Werner Kaas referred to in Appendix A, footnote 2 (PhD thesis in preparation, planned to be published in 1997).

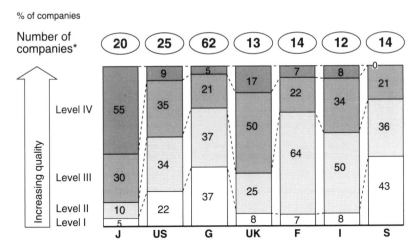

Fig. B.1 *Comparison of quality performance in the Triad*

	Key levers	Constantly improving management of key levers			
	Key levers	Level I	Level II	Level III	Level IV
Strategy and organization	1 Top management involvement				
	2 Quality objectives				
	3 QA as consultant				
	4 Flat hierarchies				
	5 Preventive focus				
'Zero defect' production as core process	6 Self-checking by workers				
	7 Projects with suppliers				
	8 Preventive QA tools				
'Design to quality' as core process	9 Controlled R&D volume				
	10 Involvement with customer				
Mobilization	11 Decision-making authority				
	12 Problem-solving by shop-floor workers				
	13 Operationalized objectives				
	14 Self-managing teams				
	15 Worker satisfaction				
		Weaknesses Average			Strengths

Fig. B.2 *Profile of quality management*

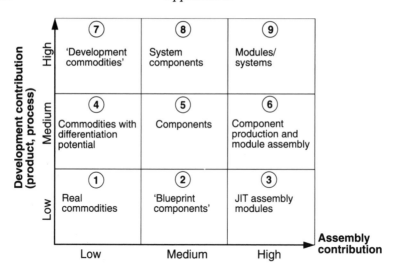

Fig. B.3 *Supplier segments according to scope of delivery*

- Its position on the *segmént matrix* will indicate what scope an auto-motive supplier has to make a development and assembly contribution to the OEM – from delivery of undifferentiated mass products in the 'commodities' segment to in-house development of complete systems or modules (Figure B.3). Features of national market structures, particularly at the supplier/OEM interface, and the degree of product modularity play an important role here (see also Chapter 1, 'Introduction'). Since increasing development and assembly contributions add new quality demands and sometimes involve the use of different levers, they have implications for the need for action.
- Finally, *productivity comparisons*, which also show marked differences between participants from different countries, also indicate the need to catch up and the improvement potential (Figures B.4 and B.5).

Like the regional perspective in the main body of the book, these country analyses do not offer statistically supported performance profiles. The numbers of participants vary too widely between countries and – with the exception of Germany – are generally too small to allow that. However, we believe that a number of informative and sometimes unexpected trends can be discerned from the strengths and weaknesses profiles for the individual countries.

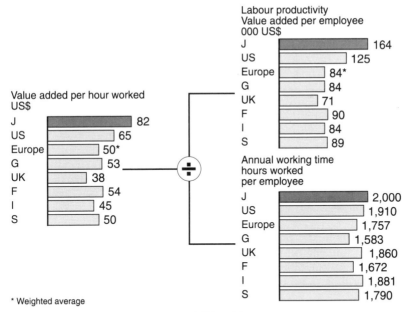

* Weighted average

Sources: Data from the participating companies; OECD statistics.

Fig. B.4 *Japan's automotive suppliers are the most productive*

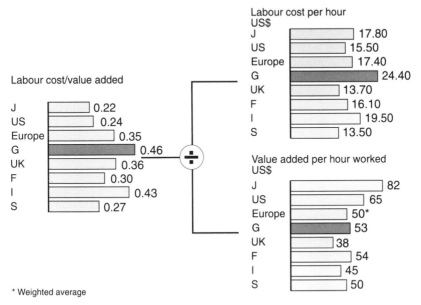

* Weighted average

Sources: Data from the participating companies; OECD statistics.

Fig. B.5 *German automotive industry suppliers have the highest share of labour costs in value added*

JAPAN

Japan is still the world champion of quality in the assembly industries, particularly in the area of stable processes. Fifty-five per cent of companies are on quality level IV, and 30 per cent on level III. Design for manufactur-ability is top class and production processes are stable, resulting in ppm values of 30 and reject and rework rates of 1.1 per cent and 1.3 per cent, respectively.

Levers Applied

The strengths of the Japanese lie in top management support for quality, good management of the two core processes, and the problem-solving capabilities of employees. Action needs to be taken in terms of giving employees more individual responsibility and removing levels of hierarchy accordingly (i.e., in terms of administrative productivity, Figure B.6). Some of the Japanese companies participating in the study have already intro-duced pilot projects in these improvement areas.

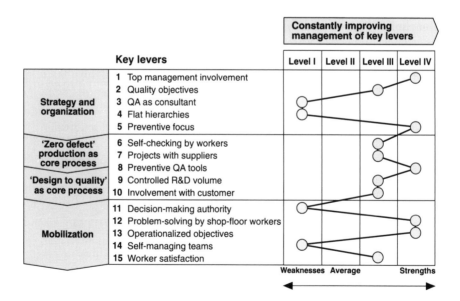

Fig. B.6 *Quality management profile of the participants from Japan*

Supplier Segments

In Japan, half the suppliers operate in those segments with a high development contribution (boxes 7, 8 and 9 in the segment matrix), more of them in the parts segment than in the systems segment. Only 12 per cent are in segments with little development contribution (boxes 2 and 3), and none in the pure commodities segment (box 1). This distribution is an indication of the development tasks transferred by the OEMs to the suppliers. In this area, the Japanese are ahead of the Americans and the Europeans. This technical competence transferred from the OEMs to the Japanese suppliers is not to be confused with the so-called end-customer competence currently being developed.

Productivity

At US$82 per hour, value added reaches its highest figure here, about 25 per cent higher than the American $65 per hour (see Figure B.4). The ratio of labour costs to value added is also the best, at 0.22 (see Figure B.5).

These excellent achievements in terms of quality and productivity could have been expected to lead to attractive levels of growth and returns in the free international market. Yet between 1987 and 1991, these ratios were, on average, only about 7.5 per cent and 3.5 per cent, respectively, for Japanese companies. This was partly because the Japanese automotive industry and its supplier industries were hit very early by the recession in the US and Japan in the late 1980s and early 1990s, and also because close bonds with the OEM mean that returns and growth are determined mainly by the OEM – under the aspect of the *Keiretsu* and its strategy.

* * *

The strength of Japanese automotive industry is based to a significant extent on the strength of the supplier industry. Important levers to be applied by Japanese suppliers (in addition to more efficient administration) could include further globalization of the sector's sales and production structures. For example, only 48 per cent of Japanese companies in the long-term study had production sites abroad, compared to about 71 per cent of the European quality companies. More intensive end-customer orientation is also an important factor for additional growth; at the same time, this will lead to a weakening of *Keiretsu* bonds.

UNITED STATES

In the US, the entry of the Japanese automotive manufacturers started a dramatic catch-up race in terms of quality, productivity, and technology. With a quality position to date of 9 per cent of suppliers at level IV and 35 per cent at level III, the Americans are, in this respect, somewhat superior to most of the Europeans. The ppm rate for OEM complaints is 748 ppm, lower than the European average of 1,010 ppm.

Levers Applied

The quality management profile of American participants in the long-term study shows strength in employee mobilization, driven by the initiative and special attention of top management (Figure B.7). Action to be taken includes complete integration of customer and supplier as well as more intensive use of preventive quality assurance tools in development, in order to design products for manufacturability and ease of assembly.

Productivity

In terms of productivity, the Americans achieved second place behind the Japanese. With about $65 of value added per hour, they are about 23 per

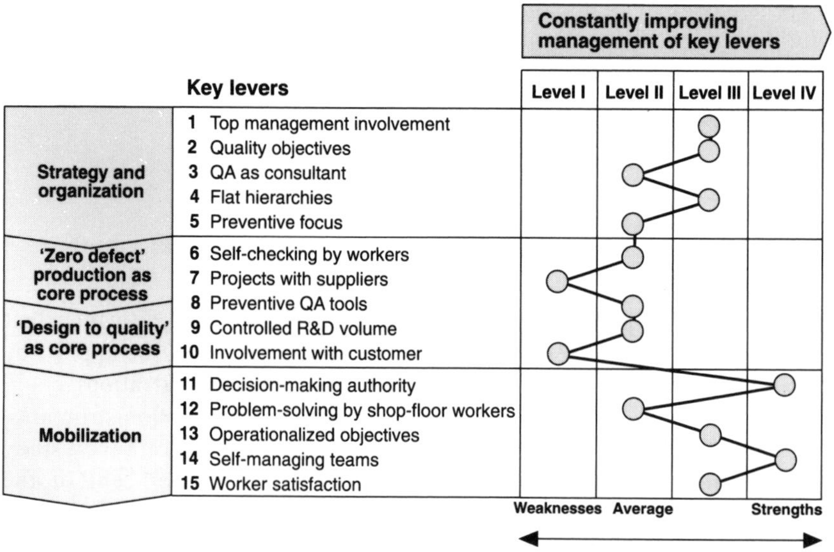

	Key levers	Constantly improving management of key levers			
		Level I	Level II	Level III	Level IV
Strategy and organization	1 Top management involvement			●	
	2 Quality objectives			●	
	3 QA as consultant		●		
	4 Flat hierarchies			●	
	5 Preventive focus		●		
'Zero defect' production as core process	6 Self-checking by workers		●		
	7 Projects with suppliers	●			
	8 Preventive QA tools		●		
'Design to quality' as core process	9 Controlled R&D volume		●		
	10 Involvement with customer	●			
Mobilization	11 Decision-making authority				●
	12 Problem-solving by shop-floor workers		●		
	13 Operationalized objectives			●	
	14 Self-managing teams				●
	15 Worker satisfaction			●	

Weaknesses — Average — Strengths

Fig. B.7 *Quality management profile of the participants from the USA*

cent ahead of the Germans (see Figure B.4) and, with a ratio of labour costs to value added of 0.24, they are again in second place behind Japan (see Figure B.5). The Americans owe their high productivity to leaner organization, the introduction of team concepts in production, and their continuous improvement process. This latter is, of course, driven primarily by Japanese (transplant) competition in the US.

The average return on sales of about 5 per cent was slightly higher than the European figure of about 4 per cent. It is interesting to note that the American parts and components manufacturers performed better than average, with returns between 7 and 12 per cent. This was primarily due to the fact that manufacturers of systems and subsystems have had little opportunity under American market conditions to improve their development complexity, specifications, or processes. As a result, only a minuscule amount of real added value could be generated for the OEM, let alone the end customer. In addition, OEMs were not prepared to reward this added value in the price.

Supplier Segments

About 30 per cent of our American participants in the systems segment (box 9 of the development and assembly contribution matrix) were affected by the squeeze on returns. However, the dramatic growth in R&D efforts in recent years, particularly among manufacturers of systems and subsystems, shows that the Americans are not content with this situation but will demand cooperation from OEMs in the future. This means that they want to exploit degrees of freedom in the design and realization of technical solutions and, at the same time, improve cost structures. About 36 per cent of the American participants were positioned in the segments with average development contribution and technological differentiation potential (boxes 4, 5 and 6), in which higher returns were earned.

✳   ✳   ✳

The Americans have already started to work on their weaknesses, either by optimizing the entire value chain from supplier to customer or by developing their technical competence (see also Chapter 5, 'Japan, Europe, and the US'). Competitive pressure from Japanese transplants in the US will spur on both OEMs and their suppliers to the necessary pace of improvement – a finding which was recently confirmed in the case of nine other industries in the Triad by a McKinsey Global Institute study. In every country, those industries marked by high and rapidly growing productivity have one thing in common: they are all in direct global competition with the best domestic and foreign firms in their sector, as a result of confrontation with imports and transplants.

GERMANY

The 62 participating German companies, which together account for about
30 per cent of their industry's sales, provide the basis for a substantiated
industry profile. Only 5 per cent of participating companies are at quality
level IV, the lowest share after Spain and Portugal. This can be seen
particularly in the ratios for process quality: German companies, with an
average reject rate of 2.8 per cent (on a unit basis) and 1,050 defective ppm
delivered to the OEM, had the second worst result after Spain and Portugal.
The fact that Germany lags behind, again just before Spain and Portugal, in
terms of design for optimum manufacturability[2] is a contributory factor.

Levers Applied

The quality management profile of the German companies shows a typical
level II position – in other words, average quality performance (Figure B.8).
The greatest need for action is in restructuring and training the supplier base
and upgrading employees' problem-solving skills. The higher-than-average
figures for R&D undertaken by suppliers for OEMs confirm the technological competence of German automotive suppliers, which also keep the end
customer well in their sights.

Supplier Segments

Forty per cent of the German companies operated in those segments that
have a high development contribution, i.e., high differentiation potential
through technological know-how (boxes 7, 8 and 9 in the matrix); 15 per
cent of them were in the classic systems segment (box 9). About one-fifth of
the German companies' development expenditure (on average 5 per cent of
sales in 1991) went on upstream development, and this is reflected in the
value to the customer: about 42 per cent of their products are superior to the
competition, the top international result for this dimension of design
quality.

But why did the German companies earn only a meager 2.9 per cent
average return during the prosperous years from 1987 to 1991? Primarily,
because about 30 per cent of the companies operate in segments with stiff
cost competition but little opportunity for technological differentiation
(boxes 1, 2 and 3 in the segment matrix). Here, a competitive cost position

---

[2] Manufacturability was measured by a scoring model which takes into account both the
application of preventive quality tools and internal assessment of the manufacturability of
products (data from top management and the production areas concerned).

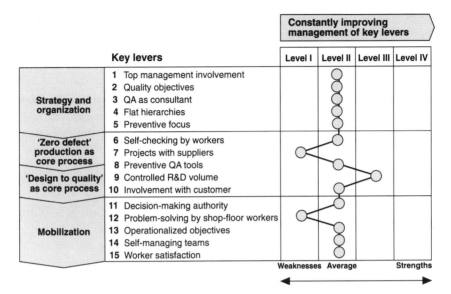

Fig. B.8 *Quality management profile of the participants from Germany*

can only be achieved through an optimized synthesis of factor costs, productivity, and process quality. But, as we have seen, cost and quality are weak areas.

Productivity

Labour productivity still stands up to European comparison, but is well behind international competition. With value added of $53 per hour worked, German suppliers earn about as much as the French ($54) and about 40 per cent more than the British, but still more than 35 per cent less than the Japanese. In terms of net annual working hours and annual labor costs, the gap compared to Japan widens to almost 50 per cent (see Figures B.4 and B.5). Two main factors prevent the Germans from drawing level on productivity: first, the number of hours worked per year which, at 1,583 hours, is the lowest; and second, labor costs which, at $24.40 on average, are the highest of all participating countries. Germany is the country with the poorest ratio of labor costs to value added, with a factor of 0.46 (see Figure B.5).

---

[3] The cost of capital includes depreciation and interest cost.

With regard to the cost of capital, too,[3] German labor costs at 4.8 are significantly higher than Japan's at 2.5 (those of other European countries lie between 4.5 and 3.7). This is particularly striking because, in relation to value added, the cost of capital in Japan is lower than in Germany (0.08 compared with 0.095). This reflects a difference in production philosophy: while German and other Western companies often invest (and sometimes even over-invest) in leading-edge technology and so need complex and expensive infrastructures (e.g., materials management, maintenance, production technology and planning, setup operatives, and machine operators), Japanese companies concentrate on stabilizing production at a high level of productivity and quality with existing, often older machinery, which allows them to cut this infrastructure. The reductions are sometimes radical.

One Japanese works manager commented, 'When you (Europeans) are thinking about equipment replacement after five to ten years, we consider that our machinery has just reached the phase of increasing optimization. Process technology is very much like your good wines – the older, the better!'

With this philosophy, the Japanese practice of strictly separating high- and low-volume products ('standard' and 'exotic' production) is very helpful. This includes the readiness to use dedicated production lines (usually older machinery) for different product lines. The employee who has to operate a number of production lines or, if necessary, shuttle back and forth between them, is then seen as a flexible resource. This production strategy was, for example, to be found among leading Japanese battery and radiator manufacturers.

Of course, productivity disadvantages – temporary ones, at least – can also be compensated for by superior technology or system solutions, but at the moment, many European (and especially German) suppliers are not – or not fully – in a position to do this. And even the restructuring of many German companies, like the entire supplier industry, will undoubtedly only compensate for some of the productivity disadvantages. Companies should also take a cautious approach to the transfer of production of labour-intensive products to low-wage economies, in Eastern Europe, for instance. This will not bring lasting success on its own. Hard work also has to be put into eliminating other major weaknesses – by methods such as complexity reduction, design to manufacture, and better work organization.

*   *   *

Without an unprecedented effort to close the quality gap, most German suppliers will go under sooner or later in the international market. The catch-up effort will need to begin with a drastic reduction in current levels of overcomplexity (e.g., in numbers of parts, subassemblies, and end products) and a focus on strategically important levers; it must continue by optimizing the entire value added chain from the supplier to the customer (concentration and integration). In addition, indirect activities should be integrated into the work of the shop-floor level, team concepts (with greater delegation of responsibility) introduced, and the problem-solving skills of employees upgraded. Finally, all this must lead to a design process which derives superior product concepts from customer requirements, and these concepts must be translated into manufacturable and easily assembled products – one of the key prerequisites for stable processes in production, and probably one of the biggest improvement opportunities for German companies.

In this way, German companies should extend their product leadership to include process leadership. Top management commitment to quality, which has been only average to date, will need to greatly increase if this is to be achieved.

GREAT BRITAIN

According to our long-term study, Great Britain leads Europe in terms of quality. At 17 per cent, British suppliers have the highest share of level IV companies after Japan and, with a further 50 per cent at level III, they are the strongest Europeans.

Levers Applied

The typical British supplier in the long-term study is a level III company (Figure B.9). Improvements in the levers still assigned to level II are under way. As in the US, the presence in Britain of Japanese transplants (the largest number of any country in Europe) provides the necessary pressure to improve and, in the light of favourable labour costs, this pressure has been exerted first and foremost on quality.

Supplier Segments

The British participants operate mainly in the components segment, about 53 per cent are in those segments with an average development contribution (boxes 4, 5, and 6 in the matrix). There are surprisingly few in the segments with low development contribution and/or small opportunities for technological differentiation (15 per cent), but just as few in the systems segment (8 per cent in box 9 in the matrix). British suppliers invest a relatively high proportion of sales (3.8 per cent) in development and, at 30 per cent, have the second highest share of products superior to the competition in Europe,

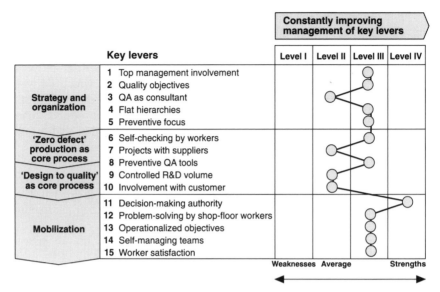

Fig. B.9 *Quality management profile of the participants from the UK*

after the Germans. This is hardly surprising, as British components and systems manufacturers have about 16 per cent of their total R&D employees working in upstream development, again the second highest share in Europe after the Germans.

Productivity

Despite a clear enough 'winner's' profile, British companies bring up the rear in terms of return on sales (2.3 per cent), and their average growth of 7.5 per cent per annum between 1987 and 1991 was also the second lowest in Europe, just beating Germany at 5.4 per cent. This is partly because British suppliers, together with their customers, were hit harder and earlier by the start of the recession in 1990–91. But the main reason, at least for the companies in our study, lay in neglect of labor productivity which, at $38 value added per hour worked, was about 30 per cent lower than the German and 54 per cent below the Japanese level (see Figure B.4). In terms of value added per employee, the gap compared to Japan is about the same, but the gap compared to Germany closes to about 15 per cent because of shorter German working hours. Despite low hourly labour costs of about $13.70, Britain's ratio of labour costs to value added of 0.36 is third from bottom in Europe (see Figure B.5).

When interpreting the productivity figures, it is important to bear in mind that some of the participating British companies were just getting up speed after a new startup, takeover, or restructuring – i.e., they were in an unusual situation with regard to productivity. To achieve the growth they wanted, the companies had invested significant amounts in the labour force up front. Internal improvements and renewed growth then ensured a rise in productivity: the fact that good quality and high productivity are not mutually exclusive but actually reinforce each other applies to British suppliers, too.

$$*\qquad*\qquad*$$

Quality has improved greatly in Britain since the beginning of the 1990s. When the Japanese car manufacturers arrived with their very strict quality requirements, upping quality levels was a matter of survival for British suppliers. British top management has now devoted itself intensely to quality, more so than that of any other country in Europe. Compared to the global leaders, the British companies still have much to do, especially in the area of productivity, but most of the surviving companies are on the right track. In the light of the favourable labour costs in Britain, productivity improvement has initially been neglected. This is a phenomenon never observed among the very top companies which, as the Japanese have shown, improve quality and productivity simultaneously.

Important levers for British suppliers include further training and involvement of shop-floor employees in problem solving, know-how building in the development department, and more supplier training. They need these actions to become acknowledged suppliers of components or systems or, with a better understanding of the end customer, to develop superior products which can be produced with zero defects by stable processes.

In each case, one imperative is a significant productivity boost to achieve internationally competitive unit costs, but also to earn returns which allow investment in building new skills or products.

FRANCE

Most of the French firms (64 per cent) are at quality level II. Twenty-two per cent are at level III and as many as 7 per cent at level IV. These figures indicate relatively stable processes, reflected in a ppm rate of 780, the second lowest OEM complaint rate in Europe after Britain. While the reject rate of 2.7 per cent is around the European average, the rework rate, at only 1.4 per cent, is very impressive. These quality ratios were first achieved partly because of pressure from Peugeot and, above all, from Renault.

Levers Applied

The French quality management profile (Figure B.10) shows that most levers are well used on average. The most important lever for improvement is more intensive employee mobilization (self-managing teams, integration of indirect tasks, delegation of responsibility, etc.) and support for the companies' own suppliers.

Supplier Segments

Most of the French companies operate in the parts segment with an average or high development contribution (28 per cent in box 4, 21 per cent in box 7 of the matrix), or manufacture components with a small development contribution (36 per cent in box 2 of the matrix). None of the participants was a genuine systems supplier.

Productivity

With average growth rates of 8.9 per cent per annum between 1987 and 1991, the French companies achieved around the industry average, and earned the second highest returns (5.6 per cent) in Europe after Spain and Portugal.

		Constantly improving management of key levers			
	Key levers	Level I	Level II	Level III	Level IV
Strategy and organization	1 Top management involvement		○		
	2 Quality objectives		○		
	3 QA as consultant		○		
	4 Flat hierarchies		○		
	5 Preventive focus		○		
'Zero defect' production as core process	6 Self-checking by workers			○	
	7 Projects with suppliers		○		
	8 Preventive QA tools		○		
'Design to quality' as core process	9 Controlled R&D volume		○		
	10 Involvement with customer		○		
Mobilization	11 Decision-making authority	○			
	12 Problem-solving by shop-floor workers		○		
	13 Operationalized objectives	○			
	14 Self-managing teams	○			
	15 Worker satisfaction	○			
		Weaknesses	Average		Strengths

Fig. B.10 *Quality management profile of the participants from France*

This can be attributed primarily to the best value added in Europe ($54 per hour worked, see Figure B.4). Together with low labour costs of about $16.10 per hour, this gives a ratio of labour cost to value added of 0.30 (see Figure B.5), the second best in Europe (compare Germany: 0.46, Japan: 0.22, US: 0.24).

* * *

Despite their relatively good quality ratios, the French companies have not yet managed to use excellent design quality to create added value for the customer, especially the end customer, and so accelerate their growth. This is reflected above all in the proportion of superior products which, at 18 per cent, is significantly below the European average of 32 per cent. The main concerns of these companies should be to push forward into levels III and IV on the basis of customer orientation and the design of superior products.

ITALY

Around half of the Italian companies in our long-term study are on level II. Their reject and rework rates are 1.7 per cent and 1.5 per cent, respectively. With 798 ppm defective (in terms of OEM complaints), the Italians are at about the same level as the French suppliers.

Levers Applied

The main strengths of the Italian quality management profile (Figure B.11) lie in its comprehensive definition of quality objectives throughout the entire business system, and in its flat hierarchies. Action needs to be taken above all in the areas of supplier training and increased employee upskilling and mobilization.

Productivity

At $45, value added per hour is about 16 per cent lower than in Germany and France (see Figure B.4). In terms of value added per employee, however, the Italians are level with the Germans because they work longer hours. Companies earn a return on sales of 4.9 per cent, above the industry average, and achieve average growth rates of about 8 per cent.

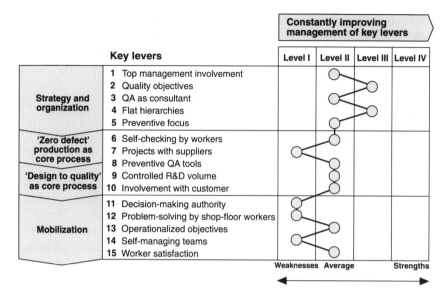

Fig. B.11 *Quality management profile of the participants from Italy*

Supplier Segments

Italy has the highest share of companies in the systems segment (25 per cent in box 9 of the matrix) or in those segments generally with a high development contribution and/or technological differentiation potential (58 per cent), as well as the smallest share in the segments with low development contribution (8 per cent). However, as the share of sales of products superior to those of the competition is only 22 per cent, significantly lower than the European average, the Italians' position in these high-tech segments is in jeopardy. With an R&D spend of only 2.7 per cent of sales and a preponderance of smaller companies, it is an open question whether the necessary critical mass in research and development can be achieved here.

We should be particularly wary of average figures in the case of Italy, because Italy had the widest performance variations within the supply industry of any country. There is an exemplary level IV company achieving world-class results, but there are also many with a great deal of catching up to do.

∗   ∗   ∗

The main levers to improve the quality level of the Italian suppliers are, in addition to employee mobilization and supplier support, primarily an improvement in design quality through stronger end-customer orientation and integration of OEMs. In the light of the meagre ratio of R&D investment to sales, a targeted increase in R&D activities is also needed. One typically Italian problem seems to be poor translation into practice of basically good ideas, such as setting quality objectives across the entire process.

SPAIN/PORTUGAL

Spain/Portugal (aggregated in the long-term study) lags the furthest behind on quality. No company was at the highest quality level, level IV. Twenty-one per cent of participants had reached level III, but the Iberian Peninsula had the highest proportion of companies (43 per cent) at the weakest level, level I. The ppm rate of 1,765 is the highest in the entire study, as is the reject rate of 4.9 per cent (rework rate: 2.0 per cent). So work still needs to be done in the area of process stability. The share of products sold which are superior to those of the competition is only 12 per cent, again the worst rating, and indicates the need to catch up in terms of design quality.

Levers Applied

The quality management profile of the Spanish and Portuguese suppliers shows that most of the levers are positioned at level I (Figure B.12); the other levers are only at level II.

Supplier Segments

Both countries have mainly profited over the past few years from the trend toward transferring labour-intensive production of parts and systems (e.g., wire harnesses) to countries with low factor costs. This is reflected in the fact that Spain and Portugal have the highest share of companies in the segment with assembly-intensive products with low differentiation opportunities and/or development contribution (box 3 in Figure B.3). On the other hand, at 13 per cent, Spain shows the highest average growth rate of any country.

Productivity

At just under 5.8 per cent, return on sales was very attractive. This can be attributed to low labour costs (the lowest figure at $13.50 per hour) and a high value added of $50 per hour (mainly due to new factories with a layout

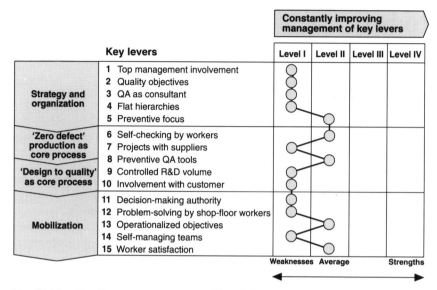

Fig. B.12 *Quality management profile of the participants from Spain and Portugal*

optimized for productivity). At 0.27, Spain also has the best ratio of labour costs to value added (see Figures B.4 and B.5). However, labour costs are also rising in Spain and Portugal, and 'factor cost competition' from Eastern Europe also entered the competitive arena some time ago. Transferring assembly of wire harnesses or sewing of seat covers to Eastern European countries long ago ceased to be regarded as a daring adventure.

✳   ✳   ✳

In general, quality orientation in Spain and Portugal is the lowest of all the countries studied. The first step on the long road to world-class quality would have to involve anchoring quality as the top priority in the minds of both management – especially top management – and employees, and focusing on prevention. This entails design to manufacture and assembly as well as employee and supplier training.

Index

243